DHAMMA
REFLECTIONS

Dhamma Reflections

Collected Essays of Bhikkhu Bodhi

Compiled by the Buddhist Publication Society
To celebrate his 70th Birthday

BUDDHIST PUBLICATION SOCIETY
KANDY • SRI LANKA

Buddhist Publication Society
54 Sangharaja Mawatha
PO Box 61
Kandy
Sri Lanka
http://www.bps.lk

First edition: 2015

National Library of Sri Lanka - Cataloguing in Publication Data

Bodhi, Bhikkhu
   Dhamma Reflections: Collected Essays on Bhikkhu Bodhi / Bhikkhu
Bodhi; ed. by Nyanatusita Bhikkhu.- Kandy: Buddhist Publication
Society Inc., 2015
   BP 436.- 290p.; 24cm.

   ISBN 978-955-24-0413-9

  i.   181.043 DDC 23   ii. Title
  ii. Nyanatusita Bhikkhu ed.

  1. Buddhist Philosophy

ISBN: 978-955-24-0413-9

Typeset at the BPS in URW Palladio Pali

Printed by
Samayawardana Printers
Colombo 10

CONTENTS

Message of Felicitation

The BPS is very grateful for all the good work that Bhikkhu Bodhi has selflessly done for it for many years. Although Bhikkhu Bodhi is no longer actively involved, the BPS continues to thrive through the hard work, commitment and vision of the current BPS editors, the BPS staff, the BPS Board of Management, and many volunteers. All these achievements have been built on what has gone before. It was the initial vision, wisdom and determination of its founding editor, Venerable Nyanaponika, fuelled by the great enthusiasm and dedication of Richard Abeyasekera, that created and sustained BPS through the first 26 years. It was then Bhikkhu Bodhi who nurtured it over the next 18 years with his gentle scholarship and dedication. That spirit continues to inspire everyone who is involved with the BPS today. It is therefore with deep gratitude and heartfelt thanks that we send our best wishes to you, Bhikkhu Bodhi.

May you have a Very Happy 70th Birthday
and
May you share your gentle loving kindness
with us many years to come

Buddhist Publication Society
Kandy, December 2014

INTRODUCTION

This volume has been published by the Buddhist Publication Society to celebrate Venerable Bhikkhu Bodhi's 70th birthday. It comprises almost all[1] of the essays written by Bhikkhu Bodhi that were published by the Buddhist Publication Society. By bringing together these fifty-three essays published over a period of thirty years they can finally get the attention that they deserve.

We are all well aware of Bhikkhu Bodhi's erudite scholarship in his translations and studies of the Buddha's discourses, but perhaps fewer of us are as cognisant of his skill in guiding us towards applying the Dhamma in everyday life. These fifty-three essays do just that. They reveal the depth and breadth of his ability to communicate the timeless teaching of the Buddha. They range from simple talks on how to incorporate the Dhamma into one's daily life, to more complex expositions of the doctrine but still with that focus of relevance to today.

The first of Bhikkhu Bodhi's essays that BPS published was in the Bodhi Leaves series, entitled *The Taste of Freedom*, in 1976. Just as this essay was his initial introduction to the BPS readership, so it is the introductory essay in this volume, wherein the essays are in chronological order. Bhikkhu Bodhi's next publication was a collection of four essays published in The Wheel Publication series, namely *Nourishing the Roots: Essays on Buddhist Ethics* in 1978 (Wheel Publication no. 259/260), which are next in this volume.

The essays from the *Buddhist Publication Society Newsletter* come next. Soon after Bhikkhu Bodhi became the Editor of BPS in 1984, a position he held for eighteen years, he introduced this newsletter to accompany the mailings of publications to BPS members. These newsletters comprised an 'editorial' in the form of a Dhamma essay, a review or two of new Dhamma books from other publishers, other items of news deemed to be of interest to the members, and a study of the Buddha's discourses. By the time Bhikkhu Bodhi retired from the position of editor in 2002, he had written some forty-two editorial essays, which form the bulk of this tribute.

The essay "Dhamma and Non-Duality" was originally published in two parts; so were "Towards a Threshold of Understanding" and "Does Rebirth Make Sense?" The essay "The Living Message of the Dhammapada" was published in the Bodhi Leaves series in 1993. It has been put among the newsletter essays to maintain the chronological order of essays.

Next comes the essays from *Facing the Future: Four Essays on the Social Relevance of Buddhism*, published as Wheel Publication no. 438/440 in 2000. The following essay, "Promoting Buddhism in Europe", was published privately in Colombo in 2000, but has nevertheless been included since it complements the *Facing the Future* essays and was written in the same period. The last essay Bhikkhu Bodhi wrote as editor of the BPS, *The Good, the Beautiful, and the True*, was published in the Bodhi Leaves series in 2001. Just as we started this volume with Bhikkhu Bodhi's first essay published in the Bodhi Leaves series, his last essay in this volume is also from this series, thus offering a fitting "final curtain."

Bhikkhu Bodhi also wrote several insightful in-depth studies on topics such as the Three Refuges and Dependent Arising that were published by the BPS in the Wheel Publications Series. Since these studies are too large too include here, they will probably be published together by the BPS as another volume that includes some of his other studies that were published in academic journals.[2]

BIOGRAPHY OF BHIKKHU BODHI

To get to know Bhikkhu Bodhi better and to understand his motivation for writing these essays, we include a biography that is made up of materials gleaned from various interviews and essays.[3]

Bhikkhu Bodhi was born in Brooklyn, New York City, on 10th December 1944 in a middle class secular Jewish family. His lay name was Jeffrey Block. He grew up in Borough Park, a Brooklyn neighbourhood that was then inhabited mainly by descendants of Jewish and Italian immigrants, and went to a public elementary school and a high school near his home. After high school he studied at Brooklyn College where he completed his Bachelor of Arts in Philosophy in 1966. In an interview[4] he recalls how he came to Buddhism while at College:

"I had become interested in Buddhism in my junior year in college. While strolling in bookshops and looking at book titles somehow I became interested in a few books on Buddhism that I could find there. I think this interest in Buddhism arose from the kind of surge or quest for some deeper understanding of human existence that was offered by the materialistic philosophy of modern American civilization, and I wasn't satisfied with my ancestral Jewish religion, and also I didn't find much long term value in Christianity. But I was drawn at an early period, say during my junior year of college to the religions of the east.

"I began reading some of the Upanishads, Bhagavadgita, then I found in the bookshops books on Buddhism by D.T. Suzuki and Alan Watts, so they were mainly on Zen Buddhism and Mahayana Buddhism. When I went to Claremont Graduate School my interest in Buddhism continued and I felt increasingly a deeper need to lead a spiritual life. At the same time I always had an underlying doubt or skepticism about any type of spiritual philosophy.

"But finally I met a Buddhist monk from Vietnam, Venerable Thich Giac Duc, who was attending the same graduate school and living in the same residence hall in which I was living. I became friends with him, and I approached him as a teacher and from him I received my first instructions in Buddhism and meditation."

Elsewhere[5] he tells the delightful story of his earlier first 'encounter' with a Buddhist monk, also Vietnamese, albeit from a distance:

"In the first week of August, 1965, after finishing summer school, I set out to travel by car from New York to California. I was twenty years old and in September would be entering my senior year at Brooklyn College. I wanted to visit a friend who was spending the summer in San Francisco and I managed to find a ride with a couple of fellow students. After a full day on the road we stopped in Madison, Wisconsin. The next morning I decided to take a walk. My steps led me through quiet streets to the University of Wisconsin campus.

"As I was approaching a mall in the middle of the campus, the door of a big stone building opened and out stepped a middle-aged man with East Asian features wearing a yellow-orange robe. He was immediately followed by a tall American man and the two walked side by side talking. At once I realized that I was looking at a Buddhist monk. I had never seen a Buddhist monk before, and in America at that time the number of Buddhist monks could probably be counted on one hand. I had just begun to read about Buddhism a few months earlier, and I knew from my reading of Hermann Hesse's *Siddhartha* that Buddhist monks wore saffron robes. Thus I could identify the person I was seeing as a bhikkhu.

"I was struck with wonder and amazement at the sight of this serene, self-composed man who radiated a lightness, inner contentment and dignity that I had never seen before in any Westerner. Just watching him walk across the mall, I was filled with joy and happiness. All too soon the two men disappeared from view into another building."

The story does not end there. It continues:

"A little more than a year later, after completing my degree at Brooklyn College, I moved to California where I entered Claremont Graduate School east of Los Angeles to begin a doctoral program in philosophy. In the spring semester a Buddhist monk from Vietnam came to study in the same university and moved in just below me in the graduate residence hall. He was not 'serene and self-composed' like the monk in Wisconsin but a 'happy-go-lucky' type. Once I got to know him, I came to like him and eventually accepted him as my first Buddhist teacher.

"One day (I think it was in November 1967) he told me that a distinguished Buddhist monk from Vietnam named Venerable Thich Minh Chau was in the U.S. and would soon be visiting Los Angeles. He invited me to accompany him to the house of the Vietnamese family with whom the distinguished monk was staying. When the Venerable Thich Minh Chau came out from his guest room, much to my surprise he looked very much indeed like the monk that I had seen two years before crossing the campus of the

University of Wisconsin. When an opportunity arose, I asked him, 'Is this your first visit to America, sir?' He replied, 'No, I was here a few years ago.' Then I asked: 'By any chance, could the Venerable have been on the campus of the University of Wisconsin in early August 1965?' And he said, 'In fact I was. I was visiting my friend Professor Richard Robinson, who started a program of Buddhist Studies there.' Then I told him about that day when I had watched him walk across the campus. He chuckled gently and said, 'So this is not the first time we are meeting.'"

Outside of Vietnam, Thich Minh Chau is known for his scholarly work, *A Comparative Study of the Pāli Majjhima Nikāya and the Chinese Madhyama Āgama*, but in Vietnam is known for his Vietnamese translations of the four collections of the Buddha's discourses (*nikāyas*) and other Pali texts. He also served as a long-term head of Vietnamese Buddhist universities and institutes.

In another interview[6] Bhikkhu Bodhi tells that his monk friend and teacher, Thich Giac Duc, taught him meditation and ordained him as a novice (*sāmaṇera*) in May 1967:

"He started me off with mindfulness of breathing, *ānāpānasati*. What is interesting is that although Vietnamese Buddhism is Mahayana, because of the proximity to Cambodia, or perhaps because it had also received a stream of transmission from Indian Mahayana and not only Chinese Mahayana coming down from south China, Vietnamese Mahayana Buddhism tends to have a stronger strain of classical Indian Buddhism within it. So the meditations he taught me were basically mindfulness of breathing, the meditation on loving kindness, and a meditation based on the Four Foundations of Mindfulness in which each foundation of mindfulness is linked up with a particular one of the four perversions or distortions. To contemplate the body as being essentially impure, to contemplate all feelings as being suffering, to contemplate every state of mind as being impermanent, and to contemplate all dhammas as being without self.

"After I became friends with him and I began the practice of meditation, my skepticism and doubts about Buddhism or the spiritual life dissipated. Since I became convinced that this is the proper path for me to follow, I asked my friend and teacher if he could give me ordination as a monk. Also, I have to confess that there was an underlying pragmatic motive as well. I would not say that was the main reason why I wanted ordination, but this was a period when America decided it had to beef up its armed forces and it was expanding its roll-call of people subject to the draft. And so I also thought it might be an extra security measure to have a formal ordination as a monk in order to be able to submit some kind of document to receive exoneration from the obligation to serve in the armed forces. ...

"I was planning to go to Asia all along, from the time that I received ordination. It was not exactly certain where I would go for ordination or training, though my Vietnamese teacher had some contact with the famous Sri Lankan monk Venerable Nārada. He was always advising me to go to Sri Lanka to ordain and to receive training."

Thich Minh Chau also advised him to go to Sri Lanka:

"A couple of years later, when Venerable Thich Minh Chau next visited the U.S. he stayed with us for a short time in our house in Claremont. Still later, when I was planning my trip to Asia to receive bhikkhu ordination and study the Dhamma, he gave me useful advice and provided me with a beautiful open letter of introduction to Buddhist authorities in Asia. I kept that letter and still have it with my belongings in Kandy. It was he who suggested that, when I go to Sri Lanka, I study with Venerable Nyanaponika Mahāthera, though I could not fulfil that aim for several years after my arrival in the island."

And so the link with Sri Lanka and Venerable Nyanaponika began. But before Bhikkhu Bodhi undertook that journey to Sri Lanka in 1972, he was to meet another monk who was to have a great significance in his life: Venerable Piyadassi Thera, a globe-trotting missionary Sri Lankan monk well known for his writings and lectures. Several of his books, such as *The Buddha's Ancient Path* were published by the BPS, of which he was the Sinhala editor for many years. It was in fact a sermon he gave in late 1957 that led to the birth of the BPS at the start of 1958. Bhikkhu Bodhi tells the story of their first meeting in a *BPS Newsletter* (No. 40, 1998):

"The story of this relationship began in 1971 when I was living at a Vietnamese Buddhist centre in Los Angeles and teaching world religions at a college in the sprawling conurbation of southern California. One day at our centre we received notice that a Buddhist monk from Sri Lanka would be coming to Los Angeles, and we invited him to stay with us and give a series of lectures on Theravada Buddhism. That Buddhist monk was none other than Venerable Piyadassi, who was then on his second world Dhamma tour. His lectures were excellent, conveying with crystal clarity and gentle humour the heart of the Buddha's teachings which he knew so well. At the end of the week, when we parted at the Los Angeles airport, Venerable Piyadassi suggested to me that one day I should come to Sri Lanka and spend time in a Buddhist monastery.

"This suggestion resonated with an idea that was already taking shape in my mind, and thus the following year, when I decided to come to Asia to enter the Saṅgha, I wrote to Venerable Piyadassi to remind him of his invitation. In reply he gave me the name and address of a 'senior prelate,' Venerable Balangoda Ānanda Maitreya. At first I hesitated to contact this elder, for he was already 76 years old and I feared that at such an age he might not be fit enough to teach me. Little did I realize I was being introduced to a monk of such amazing strength and vitality that he would still be striding the globe well into his 100th year. In any case, I took the chance and wrote to him, and his welcoming reply set me on a 'journey to the East' that culminated in my ordination as a bhikkhu and a three-year tutelage under him at his small village temple near Balangoda."

After his first teacher, Thich Giac Duc, finished his doctorate degree and went back to Vietnam, Bhikkhu Bodhi went to live with another Vietnamese monk, Venerable Thich Thien An, at the International Buddhist Meditation Centre in Los Angeles. Bhikkhu Bodhi received his PhD from Claremont Graduate School in February 1972. His dissertation was on the theory of primary and secondary qualities in the philosophy of the British empiricist philosopher John Locke. While he was working on his dissertation, and for several months after completing it, he taught part-time at California State University at Fullerton in order to pay back his student debt. At the Philosophy Department of this university he taught a course on World Religions. When his debt had been paid off, he left the United States for Asia. His intention was first to study Buddhism and then to meditate. In an interview he tells:[7]

"I never intended to become a Buddhist scholar or a translator of Pali texts; in fact, I do not consider myself a serious scholar of Buddhism even now. I was initially attracted to Buddhism through the practice of meditation. It was my first teacher, Venerable Giac Duc, who impressed on me the need for systematic study of the Dhamma to serve as a proper foundation for both meditation practice and for teaching the Dhamma in the West. When I went to Sri Lanka and took ordination, my original intention was to study the texts for several years and then go off to meditate."

In August 1972 he flew to Thailand and spent one week at a meditation monastery called Wat Pleng Vipassana in Bangkok. From there he went to Vietnam in order to visit his friend and teacher Thich Giac Duc. Because of the civil war Vietnam was in a rather hectic, chaotic state and the monks were very uncertain about the future of Buddhism and the country. He stayed in Vietnam for two months, mostly in Saigon, and then went on to Sri Lanka:[8]

"I was still a Mahayana novice (*sāmaṇera*) and I arrived in Sri Lanka wearing my Vietnamese style robe. My teacher wanted me to wear the yellow robe when I came to Sri Lanka since with the brown robe I might not have been recognized as a Buddhist monk. So I wore this flowing yellow robe. After a week or so in Colombo I went out to Balangoda to stay at the monastery of my ordination teacher: Venerable Balangoda Ānanda Maitreya. A few weeks later, in November 1972, I took a new ordination into the Theravada Order as a sāmaṇera, and then I took the Upasampadā (bhikkhu ordination) in May 1973."

The Venerable Ānanda Maitreya, besides being the foremost Sinhalese scholar-monk fluent in English was also a very gentle and lovable person. He had a comprehensive knowledge of the Pali language and of the Tipiṭaka and its commentaries. To the newly ordained monk, the breadth and depth of his preceptor's knowledge was inspiring: "It was with him that I began my study of Pali ... Once I'd learned enough Pali ... we went through certain texts together. We started with the first part of the Saṃyutta Nikāya, the collection with verses, then we went through some suttas in the Majjhima Nikāya, then he took me through the *Abhidhammatthasaṅgaha*."

Like many other Western monks in Sri Lanka before him, Bhikkhu Bodhi revelled in the challenge of understanding the teachings of the Buddha without the intermediary of a translator. This tradition started with the Venerable Nyanatiloka, one of the first Westerners to become a Theravada Buddhist monk. In 1912 Nyanatiloka founded a monastery called the Island Hermitage, where he ordained many Western monks. Since the early translations of the Pali Canon were unreliable, Nyanatiloka stressed the importance of learning Pali to gain a proper understanding of the Buddha's teachings. He therefore personally taught Pali to his pupils, including Nyanaponika and Ñāṇamoli. A book describing Nyanatiloka's life and achievements has recently been published by BPS—it is an amazing story.[9]

In an email interview published in an American Buddhist magazine,[10] Bhikkhu Bodhi explains his motivation for studying and translating the Pali Buddhist scriptures and why it became his life's work.

"During the period immediately preceding my departure for Asia and ordination as a monk in 1972, the interest in Buddhism among young Americans tended to be anti-intellectual. While most Westerners who went to Asia in quest of Theravada teachings found themselves in forest monasteries in Thailand or meditation centers in Burma, my karmic connections led me to Sri Lanka and to teachers who were steeped in the scriptures and were ready to guide a Western student eager to learn them.

"When I started to read the Pali suttas, I was exhilarated by their clarity, intellectual rigor, delicate beauty and subtle emotional fervor, which shimmers just beneath their tranquil surface. I started translating suttas and passages from the commentaries simply to make them intelligible to myself, not to publish them. In time, though, I came to see that Western Buddhism was characterized by a gaping void: lack of a clear knowledge of the Buddha's own teachings. I thus thought it extremely important that the suttas be translated in lucid, contemporary language accompanied by a body of annotations that brings out their deeper meanings and practical relevance. This to date has been my life's work.

"Many new Western Buddhists take the word practice as almost synonymous with meditation and then drive a sharp wedge between study and practice. They assume that if a monk is devoted to scholarship, he can't be a serious practitioner, as if scholarship were somehow antithetical to real practice. I have to admit that my own meditation practice has fallen far short of my ideal, but I ascribe this largely to a chronic health condition (a personal karmic obstacle with which I must deal) rather than to a dedication to scholarship and a concern to translate the Buddhist scriptures.

"We should remember that in Buddhist Asia down through the centuries, in virtually all traditions, the main task of the monastic order has been the preservation and transmission of the Buddhist teachings. This was done primarily through the intensive study, investigation and propagation of Buddhist scriptures and philosophy. This has formed the foundation stone upon which all higher achievements in Buddhist practice have rested, the skeleton that has supported the muscles and organs of Buddhism. ... What can be said unequivocally is that scholarly knowledge without practical application is barren; vigorous meditation practice without the guiding light of clear conceptual understanding is futile. Without knowledge of the texts, I fear, within a couple of generations a practice tradition will easily become diluted, chewed up and digested by the surrounding culture, especially when that culture is a theistic or a materialistic one.

"When I first began to read Buddhist texts while I was in graduate school, I was naturally impressed by the Buddha's teachings on dependent origination, the five aggregates, nonself, etc., which take us to the heart of the Dhamma. But one of the suttas that made the strongest impressions on me is not to be found among these deep texts on meditation and realization. When I read the suttas on dependent origination and nonself, I thought: the Buddha is certainly enlightened, but maybe not perfectly so. However, when I came to the Sigālaka Sutta (Dīgha Nikāya Sutta 31) my doubts were dispelled. When I read this sutta, particularly the section on 'worshipping the six directions,' and saw how one who had fathomed the deepest truths of existence could also teach in detail parents how to bring up their children, a husband and a wife how to love and respect each other, and an employer how to care for his workers, I then knew: This teacher is indeed perfectly enlightened. To my mind, this sutta showed that the Buddha possessed not only the 'ascendant wisdom' that rises up to the highest truth, but the 'descending wisdom' embraced by compassion that drops down again to the level of the world and, in the light of the fullest realization, teaches and guides others in the way that suits them best. ...

"I also want to emphasize that the suttas stem from the earliest period of Buddhist literary history and thus constitute the common heritage of the entire Buddhist tradition. So to study them is not a task solely for followers of Theravada Buddhism or of Theravada-based *vipassanā*: it is a task, indeed a responsibility, of Buddhists belonging to all schools who want to understand the taproot of Buddhism."

Shortly after his ordination, Bhikkhu Bodhi first met Venerable Nyanaponika when both were visiting the Island Hermitage for the annual Kathina ceremony. Venerable Nyanaponika was a well-known, learned senior German monk, a close disciple of Nyanatiloka Thera, and the author of the first popular book on Theravāda Buddhist mindfulness meditation in English, *The Heart of Buddhist Meditation*. He also wrote several other books which were published by the Buddhist Publication Society, of which he was the editor and president. The two monks, who were both from a Jewish background, shared a fascination for the Buddha's teachings and for conveying them accurately in the English language. Bhikkhu Bodhi had some discussions with Venerable Nyanaponika and after returning to Balangoda occasionally wrote to him to get his views about points on Dhamma. In the 1970s Venerable Nyanaponika would go to Europe each spring for a month or two and in 1974 he asked Bhikkhu Bodhi if he could come and look after the Forest Hermitage in his absence. In this way the two monks became friends. Venerable Nyanaponika played a crucial role in Bhikkhu Bodhi's spiritual development:

"My greatest inspiration in my life as a Buddhist monk has been the person who served as my mentor during my years in Sri Lanka, the German elder Venerable Nyanaponika Thera. It was his clear comprehension of the intersection between the ancient Buddhist teachings of the Pali Canon and the compelling needs of our time that gave me the perspective and sense of direction that has guided my own development as a Buddhist monk and teacher."[11]

In 1975 Bhikkhu Bodhi stayed for ten months at the Maha Bodhi Society in Bangalore, India. At Balangoda he had met an Indian monk from the Maha Bodhi Society monastery who was returning to India and had invited him to come along with him. Bhikkhu Bodhi found his stay at the Maha Bodhi Society quite inspiring because the teacher and abbot, Venerable Ācariya Buddharakkhita, spoke English very fluently, had a very good understanding and knowledge of Dhamma, and would give good Dhamma talks each week. At that time there five or six monks there, including an American and a Swedish monk, Bhikkhu Lakkhaṇa:

"At that time Bhikkhu Lakkhaṇa was very into Abhidhamma, and I was into the study of suttas. And so Ācariya Buddharakkhita had Bhikkhu Lakkhaṇa teach the Abhidhamma to all the monks and he had me teach the suttas to all the monks. Even though I didn't have much knowledge at the time, it really forced me to prepare talks on the suttas and to study the suttas carefully and learn how to explain them. Occasionally Ācariya Buddharakkhita would ask us to give the Sunday public Dhamma talk in place of himself, and that forced us to learn how to give public discourses."[12]

At the end of 1975 Bhikkhu Bodhi went back to the Forest Hermitage due to problems with getting his Indian visa renewed. He then stayed almost two years with Venerable Nyanaponika. Bhikkhu Khantipālo, a senior English Buddhist monk ordained in Thailand and author of several popular books on Buddhism, also stayed at the Forest Hermitage from April 1976 until early 1977. Venerable Nyanaponika hoped that Bhikkhu Khantipālo would take over the editorship of the BPS, but instead he worked on a compilation of discourses from Bhikkhu Ñāṇamoli's translation of the Majjhima Nikāya and then went to Australia to promote the Dhamma there.

A difficult time had arrived in Bhikkhu Bodhi's monastic life:

"When I took ordination, my parents were extremely upset with this. And they would write to me frequently, sometimes angry letters, sometimes letters of grief and sorrow, sometimes letters critical of Buddhism and of myself, sometimes letters pleading with me to go back. And so I actually decided that I wouldn't be able to continue as a monk and that I would disrobe and go back to the United States. I told this decision to Venerable Nyanaponika and he regretted it very much. But he thought that I had to make my own decisions and didn't try to compel me, though he felt that I would have been justified in continuing as a monk rather than conceding to my parent's wishes. But I felt that maybe this was necessary to do.

"I actually fixed the date that I would disrobe and was already making arrangements with my parents to get the ticket for the trip back to the United States. It was about two or three weeks away from the time I was scheduled to disrobe and one day I was sitting up in my room and was thinking that the whole purpose of my life was to live as a Buddhist monk and if I were to disrobe just to satisfy my parent's wishes it would be like nullifying all that was of value and of meaning, of significance in my own life, just to fulfill their expectations. When I told this to Venerable Nyanaponika he said 'in that case go back but go back as a monk', and I thought 'why not'.

"I went back to the United States as a monk in August 1977. When my parents, who were expecting me to come down in lay clothes, saw me coming in my saffron robes with an alms bowl on my back and the monk's umbrella in my hand, my mother said to my father, 'that's not our son, let's go' and she actually started to walk away from the airport but my father held her back and they took me home. This is what my father told me later, they had seen me before I saw them."

After staying with this parents for a short period, he went to stay at the Lamaist Buddhist Monastery in New Jersey where he studied Tibetan and Sanskrit so as to be able to study some aspects of Indian Mahayana Buddhism. From 1979 until 1982 he stayed at the Washington Buddhist Vihara in Washington D.C.

"Then I felt that I wanted to go back to Asia in order to do more intensive training and meditation. My original plan was to go to Burma and to practice meditation with Mahasi Sayadaw. ... Several years earlier, Burma started to loosen up its visa policy and they were giving long term residence visas to foreigners who would come and stay at Buddhist monasteries and meditation centers just for the purpose of practicing meditation, or studying Buddhism. And so I was hoping to ride in on that wave. But just when I started to make the application, Burma went through one of its paranoid phases and threw all the foreigners out of the country and was refusing to give any long term visas. ... Then I had to reroute my trip and so I decided to come back to Sri Lanka."[12]

In May 1982 Bhikkhu Bodhi returned to Sri Lanka. After spending several months with Venerable Nyanaponika at the Forest Hermitage, he went to stay at a renowned forest meditation monastery called Meetirigala Nissarana Vanaya. For two years he practised meditation there under the guidance of the accomplished meditation teacher Venerable Ñāṇarāma. On and off he went back to Kandy to stay with Venerable Nyanaponika, who was in his 80s and was getting quite weak. In 1984 he therefore decided to live continuously at the Forest Hermitage to help the old monk: "I felt that I should go to stay with him to look after him. About a month after I came to stay with him, he told me that he would like to pass on the editorship of the Buddhist Publication Society to me. I wasn't quite prepared to take it but I agreed to do so."

In another interview[13] Bhikkhu Bodhi relates his initial reaction to the request: "I replied: 'Bhante, I agreed to be the editor when you pass away, but at this point I don't think I'm ready.' He said, 'I'm now eighty-two and it's time I retire. I'm going to recommend you.' That night, as I lay in bed, I considered fleeing through the forest, but I couldn't leave this old monk alone in the Hermitage."

The Buddhist Publication Society (BPS) was founded in 1958 at the Forest Hermitage in Kandy, where Venerable Nyanatiloka and his pupil Venerable Nyanaponika had gone to live a few years earlier to get away from the low country heat that prevailed at the Island Hermitage. The founding of a Buddhist publication society had been an idea mooted earlier, but it was the Venerable Nyanaponika (who had already made a detailed suggestion for a Buddhist publication house in a memorandum presented at the Sixth Council in Burma in 1956),[14] and two lay persons, Mr A.S. Karunaratna and Mr Richard Abeyasekera, who made it a reality. Bhikkhu Bodhi tells the story of the founding of the BPS—on New Year's Day in 1958—in the *BPS Newsletter* that celebrated its 50th Anniversary (No. 50, 2008).

> "The idea of creating such a society first took shape in late 1957 in the mind of a prominent Kandyan lawyer, A.S. Karunaratna, a former mayor of the town. One day, while he was printing a small booklet on Buddhism to be distributed free in memory of a deceased relative, the thought occurred to him of issuing a series of such publications—small paperbound booklets in English on various aspects of the Dhamma that could be distributed throughout the world.
>
> "Karunaratna discussed this idea with his friend, a retired school master named Richard Abeyasekera, who took it up with enthusiasm. Together, they approached the German-born scholar-monk, Venerable Nyanaponika Thera, and asked him to serve as editor for this undertaking. The three constituted themselves into an informal society, with Venerable Nyanaponika as honorary secretary (later president), Karunaratna as honorary treasurer, and Abeyasekera as assistant secretary (later general secretary).
>
> "Originally the founders intended to issue only a limited series of booklets in English on basic Buddhism and then to end this venture into the publishing world. However, the formative period of the BPS coincided

with the unexpected upsurge of a world-wide interest in the Dhamma, and as this interest escalated so did the demand for authentic Buddhist literature. Thus the BPS found its first publications greeted with an enthusiastic welcome, both in Asia and the West. Encouraged by this reception, its founders abandoned their original limited aim and instead embarked on an ongoing publishing programme which still continues to grow."

As mentioned above, the BPS had by this time already published several of Bhikkhu Bodhi's Sutta translations and essays and Venerable Nyanaponika naturally considered him the most suitable candidate to take on the demanding task. In 1988, Venerable Nyanaponika resigned from the presidency of BPS and Bhikkhu Bodhi took on that mantle as well:

"I lived on constantly at the Forest Hermitage with Venerable Nyanaponika, very rarely leaving the place and looking after him quite diligently. He remained in quite good health up till the last few weeks of his life, but he was getting weaker and his eyesight had deteriorated. By about late 1989 he was not able to read anymore. So each evening we would have our evening tea and I would read to him for about one hour from various books. I would also record what I read so that later he could listen again and also tried to obtain tapes from various teachers for him to listen to."[15]

Conditions at the Forest Hermitage—an old house located in the middle of a tropical forest reserve—were not easy. There were water shortages and there was no electricity. Until 1984, when the first solar panel was installed on the roof, Venerable Nyanaponika and Bhikkhu Bodhi were working at night with kerosene lamps. They did all of their writing by hand or on an old typewriter. In the mid-nineteen nineties Bhikkhu Bodhi got his first laptop, on which he could work a few hours a day as long as the battery lasted. Scripts, messages and letters had to be carried by hand to and from the main BPS office in Kandy town. There was no telephone at the Hermitage until the late 1990s, when mobile phones became available in Sri Lanka. Nevertheless, despite the hard conditions and Bhikkhu Bodhi's health problems, the BPS flourished under his guidance, publishing a steady stream of new books in both English and Sinhala, reprinting old favourites, as well as producing some 60 booklets in both the Bodhi Leaves series and The Wheel series over the 18 years he held the position—*plus* producing the *BPS Newsletter* and writing the essays that form a large part of this small volume. At the same time, with Venerable Nyanaponika's encouragement he began working on translations of Suttas, first individual Suttas together with their commentaries and subcommentaries and then complete collections (*nikāya*) of Suttas, of which the first one was the Majjhima Nikāya.

To take up that story we need to go back several years, namely the late 1940s. After the war, an Englishman came to Sri Lanka and ordained with Venerable Nyanatiloka at the Island Hermitage. This was Venerable Ñāṇamoli. He rapidly acquired a great command of Pali and a wide knowledge of the Canon and post-canonical literature. By 1956, he had translated the entire *Visuddhimagga* into English, which is published by the BPS as *The Path of Purification*. When he died in 1960, "three thick, hand-bound notebooks containing a handwritten translation of the entire Majjhima Nikāya were found among his effects."[16] In the 1970s, another English monk, Bhikkhu Khantipālo, who had been ordained in Thailand, took Ñāṇamoli's notebooks during his stay at the Forest Hermitage and revised and arranged 90 of the 152 suttas. These were published in 1976/77 in Bangkok in three volumes under the title *A Treasury of the Buddha's Words*. In an interview[17] Bhikkhu Bodhi explains how he started translation Suttas and how the English translations of the Majjhima Nikāya came about:

"Actually the proposal for the translation of the Saṃyutta Nikāya came out even earlier than the Majjhima Nikāya. Bhikkhu Khantipālo initiated that. He felt that there was an urgent need for a new translation of the Saṃyutta Nikāya, and I had already started translating suttas from the Canon and attaching to them translations of large portions of the commentary and sub-commentary. ... I did this on the urging of Venerable Nyanaponika as he was very keen to have this done. Many years earlier he had translated large portions of the commentary and sub-commentary to the Brahmajāla Sutta, which he had kept in a notebook. I really learned very much, reading and understanding the commentaries and sub-commentaries from these notebooks of Venerable Nyanaponika. The style of the commentaries and sub-commentaries, particularly the *Ṭīkās*, can be quite difficult because the sub-commentator writes in the style of the classical Sanskrit commentator: very terse and using very complex sentences with a lot of abstract nouns linked together by various indirect cases. So it is quite a project to translate a sub-commentary. ... I first put together translations of the Brahmajāla Sutta with the commentary and sub-commentary. It is called *The Discourse on the All Embracing Net of Views*. After that I did the Mūlapariyāya Sutta and its commentary and sub-commentary, called *The Root of Existence*, then the Mahānidāna Sutta, *The Great Discourse on Causation*, and the Sāmaññaphala Sutta, *The Discourse on the Fruits of Recluseship*."[18]

Bhikkhu Khantipālo liked Bhikkhu Bodhi's translations and in 1985 proposed that he should do a new translation of the Saṃyutta Nikāya for the Pali Text Society. However, at just about that same time Wisdom Publications had written to Venerable Nyanaponika asking him whether he could make a complete translation of the Majjhima Nikāya, editing the sixty remaining discourses that Venerable Ñāṇamoli had translated and adding them to the ninety suttas that Bhikkhu Khantipālo had already done. Since Venerable Nyanaponika was in his mid-eighties he could not undertake this project, and instead asked Bhikkhu Bodhi if he would be willing to do it. In 1985 he started. With the approval of Venerable Nyanaponika, Bhikkhu Bodhi changed some of the terminology in Venerable Ñāṇamoli's translations as he felt that it was too experimental and incomprehensible to ordinary readers in English. Although he finished the work in 1989, due to the manually typed scripts having to be entered into digital format, it was only published by Wisdom Publishers in 1995 under the title *The Middle Length Discourses of the Buddha*.

When Venerable Nyanaponika passed away in 1994, Bhikkhu Bodhi wrote in the next *BPS Newsletter*: "… with the passing of Venerable Nyanaponika I have lost my life's closest friend, my teacher and spiritual guide. The last ten years, during which I had the privilege to live with him and to look after him at the Forest Hermitage, were indeed a blessing."[19]

Bhikkhu Bodhi continued to live at the Forest Hermitage until 2001. In 1989 he started on his translation of the Saṃyutta Nikāya, a task that was to take ten years. It was published as *Connected Discourses of the Buddha* by Wisdom Publications in 2000. It carries a fitting dedication to the memory of his teacher, Ānanda Maitreya Mahānāyaka Thera, and "to the memories of my chief *kalyāṇamittas* in my life as a Buddhist monk, Venerable Nyanaponika Mahāthera (1901–1994) and Venerable Piyadassi Nāyaka Thera (1914–1998)".[20] Venerable Ānanda Maitreya and Venerable Piyadassi had both passed away in 1998. Bhikkhu Bodhi has written a tribute to both of these men in his eulogy "A Time for Parting" in *BPS Newsletter* No. 40, 1998.

From 1990 until 2001 Bhikkhu Bodhi frequently gave talks at the Buddhist Publication Society. In the weekly talks he explained the Buddha's discourses from the Majjhima Nikāya. His reputation as a speaker spread. In 1995 he gave a speech called "Venerable Nyanaponika Mahāthera: German Emissary of the Dhamma in Sri Lanka" at the symposium "Wilhelm Geiger and the Study of Sri Lanka" in Colombo. His talk on the promotion of Buddhism in Europe, given at a seminar in Colombo in 2000, is included in this book as essay 52. In May 2000, at the first official Vesak celebration at the United Nations headquarters at New York, he gave the keynote address, "The Buddha and His Message: Past, Present, and Future" explaining the significance of Vesak and the relevance of the Buddha's teachings to the modern world.[21]

For a long time, from early 1977 onwards, Bhikkhu Bodhi has suffered from a chronic head pain condition for which he had not been able to find a remedy in Sri Lanka. Since the conditioned had worsened and was quite an obstruction to his work and other activities, he left Sri Lanka in June 2001 to seek a cure. He stayed in Singapore until March 2002 to undergo various medical treatments. From there he went to Germany for a few weeks to visit a neurologist recommended to him by a German Buddhist friend, then went on to the USA to visit his father. While taking a treatment from a New York headache clinic on the recommendation of his father, he decided to stay on in the USA: "Two thoughts grew increasingly compelling in my mind: first, that I should be closer to my father in his old age; and second, that I might be able to contribute more to the Dhamma here in America than in Sri Lanka."[22] He also saw that his treatment would be a slow and extended process and realized that he could obtain medical care for his condition more easily in the USA than would be possible in Sri Lanka. Earlier in the year he had already formally retired as editor for the Buddhist Publication Society, and thus he felt that he was no longer obliged to reside in Sri Lanka. During his first weeks in the U.S., he stayed in the crowded and bustling New York Buddhist Vihara, but then met by chance an old Chinese Dharma master called Jen Chun and his translator who invited him to visit their monastery in New Jersey:

"I expected it to be a busy devotional temple in a run-down urban ghetto, but to my pleasant surprise it turned out to be a serious study monastery located on quiet and spacious grounds in rural New Jersey, with wooded hills all around and herds of deer grazing on the lawns. Master Jen Chun and I took an immediate liking to each other, and he invited me to stay as long as I wish."

In July 2002 he went to stay at Bodhi Monastery. That he was a Theravāda monk was no problem:

"In ancient India it was not rare for monks of different Buddhist schools to dwell peacefully in the same monastery. I have found Master Jen Chun to be one of the most admirable monks I have ever known: vastly learned, with profound understanding of Buddhism, yet utterly simple, humble, and selfless; strict in discipline yet always bubbling with laughter and loving kindness. He is, moreover, an authority on the Āgamas, a body of literature in the Chinese Tripiṭaka that corresponds to the Pali Nikāyas. Thus I find his approach quite congruent with my own. He has asked me to give teachings at the monastery on the Pali suttas and the Pali language, and the resident monks and many lay followers are keen to attend both courses. ... The place, incidentally, is named Bodhi Monastery, but it is sheer coincidence that I wound up at a monastery that bears my name."[22]

The teacher of Master Jen Chun (1919–2011), Master Yin Shun (1906–2005) is widely regarded as the foremost Chinese scholar-monk of the past century. He was a pupil of Master Tai Hsu—a famous Chinese Buddhist monastic reformer of the early 20th century. In an interview given in 2011 Bhikkhu Bodhi tells that through his affiliation with Chinese Buddhists in the USA, he has been greatly inspired by these three masters who "emphasized what Yin Shun called 'Buddhism for the human realm,' an approach that advocates a fusion of the 'world-transcending' aspect of the Dharma with its capacity for world transformation and the ennoblement of human life in our concrete existential situation."[23]

In order to avoid administrative work and seeking more seclusion, he moved in 2007 to Chuang Yen Monastery. This Chinese Buddhist monastery is located in a woodlands area at Carmel in the beautiful and quiet Hudson River Valley in upstate New York. Here he lives in the secluded Tai Hsu Hermitage, where he continues to work on translations of the Buddha's discourses. In 2005 Wisdom Publications published his anthology of sutta passages called *In the Buddha's Words* and in 2012 a complete translation of the Aṅguttara Nikāya, entitled *The Numerical Discourses of the Buddha*. Besides giving occasional teachings at the Chuang Yen Monastery and Bodhi Monastery, he is president of the Buddhist Association of the United States.

In 2007 Bhikkhu Bodhi participated in a conference in Hamburg called "Buddhist Women's Role in the Sangha" and presented the paper "The Revival of Bhikkhunī Ordination in the Theravāda Tradition". In the paper he discusses the textual and ethical considerations that support the claim that bhikkhunī ordination should be restored, and how the ordination can best be done in accordance with the stipulations of the Vinaya. The paper has been published[24] and has received a lot of attention. He concludes:

"… the revival of a Theravāda Bhikkhunī Sangha can be seen as an intrin-sic good that conforms to the innermost spirit of the Dhamma, helping to bring to fulfillment the Buddha's own mission of opening 'the doors to the Deathless' to all humankind, to women as well as to men. At the same time, the existence of a Bhikkhunī Sangha can function as an instrumental good. It will allow women to make a meaningful contribution to Buddhism in many of the ways that monks do … and perhaps in certain ways that will be unique to female renunciants, for example, as counselors and guides to women lay followers. A Bhikkhunī Sangha will also win for Bud-dhism the respect of high-minded people in the world, who regard the absence of gender discrimination as the mark of a truly worthy religion in harmony with the noble trends of present-day civilization."

In 2007 Bhikkhu Bodhi also wrote another influential essay, "A Challenge to Buddhists" which was published in *Buddhadharma*, a popular North American Buddhist magazine. The inspiration for this essay was what Bhikkhu Bodhi regards as the overly inward focus of American Buddhism and its lack of outwards directed compassion. These are a few extracts from the essay:

"If Buddhism in the West becomes solely a means to pursue personal spiritual growth, I am apprehensive that it may evolve in a one-sided way and thus fulfill only half its potential. Attracting the affluent and the educated, it will provide a congenial home for the intellectual and cultural elite, but it will risk turning the quest for enlightenment into an private journey that, in the face of the immense suffering which daily hounds countless human lives, can present only a resigned quietism. …

"The Buddha's mission, the reason for his arising in the world, was to free beings from suffering by uprooting the evil roots of greed, hatred, and delusion. These sinister roots don't exist only in our own minds. Today they have acquired a collective dimension and have spread out over whole countries and continents. To help free beings from suffering today therefore requires that we counter the systemic embodiments of greed, hatred, and delusion.

"In each historical period, the Dharma finds new means to unfold its potentials in ways precisely linked to that era's distinctive historical conditions. I believe that our own era provides the appropriate historical stage for the transcendent truth of the dharma to bend back upon the world and engage human suffering at multiple levels—even the lowest, harshest, and most degrading levels—not in mere contemplation but in effective, relief-granting action illuminated by its own world-transcending goal.

"The special challenge facing Buddhism in our age is to stand up as an advocate for justice in the world, a voice of conscience for those victims of social, economic, and political injustice who cannot stand up and speak for themselves. This, in my view, is a deeply moral challenge marking a watershed in the modern expression of Buddhism. I believe it also points in a direction that Buddhism should take if it is to share in the Buddha's ongoing mission to humanity."

To meet the challenge, in 2008 Bhikkhu Bodhi and several of his American students set up Buddhist Global Relief, a non-profit group dedicated to supporting hunger relief, sustainable agriculture, and education in countries suffering from chronic poverty and malnutrition. He explains it as an attempt among present-day Buddhists to give concrete expression to a Buddhist sense of conscience and compassion in redressing one of the most poignant manifestations of social and economic injustice: the widespread persistence of chronic hunger and malnutrition.[26] Buddhist Global Relief is comparable to similar Christian and Jewish relief organisations that are not missionary movements aimed at proselytizing but relief organizations that provide relief and development aid to the people of the developing world regardless of race, religion, or nationality while also tackling the causes of poverty and injustice. Bhikkhu Bodhi explains:[27]

"I lived in Sri Lanka for about twenty-three years. There I observed that the Buddhist temple is the social and cultural hub of the community, and the resident monks are the ones who take the initiative in looking after the well-being of the people, regardless of religion and ethnicity. But as Buddhism is rooting itself in the U.S., I see a danger that it might become an elitist methodology for discovering inner peace, or for living happily in the here and now, at the cost of its capacity for transforming broader systemic causes of suffering. It seems to me that both the ultimate liberative goal of the Buddha's teaching, and the active compassionate application of the Dharma to the alleviation of socially caused suffering, are at risk of being pushed to the sidelines in favor of a 'feel good about yourself' version of Buddhism, or a Buddhism that functions as a mere existential psychotherapy. This risk is especially serious as Buddhism becomes integrated into mainstream American culture. Buddhist Global Relief aims to provoke a sense of what I call 'conscientious compassion', the attempt to give active expression to compassion through concrete measures aimed at alleviating real human suffering even of the most demeaning kind."

In connection with his work for Buddhist Global Relief, Bhikkhu Bodhi also tries to raise awareness about the dangers of climate change due to global warming and its underlying cause, the materialistic economical paradigm. In a recent essay called "Moving from a Culture of Death to a Culture of Life"[28] he writes:

"The distinctive mark of the dominant paradigm is the locating of all value in monetary wealth. ... The model posits the goal of the economy to be continuous growth, based on the madcap premise of infinite growth on a finite plane. ... This system flourishes by inciting in people insatiable desires for the consumption of material commodities. Its blueprint is the simple 'throughput' sequence by which resources and labor are converted into goods that are converted into monetary wealth and material waste. All these factors functioning in unison churn out the devastation we see around us, signs of a planet in peril. We're living in a world weighed down by 'the culture of death,' both literally and figuratively. Amid unimaginable luxury, almost 900 million people must endure chronic hunger and malnutrition. Easily cured diseases turn fatal. The gap between the super-rich elite and everyone else grows wider. And climate disruption claims tens of millions of lives each year. Unless we change direction fast, the final outcome could well be the collapse of human civilization as we know it. ..."

In 2009, Bhikkhu Bodhi co-authored the "Buddhist Declaration on Climate Change"—a pan-Buddhist declaration on climate change endorsed by the Dalai Lama and other Buddhist leaders.[29] In an interview[30] he tells more about the measures that he believes need to be taken:

"... Being a Buddhist committed to both a spiritual life and social justice, I believe that to preserve human civilization, we need fundamental and radical measures that strike a deeper level than mere pragmatic technological fixes to runaway greenhouse gas emissions. These would include especially the development of a universal sense of social responsibility, a commitment to ensure that people everywhere can obtain the basic requisites of survival: clean water, nutritious food, education, peaceful means of conflict resolution, and satisfactory health care. This would entail that we adopt, as a matter of national priority, a policy of generosity aimed at promoting the well-being of the entire global community. Some might balk at the expense this would involve, but in reality it would require but a mere fraction, less than 5%, of the vast expenditures we make to conduct wars and produce weaponry. ..."

Bhikkhu Bodhi's present role as a Buddhist advocate for social justice is, in a way, a fulfilment of his initial practice in the Vietnamese Mahayana tradition, enhanced by wisdom developed through his great knowledge of the Buddha's discourses that were preserved in the Sri Lankan Theravada tradition and his extensive knowledge of Western philosophy. In accordance with his own path of practice, Bhikkhu Bodhi encourages us to develop inner wisdom through understanding and practising the Buddha's message as found in the Buddha's discourses, as well as to develop compassion for others through conscientious social action. Bhikkhu Bodhi truly is a shining, modern embodiment of the universal Buddhist ideals of wisdom and compassion.

oOo

NOTES

1. The four essays specifically directed to the BPS members, such as the eulogy of Ven. Nyanaponika Thera, are not included.
2. This introduction and the following biography were written by Judy Caughley and Bhikkhu Nyanatusita.
3. All the interviews and essays are available on the internet. Included are also a few details that Bhikkhu Bodhi supplied in emails to the editor of this volume.
4. "An Interview with Ven. Bhikkhu Bodhi" by Ven. Kantasīlo, held at Wat Palelai, Singapore, on June 20, 2001.
5. Published in *Parabola Magazine*, Winter 2009. Available at bodhimonastery.org.
6. "An Interview with Ven. Bhikkhu Bodhi" by Ven. Kantasīlo, 2001.
7. "Climbing to the Top of the Mountain: An interview with Bhikkhu Bodhi" *Insight Journal* Vol. 19, fall 2002.
8. "An Interview with Ven. Bhikkhu Bodhi" by Ven. Kantasīlo.
9. Bhikkhu Nyanatusita and Hellmuth Hecker, *The Life of Ñāṇatiloka Thera: The Biography of a Western Buddhist Pioneer,* BPS, Kandy, 2009.
10. "Translator for the Buddha: An Interview with Bhikkhu Bodhi", *Inquiring Mind,* 2006.
11. "Interview with Ven. Bhikkhu Bodhi" by Maia, Sept. 2011. at jizochronicles.com.
12. "An Interview with Ven. Bhikkhu Bodhi" by Ven. Kantasīlo, 2001.
13. In "Profile: Buddhist Publication Society", *Buddhadharma* 2010.
14. See Bhikkhu Nyanatusita and Hellmuth Hecker, *The Life of Ñāṇatiloka Thera: The Biography of a Western Buddhist Pioneer,* BPS, Kandy, 2009: 248–250.
15. "An Interview with Ven. Bhikkhu Bodhi" by Ven. Kantasīlo, 2001.
16. Bhikkhu Ñāṇamoli and Bhikkhu Bodhi, *The Middle Length Discourses of the Buddha*, Wisdom Publications, Boston 1995.
17. "Translator for the Buddha: An Interview with Bhikkhu Bodhi", *Inquiring Mind,* 2006.
18. These works were first published by the BPS in 1978, 1980, 1984, 1989.
19. *BPS Newsletter* No. 28, 3rd mailing 1994. Available at www.bps.lk.
20. Bhikkhu Bodhi, *The Connected Discourses of the Buddha*, Boston 2000.
21. Available from the BPS in printed as well as digital format (www.bps.lk).
22. "Climbing to the Top of the Mountain" *Insight Journal* Vol. 19, fall 2002.
23. "Interview with Ven. Bhikkhu Bodhi" by Maia, Sept. 2011, at jizochronicles.com.
24. It was published as a book in Penang 2009. It was also published in *Dignity and Discipline: Reviving Full Ordination for Buddhist Nuns*, Boston 2010.
25. "Conscientious Compassion", *Helping Hands*, Volume 1, No. 2, Summer 2009.
26. "Bhikkhu Bodhi: The Elephant Journal Interview" by Rev. Danny Fisher, 2010.
27. *Helping Hands*, Volume 6, No. 3, Fall 2014.
28. Available at www.ecobuddhism.org/bcp/all_content/buddhist_declaration.
29. "Bhikkhu Bodhi: The Elephant Journal Interview" by Rev. Danny Fisher, 2010.

COLLECTED ESSAYS OF BHIKKHU BODHI

1. THE TASTE OF FREEDOM

The clarion call of our present age is, without doubt, the call for freedom. Perhaps at no time in the past history of mankind so much as at present has the cry for freedom sounded so widely and so urgently, perhaps never before has it penetrated so deeply into the fabric of human existence.

In response to man's quest for freedom, far-reaching changes have been wrought in almost every sphere of his activity—political, social, cultural and religious. The vast empires which once sprawled over the earth, engulfing like huge mythical sea-monsters the continents in their grasp, have crumbled away and disintegrated, as the peoples over whom they reigned have risen up to repossess their native lands—in the name of independence, liberty and self-rule.

Old political forms such as monarchy and oligarchy have given way to democracy—government by the people—because every man demands the right to contribute his voice to the direction of his collective life. Long-standing social institutions which kept man enthralled since before the dawn of history—slavery, serfdom, the caste-system—have now disappeared, or are rapidly disappearing, while accounts of liberation movements of one sort or another daily deck the headlines of our newspapers and crowd the pages of our popular journals.

The arts, too, bear testimony to this quest for greater freedom: free verse in poetry, abstract expression in painting and atonal composition in music are just a few of the innovations which have toppled restrictive traditional structures to give the artist open space in his drive for self-expression. Even religion has not been able to claim immunity from this expanding frontier of liberation. No longer can systems of belief and codes of conduct justify themselves, as in the past, on the grounds that they are commanded by God, sanctified by scripture or prescribed by the priesthood. They must now be prepared to stand out in the open, shorn of their veils of sanctity, exposed to the critical thrust of the contemporary thinker who assumes for himself the right to free inquiry and takes his own reason and experience for his court of final appeal. Freedom of speech, freedom of the press and freedom of action have become the watchwords of our public life, freedom of thought and freedom of conscience the watchwords of our private life. In any form in which it obtains, freedom is guarded as our most precious possession, more valuable than life itself. "Give me liberty or give me death," an American patriot exclaimed two hundred years ago. The succeeding centuries have echoed his demand.

As though in response to mankind's call for wider frontiers of freedom, the Buddha offers to the world his Teaching, the Dhamma, as a pathway to liberation as applicable today as it was when first proclaimed twenty-five centuries ago.

"Just as in the great ocean there is but one taste—the taste of salt—so in this Doctrine and Discipline *(dhammavinaya)* there is but one taste—the taste of freedom": with these words the Buddha vouches for the emancipating quality of his doctrine.

Whether one samples water taken from the surface of the ocean, or from its middling region, or from its depths, the taste of the water is in every case the same—the taste of salt. And again, whether one drinks but a thimble-full of ocean water, or a glass-full, or a bucket-full, the same salty taste is present throughout. Analogously with the Buddha's Teaching, a single flavour—the flavour of freedom *(vimuttirasa)*—pervades the entire Doctrine and Discipline, from its beginning to its end, from its gentle surface to its unfathomable depths. Whether one samples the Dhamma at its more elementary level—in the practice of generosity and moral discipline, in acts of devotion and piety, in conduct governed by reverence, courtesy, and loving-kindness—or at its intermediate level in the taintless supramundane knowledge and deliverance realized by the liberated saint, in every case the taste is the same—the taste of freedom.

If one practises the Dhamma to a limited extent, leading a household life in accordance with righteous principles, then one experiences in return a limited measure of freedom; if one practices the Dhamma to a fuller extent, going forth into the homeless state of monkhood, dwelling in seclusion adorned with the virtues of a recluse, contemplating the rise and fall of all conditioned things, then one experiences a fuller measure of freedom; and if one practices the Dhamma to its consummation, realising in this present life the goal of final deliverance, then one experiences a freedom that is measureless.

At every level the flavour of the Teaching is of a single nature, the flavour of freedom. It is only the degree to which this flavour is enjoyed that differs, and the difference in degree is precisely proportional to the extent of one's practice. Practise a little Dhamma and one reaps a little freedom, practise abundant Dhamma and one reaps abundant freedom. The Dhamma brings its own reward of freedom, always with the exactness of scientific law.

Since the Dhamma proposes to provide a freedom as complete and perfect as any the modern world might envisage, a fundamental congruence appears to obtain between man's aspiration for expanding horizons of liberty and the possibilities he might realize through the practice of the Buddha's Teaching. Nevertheless, despite this concordance of ends, when our contemporaries first encounter the Dhamma they often find themselves confronted at the outset by one particular feature which, clashing with their familiar modes of thought, strikes them intellectually as a contradiction and emotionally as a stumbling block. This is the fact that while the Dhamma purports to be a pathway to liberation, a Teaching pervaded throughout by 'the taste of freedom,' it yet requires from its followers the practice of a regimen that seems the very antithesis of freedom—a regimen built upon discipline, restraint and self-control. "On the one hand we seek freedom," our contemporaries object, "and on the other we are told that to reach this freedom, our deeds, words and thoughts must be curbed and controlled." What are we to make of this astonishing thesis the Buddha's Teaching appears to advance: that to achieve freedom, freedom must be curtailed? Can freedom as an end really be achieved by means that involve the very denial of freedom?

The solution to this seeming paradox lies in the distinction between two kinds of freedom—between freedom as license and freedom as spiritual autonomy. Contemporary man, for the most part, identifies freedom with license. For him, freedom means the license to pursue unhindered his impulses, passions and whims. To be free, he believes, he must be at liberty to do whatever he wants, to say whatever he wants and to think whatever he wants. Every restriction laid upon this license he sees as an encroachment upon his freedom; hence a practical regimen calling for restraint of deed, word and thought, for discipline and self-control, strikes him as a form of bondage. But the freedom spoken of in the Buddha's Teaching is not the same as license. The freedom to which the Buddha points is spiritual freedom—an inward autonomy of the mind which follows upon the destruction of the defilements, manifests itself in an emancipation from the mould of impulsive and compulsive patterns of behaviour, and culminates in final deliverance from *saṃsāra*, the round of repeated birth and death.

In contrast to license, spiritual freedom cannot be acquired by external means. It can only be attained inwardly, through a course of training requiring the renunciation of passion and impulse in the interest of a higher end. The spiritual autonomy that emerges from this struggle is the ultimate triumph over all confinement and self-limitation; but the victory can never be achieved without conforming to the requirements of the contest—requirements that include restraint, control, discipline and, as the final price, the surrender of self-assertive desire.

In order to bring this notion of freedom into clearer focus, let us approach it via its opposite condition, the state of bondage, and begin by considering a case of extreme physical confinement. Suppose there is a man locked away in a prison, in a cell with dense stone walls and sturdy steel bars. He is tied to a chair—his wrists bound together by rope behind his back, his feet locked in shackles, his eyes covered by a blindfold and his mouth by a gag. Suppose that one day the rope is unfastened, the shackles loosened, the blindfold and gag removed. Now the man is at liberty to move about the cell, to stretch his limbs, to speak, and to see. But though at first he might imagine that he is free, it would not take him long to realize that true freedom is still as distant as the clear blue sky beyond the stone walls and steel bars of his cell.

But suppose, next, that we release the man from prison, set him up as a middle-class householder, and restore to him his full body of rights as a citizen of the state. Now he can enjoy the social and political freedom he lacked as a prisoner; he can vote, work and travel as he likes; he can even hold public office. But there still remains—in the form of his responsibilities, his burden of duties, his limitations of power, pleasure and prestige—a painful discrepancy between the freedom of license for which he might personally yearn, and the actuality of the situation which circumstances has doled out to him as his drearisome lot. So let us, as a further step, lift our man up from this middle-class routine, and install him, to his pleasant surprise upon the throne of a world monarch, a universal emperor exercising sovereignty over all the earth. Let us place him in a magnificent palace, surrounded by a hundred wives more beautiful than lotus-flowers, possessed of limitless resources of gold, land and gems, endowed with the most sublime pleasures of the five senses. All power is his, all enjoyment, fame, glory and wealth. He needs only express his will for it to be taken as command, need only utter a wish for it to be translated into deed. No obstruction to his freedom of license remains. But still the question stands: is he truly free? Let us consider the issue at a deeper level.

Three kinds of feeling have been pointed out by the Buddha: pleasant feeling, painful feeling and neutral feeling (i.e., feeling which is neither pleasant nor painful). These three classes exhaust the totality of feeling, and one feeling of one class must be present on any given occasion of experience. Again, three mental factors have been singled out by the Buddha as the subjective counterparts of the three classes of feeling and described by him as *anusaya*, latent tendencies which have been lying dormant in the subconscious mental continua of sentient beings since beginningless time, always ready to crop up into a state of manifestation when an appropriate stimulus is encountered, and to subside again into the state of dormancy when the impact of the stimulus has worn off. These three mental factors are lust (*rāga*), repugnance (*paṭigha*), and ignorance (*avijjā*), psychological equivalents of the unwholesome roots of greed (*lobha*), hatred (*dosa*), and delusion (*moha*).

When a worldling, with a mind untrained in the higher course of mental discipline taught by the Buddha, experiences a pleasant feeling, then the latent tendency to lust springs up in response—a desire to possess and enjoy the object serving as stimulus for the pleasant feeling. When a worldling experiences a painful feeling, then the latent tendency to repugnance comes into play, an aversion toward the cause of the pain. And when a worldling experiences a neutral feeling, then the latent tendency to ignorance—present but recessive on occasions of lust and aversion—rises to prominence, shrouding the worldling's consciousness in a cloak of dull apathy.

On whatever occasion the three latent tendencies to lust, repugnance and ignorance are provoked by their corresponding feelings from their dormant condition into a state of activity, if a man does not make an effort to dispel them, does not strive to restrain, remove and abandon them and bring them to nought, then they will persist in consciousness. If, as they persist in consciousness, he repeatedly yields to them, endorses them and continues to cling to them, they will gather momentum, come to growth, and like a ball of flame flung upon a haystack, flare up from their initial phase as feeble impulses into powerful obsessions which usurp from a man his capacity for self-control. Then, even if a man be like our hypothetical subject, an emperor over the earth, he is inwardly no longer his own master but a servant at the bidding of his own defilements of mind.

Under the dominance of lust he is drawn to the pleasant, under the dominance of hate he is repelled by the painful, under the dominance of delusion he is confused by the neutral. He is bent up by happiness, bent down by sorrow, elated by gain, honour, and praise, dejected by loss, dishonour, and blame. Even though he perceives that a particular course of action can lead only to his harm, he is powerless to avoid it; even though he knows that an alternative course of action is clearly to his advantage, he is unable to pursue it. Swept on by the current of unabandoned defilements, he is driven from existence to existence through the ocean of *saṃsāra*, with its waves of birth and death, its whirlpools of misery and despair. Outwardly, he may be a ruler over all the world, but in the court of consciousness he is still a prisoner. In terms of license he may be completely free, but in terms of spiritual autonomy he remains a victim of bondage in its most desperate form: bondage to the workings of a defiled mind.

Spiritual freedom, as the opposite of this condition of bondage, must therefore mean freedom from lust, hatred and delusion. When lust, hatred and delusion are abandoned in a man, cut off at the root so that they no longer remain even in latent form, then a man finds for himself a seat of autonomy from which he can never be dethroned, a position of mastery from which he can never be shaken. Even though he be a mendicant gathering his alms from house to house, he is still a king; even though he be locked behind bars of steel, he is inwardly free. He is now sovereign over his own mind, and as such over the whole universe; for nothing in the universe can take from him that deliverance of heart which is his inalienable possession. He dwells in the world among the things of the world, yet stands in perfect poise above the world's ebb and flow. If pleasant objects come within range of his perception he does not yearn for them, if painful objects come into range he does not recoil from them. He looks upon both with equanimity and notes their rise and fall. Toward the pairs of opposites which keep the world in rotation he is without concern, the cycle of attraction and repulsion he has broken at its base. A lump of gold and a lump of clay are to his eyes the same; praise and scorn are to his ears empty sounds. He abides in the freedom he has won through long and disciplined effort. He is free from suffering, for with the defilements uprooted no more can sorrow or grief fall upon his heart; there remains only that perfect bliss unsullied by any trace of craving.

He is free from fear, from the chill of anxiety which even kings know in their palaces, protected by bodyguards inside and out. And he is free from disease, from the sickness of the passions, vexing and feverish, that tie the mind in knots, from the sickness of *saṃsāra* with its rounds of defilement, action and result. He passes his days in peace, pervading the world with a mind of boundless compassion, enjoying the bliss of emancipation or teaching fellow wayfarers the path he himself has followed to the goal, in the calm certain knowledge that for him the beginningless trail of repeated births and deaths has been brought to a close, that he has reached the pinnacle of holiness and effected the cessation of all future becoming.

In its fullness, the freedom to which the Buddha points as the goal of his Teaching can only be enjoyed by him who has made the realization of the goal a matter of his own living experience. But just as salt lends its taste to whatever food it is used to season, so does the taste of freedom pervade the entire range of the Doctrine and Discipline proclaimed by the Buddha, its beginning, its middle and its end. Whatever our degree of progress may be in the practice of the Dhamma, to that extent may the taste of freedom be enjoyed. It must always be borne in mind, however, that true freedom—the inward autonomy of the mind—does not descend as a gift of grace. It can only be won by the practice of the path to freedom, the Noble Eightfold Path.

From Bodhi Leaves No. 71; first published in 1976.

2. Nourishing the Roots

The course of spiritual training taught by the Buddha is a double process of self-transformation and self-transcendence issuing in complete emancipation from suffering. The process of self-transformation involves the elimination of unwholesome mental dispositions and their replacement by pure dispositions conducing to the benefit of oneself and others; the process of self-transcendence focuses on the abandoning of egocentric notions by seeing with direct insight the essenceless nature of the bodily and mental processes we normally take to be 'I' and 'mine.' When this double process is brought to its culmination, suffering is extinguished, for with the awakening of wisdom the basic root of suffering—craving backed by blinding ignorance—falls away never to rise again.

Because the unwholesome tendencies and selfish clinging spring from seeds buried deep in the bottom-most strata of the mind, to eradicate these sources of affliction and nurture the growth of the liberating vision of reality the Buddha presents his teaching in the form of a gradual training. Buddhist discipline involves gradual practice and gradual attainment. It does not burst into completeness at a stroke, but like a tree or any other living organism, it unfolds organically, as a sequence of stages in which each stage rests upon its predecessor as its indispensable foundation and gives rise to its successor as its natural consequent. The principal stages of this gradual training are three: the training in *sīla* or virtue, the training in *samādhi* or concentration, and the training in *paññā* or wisdom. If we follow through the comparison of the Buddhist discipline to a tree, faith *(saddhā)* would be the seed, for it is faith that provides the initial impulse through which the training is taken up, and faith again that nourishes the training through every phase of its development. Virtue would be the roots, for it is virtue that gives grounding to our spiritual endeavours just as the roots give grounding to a tree. Concentration would be the trunk, the symbol of strength, non-vacillation, and stability. And wisdom would be the branches, which yield the flowers of enlightenment and the fruits of deliverance.

The vigour of the spiritual life, like the vigour of a tree, depends upon healthy roots. Just as a tree with weak and shallow roots cannot flourish but will grow up stunted, withered and barren, so a spiritual life devoid of strong roots will also have a stunted growth incapable of bearing fruit. To attempt to scale the higher stages of the path it is essential at the outset to nourish the proper roots of the path; otherwise the result will be frustration, disillusionment, and perhaps even danger. The roots of the path are the constituents of *sīla*, the factors of moral virtue. These are the basis for meditation, the ground for all wisdom and higher achievement.

To say that *sīla* is the precondition for success, however, does not mean, as is too often believed in conservative Buddhist circles, that one cannot begin to meditate until one's *sīla* is perfect. Such a stipulation would make it almost impossible to start meditation, since it is the mindfulness, concentration, and wisdom of the meditative process that bring about the gradual purification of virtue. But to say that virtue is the basis of practice does mean that the capacity for achievement in meditation hinges upon the purity of our *sīla*. If our roots of virtue are weak, our meditation will likewise be weak. If our actions repeatedly clash with the basic principles of right conduct, our attempts to control the mind in the discipline of meditation will turn into a self-defeating enterprise, since the springs of our conduct will be the same defiled states of mind the meditation is intended to eliminate.

Only when we secure our cultivation upon the foundation of blameless principles of right action can the inward endeavour of meditation prosper and issue in success. With true principles of conduct as the base, the roots of virtue will give birth to the trunk of concentration, the concentrated mind shoot forth the branches of wisdom, and the branches of wisdom yield the flowers and fruits of enlightenment, culminating in total freedom from bondage. Therefore, just as a skilful gardener brings a sapling to growth by first tending to the roots, so the earnest seeker of enlightenment should begin his cultivation by tending to the roots of his practice—that is, to his *sīla* or moral virtue.

The Pāli word *sīla* originally meant simply conduct. But in the context of the Buddhist spiritual training the term is used to signify only a specific kind of conduct, i.e., good conduct, and by an extension of meaning, the type of character for which such conduct stands, i.e., good character. Hence *sīla* means both moral conduct, a body of habits governed by moral principles, and moral virtue, the interior quality the regular observance of these principles is intended to produce.

Both shades of meaning are essential to understand the place of *sīla* in the spectrum of Buddhist discipline. *Sīla* in the former sense consists in the non-transgression through body or speech of the basic precepts regulating the moral life. It is moral discipline in deed and word, beginning as the inhibition of immoral impulses seeking an outlet through body and speech, and developing into the habitual conformation to the principles of righteous conduct. But the full range of *sīla* is not exhausted by mere outward behavioural control, for the term has in addition a deeper, more psychological significance. In this second sense *sīla* is moral purity, the inner purification of character which results from a life consistently moulded upon moral principles. This aspect of *sīla* places the stress on the subjective, motivational side of action. It looks not towards the outward act itself, but towards the rectitude of mind from which good conduct springs.

Upon inspection *sīla* thus reveals itself to be a two- dimensional quality: it contains an external dimension consisting in purification of conduct, and an internal dimension consisting in purification of character. However, in the Teaching of the Buddha, these two dimensions of experience, the internal and the external, are not torn apart and consigned to separate, self-sufficient domains. They are recognized, rather, to be two facets of a single whole, complementary poles of a unified field which mirror one another, implicate one another, and penetrate one another with their own respective potentialities of influence. Actions performed by body and speech are not, from the Buddhist standpoint, so many detachable appendages of a distinct spiritual essence, but concrete revelations of the states of mind which stand behind them as their activating source. And states of mind, in turn, do not remain closed up in a purely mental isolation, but spill forth according to the play of circumstances from the fountain of consciousness where they arise, through the channels of body, speech and thought, out into the world of inter-personally significant events. From the action we can infer the state of mind, and from the state of mind we can predict the probable course of action. The relationship between the two is as integral as that between a musical score and its orchestrated performance on the concert stage.

Because of this mutual dependence of the two domains, moral conduct and purity of character lock up with one another in a subtle and complex interrelationship. The fulfilment of the purification of virtue requires that both aspects of *sīla* be realized: on the one side, behaviour of body and speech must be brought into accord with the moral ideal; on the other, the mental disposition must be cleansed of its corruptions until it is impeccably pure. The former without the latter is insufficient; the latter without the former is impossible. Between the two, the internal aspect is the more important from the standpoint of spiritual development, since bodily and verbal deeds acquire ethical significance primarily as expressions of a corresponding disposition of mind. In the sequence of spiritual training, however, it is moral discipline that comes first. For at the beginning of training, purification of character stands as an ideal which must be reached; it is not a reality with which one can start.

According to the Buddhist principle of conditionality, the actualization of any given state is only possible through the actualization of its appropriate conditions, and this applies as much to the achievement of the various stages of the training as to the bare phenomena of matter and mind. Since beginningless time the consciousness-continuum has been corrupted by the unwholesome roots of greed, hatred and delusion; it is these defilements which have functioned as the source for the greatest number of our thoughts, the ground for our habits, and the springs for our actions and general orientation towards other people and the world as a whole. To uproot these defiling afflictions at a single stroke and reach the peak of spiritual perfection by a mere act of will is a well-near impossible task. A realistic system of spiritual training must work with the raw material of human nature; it cannot rest content merely with postulated paragons of human excellence or demands for achievement without showing the method by which such demands can be realized.

The Buddha rests his teaching upon the thesis that with the right method we have the capacity to change and transform ourselves. We are not doomed to be for ever burdened by the weight of accumulated tendencies, but through our own effort we can cast off all these tendencies and attain a condition of complete purity and freedom. When given the proper means in the context of right understanding, we can bring about radical alterations in the workings of consciousness and mould a new shape out of the seemingly immutable stuff of our own minds.

The first step on this path is the purification of character, and the efficient means for the restructuring of character the Buddha provides in the observance of *sīla* as a set of precepts regulating bodily and verbal conduct. *Sīla* as moral discipline, in other words, becomes the means for inducing *sīla* as moral virtue. The effectiveness of this measure stems from the reciprocal interlocking of the internal and external spheres of experience already referred to. Because the inner and outer domains are mutually implicated, the one can become the means for producing deep and lasting changes in the other. Just as a state of mind expresses itself outwardly in an action—in deed or speech—so too the avoidance and performance of certain actions can recoil upon the mind and alter the basic disposition of the mental life. If mental states dominated by greed and hatred can engender deeds of killing, stealing, lying, etc., then the abstinence on principle from killing, stealing and lying can engender a mental disposition towards kindliness, contentment, honesty and truthfulness. Thus, although *sīla* as moral purity may not be the starting point of spiritual training, conformity to righteous standards of conduct can make it an attainable end.

The medium which bridges the two dimensions of *sīla*, facilitating the translation of outward behaviour into inner purity, is volition or *cetanā*. Volition is a mental factor common to every occasion of experience, a universal concomitant of every act of consciousness. It is the factor which makes experience teleological, i.e., oriented to a goal, since its specific function is to direct its associated factors towards the attainment of a particular end. All action *(kamma)*, the Buddha teaches, is in essence volition, for the act itself is from the ultimate standpoint a manifestation of volition through one of the three doors of action—body, speech or mind: "It is volition, bhikkhus, that I call action. For having willed, one performs an action through body, speech, or mind."

Volition determines an action as being of a definite sort, and thence imparts to action its moral significance. But since volition is invariably present in every state of consciousness, it is in its own nature without ethical distinctiveness. Volition acquires its distinctive ethical quality from certain other mental factors known as roots (*mūla*), in association with which it always arises on occasions of active experience. Roots are of two morally determinate kinds: unwholesome (*akusala*) and wholesome (*kusala*). The unwholesome roots are greed, hatred and delusion; the wholesome roots are non-greed, non-hatred and non-delusion. These latter, though expressed negatively, signify not merely the absence of the defiling factors, but the presence of positive moral qualities as well; generosity, loving-kindness and wisdom, respectively.

When volition is driven by the unwholesome roots of greed, hatred and delusion, it breaks out through the doors of the body and speech in the form of evil deeds—as killing, stealing and fornication, as lying, slander, harsh speech and gossip. In this way the inner world of mental defilement darkens the outer world of spatio-temporal extension. But the defiled trend of volitional movement, though strong, is not irrevocable. Unwholesome volition can be supplanted by wholesome volition, and thence the entire disposition of the mental life made subject to a reversal at its foundation. This redirecting of volition is initiated by voluntarily undertaking the observance of principles of conduct belonging to a righteous order—by willing to abstain from evil and to practise the good. Then, when volition tending to break out as evil action is restrained and replaced by volition of the opposite kind, by the will to behave virtuously in word and deed, a process of reversal will have been started which, if followed through, can produce far-reaching alterations in the moral tone of character. For acts of volition do not spend their full force in their immediate exercise, but rebound upon the mental current which gave birth to them, re-orienting that current in the direction towards which they point as their own immanent tendency: the unwholesome volitions towards moral depravation, and the wholesome volitions towards moral purification. Each time, therefore, an unwholesome volition is supplanted by its wholesome opposite, the will to the good is strengthened.

A process of factor substitution, built upon the law that incompatible mental qualities cannot be simultaneously present on a single occasion of experience, then completes the transformation through the efficacy of the associated roots. Just as unwholesome volitions invariably arise in association with the unwholesome roots—with greed, hatred and delusion—so do wholesome volitions inevitably bring along with them as their concomitants the wholesome roots of non-greed, non-hatred and non-delusion. Since opposite qualities cannot co-exist, the replacement of unwholesome volition by wholesome volition at the same time means the transposition of the unwholesome and the wholesome roots. Continually called into play by the surge of volition, the wholesome roots "perfume" the mental stream with the qualities for which they stand—with generosity, loving-kindness and wisdom; and these, as they gather cumulative force, come to prominence as regular propensities of the personality, eclipsing the inclination towards the unwholesome. In this way the exercise of wholesome volitions on repeated and varied occasions effects a transformation of character from its initial moral susceptibility to a pitch of purity where even the temptation to evil remains at a safe remove.

Though volition or *cetanā* is the primary instrument of change, the will in itself is indeterminate, and requires specific guidelines to direct its energy towards the actualization of the good. A mere 'good will,' from the Buddhist standpoint, is altogether inadequate, for despite the nobility of the intention, as long as the intelligence of the agent is clouded with the dust of delusion, the possibility always lies open that laudable motives might express themselves in foolish or even destructive courses of action. This has been the case often enough in the past, and still stands as the perennial bugbear of the ethical generalist. According to the Buddhist outlook, goodness of will must be translated into concrete courses of action. It must be regulated by specific principles of right conduct, principles which, though flexible in their application, possess normative validity independently of any historical culture or existing scheme of values, entirely by virtue of their relation to a universal law of moral retribution and their place in the timeless path of practice leading to deliverance from suffering and the saṃsāric round.

To guide the will in its aspiration for the good, the Buddha has prescribed in definite and lucid terms the factors of moral training which must be fulfilled to safeguard progress along the path to enlightenment. These factors are comprised in the three items which make up the aggregate of virtue in the Noble Eightfold Path: namely, right speech, right action, and right livelihood. Right speech is the avoidance of all harmful forms of speech—the abstinence from falsehood, slander, harsh speech and idle chatter. The speech of the aspirant must be constantly truthful, conducive to harmony, gentle and meaningful. Right action applies a brake upon unwholesome bodily action, by prescribing abstinence from the destruction of life, from stealing, and from sexual misconduct; the latter means incelibacy in the case of monks, and adultery and other illicit relations in the case of householders. The behaviour of the aspirant must always be compassionate, honest and pure. And right livelihood requires the avoidance of trades which inflict harm and suffering upon other living beings, such as dealing in meat, slaves, weapons, poisons and intoxicants. Avoiding such harmful trades, the noble disciple earns his living by a peaceful and righteous occupation.

The training factors embedded in these components of the Noble Eightfold Path simultaneously inhibit the base, ignoble and destructive impulses of the human mind and promote the performance of whatever is noble and pure. Though worded negatively, in terms of the types of conduct they are intended to shut out, they are positive in effect, for when adopted as guidelines to action, they stimulate the growth of healthy mental attitudes which come to expression as beneficent courses of conduct. Intensively, these training rules reach into the recesses of the mind, blunt the force of unwholesome volition, and redirect the will to the attainment of the good. Extensively, they reach into the commotion of man's social existence, and arrest the tide of competition, exploitation, grasping, violence and war. In their psychological dimension they confer mental health, in their social dimension they promote peace, in their spiritual dimension they serve as the irreplaceable foundation for all higher progress along the path to emancipation. Regularly undertaken and put into practice, they check all mental states rooted in greed, hatred and delusion, promote actions rooted in non-greed, non-hatred and non-delusion, and lead to a life of charity, love and wisdom.

From this it will be seen that from the Buddhist point of view formulated rules of conduct are not superfluous accessories to a good will, but necessary guidelines to right action. They are an essential part of the training, and when implemented by the force of volition, become a fundamental means to purification. Especially in the context of the practice of meditation, the training precepts prevent the eruption of defiled actions destructive to the purpose of the meditative discipline. By following carefully the prescribed rules of conduct, we can rest assured that we are avoiding at least the coarser expressions of greed, hatred and delusion, and that we will not have to face the obstacle of guilt, anxiety and restlessness that comes in the trail of regular moral transgressions.

If we return to our earlier comparison of the Buddhist discipline to a tree, and take virtue to be the roots, then the principles of right conduct become the soil in which the roots grow. Just as the soil contains the nutritive essences required for the tree to sprout and flourish, so do the precepts contain the nutriment of purity and virtue required for the growth of the spiritual life. The precepts embody the natural conduct of the arahant or perfected saint. For the arahant, his conduct flows outward as the spontaneous expression of his innate purity. By his very nature, all his deeds are flawless, free from blemish. He cannot follow any course of action motivated by desire, ill will, delusion or fear—not through any forced conformity to rules, but by the very law of his being.

The worldling, however, is not immune from the possibility of immoral conduct. To the contrary, because the unwholesome roots remain firmly planted in the makeup of his mind, he is constantly prone to the temptation to moral transgression. He is liable to kill, steal, commit adultery, lie, drink, etc.; and in the absence of any sound moral code prohibiting such actions, he will often succumb to these liabilities. Hence the necessity of providing him with a set of ethical principles built upon the pillars of wisdom and compassion, by which he can regulate his actions and conform to the natural, spontaneous behaviour of the Liberated One.

A precept is, therefore, from the Buddhist perspective much more than a prohibition imposed upon conduct from without. Each precept is a tangible expression of a corresponding attitude of mind, a principle which clothes in the form of concrete action a beam of the light of inward purity. The precepts render visible the invisible state of purification. They make it accessible to us by refracting it through the media of body and speech into specific rules of conduct we can apply as guides to action when we find ourselves in the diverse situations they are designed to cover. By bringing our conduct into harmony with the precepts, we can nourish the root of our spiritual endeavours, our virtue. And when virtue is made secure, the succeeding stages of the path unfold spontaneously through the law of the spiritual life, culminating at the crest in the perfection of knowledge and the serene azure of deliverance. As the Master says:

> "For one who is virtuous, bhikkhus, endowed with virtue, no deliberate volition need be exerted: "Let freedom from remorse arise in me." This is the natural law, bhikkhus, that freedom from remorse arises in one who is virtuous, endowed with virtue.
>
> "For one who is free from remorse, no deliberate volition need be exerted: "Let gladness arise in me." This is the natural law, bhikkhus, that gladness arises in one free from remorse.
>
> "For one who is gladdened, no deliberate volition need be exerted: "Let rapture arise in me." This is the natural law, bhikkhus, that rapture arises in one who is gladdened.
>
> "For one filled with rapture, no deliberate volition need be exerted: "Let my body become tranquil." This is the natural law, bhikkhus, that for one filled with rapture the body becomes tranquil.
>
> "For one tranquil in body, no deliberate volition need be exerted: "May I experience bliss." This is the natural law, bhikkhus, that one tranquil in body experiences bliss.
>
> "For one who is blissful, no deliberate volition need be exerted: "Let my mind become concentrated." This is the natural law, bhikkhus, that for one who is blissful the mind becomes concentrated.

"For one who is concentrated, no deliberate volition need be exerted: "May I know and see things as they really are." This is the natural law, bhikkhus, that one who is concentrated knows and sees things as they really are.

"For one knowing and seeing things as they really are, no deliberate volition need be exerted: "May I become disenchanted and dispassionate." This is the natural law, bhikkhus, that one knowing and seeing things as they really are becomes disenchanted and dispassionate.

"For one who has become disenchanted and dispassionate, no deliberate volition need be exerted: "May I realize the knowledge and vision of deliverance." This is the natural law, bhikkhus, that one who is disenchanted and dispassionate realizes the knowledge and vision of deliverance...

"Thus, bhikkhus, one stage flows into the succeeding stage, one stage comes to fulfilment in the succeeding stage, for crossing over from the hither shore to the beyond."

Aṅguttara Nikāya 10:2

From Nourishing the Roots: Essays on Buddhist Ethics, *Wheel Publications No. 259–260, first published in 1978.*

3. MIND AND THE ANIMATE ORDER

As we cast our gaze out upon the landscape of animate nature, it does not take long before our attention is struck by the tremendous diversity of forms the animate order displays. The folds of nature's lap, we find, teem with a multitude of living beings as staggering in their range of specific differentiation as in the sheer impression of their quantitative force. Before our eyes countless varieties of creatures—insects and reptiles, fish and birds, mammals domestic and wild—turn the earth with its seas and skies into a complex metropolis, throbbing with the pulse of sentient life. But realms of being beyond sight—vouched for by spiritual cosmology, folklore and the reports of seers—are no less crowded, and no less diversified in their composition. According to this testimony, gods, Brahmas, angels and demons populate boroughs of the city of life invisible to fleshly eyes, while other creatures, such as fairies, ghosts and goblins, fill up unfamiliar pockets of the same borough.

The human world, again, is itself far from homogeneous. The family of man breaks down into a great diversity of types—into people black, white, brown, yellow and red, dividing still further, according to their fortunes and faculties, into the long-lived and the short-lived, the healthy and the sickly, the successful and the failures, the gifted and the deprived. Some people are intelligent, others are dull-witted, some are noble, others ignoble, some are spiritually evolved, others spiritually destitute. Human beings range all the way from mental retards who can manage their bodily needs only with great difficulty, to sages and saints who can comprehend the deepest secrets of the universe and lift the moral outlook of their less acute brothers and sisters to heights undreamed of in the common stream of thought.

To the thinker who would dig below the surface presentations and discover the reasons for the manifest phenomena, the question naturally arises why life exhibits itself in such variegated apparel. Reflection upon this question has given birth to a multitude of schools of thought, religious and philosophical, each offering its own speculations as the key to unravel the riddle of nature's kaleidoscopic design. In the intellectual history of humanity, the two dominant positions around which these schools cluster are theism and materialism. Pitted against one another by their antithetical tenets, the two have come down in different guises from ancient times even to the present. Theism refers the diversity of sentient life, including the disparities of fortune evident in the human world, to the will of God. It is God, the theist holds, the omnipotent, omniscient author of the universe, who creates through the fiat of his will the variety of natural forms, allots to beings their respective shares of happiness and suffering, and divides people into the high and the low, the fortunate and the miserable.

Materialism, in contradistinction, rules out any recourse to an extraterrestrial agency to account for the differentiation in the faculties and capacities found amongst living beings, and attempts to provide in its place a system of explanation which works exclusively with naturalistic principles, pertaining to the material order. The entire gamut of living forms together with all life's modes of expression, the materialist claims, can be effectively reduced in the end to the adventures of matter governed by physical, chemical and biological laws. Even consciousness represents, for the materialist, only a secondary superstructure built upon a material base devoid of any larger significance in itself.

It is not our present purpose here to examine at length these two rival doctrines. Let it suffice to note that both, in different ways, throw into jeopardy the postulate of a progressive spiritual evolution of beings by withholding, implicitly or explicitly, the necessary condition for such a course of evolution— namely, an inwardly autonomous will which finds in the diversity of the sentient order the field for the working out of its own potentialities for growth and transformation, in accordance with laws governing freely chosen possibilities of action.

Theism withholds this condition by its basic postulate of an omnipotent deity directing the entire field of nature from above. If all of nature runs its course in obedience to divine command, then the individual will, which belongs to the natural order, must be subject to the same divine supervision as the rest of animate nature. The autonomy of the individual will and its direct impact on the sentient sphere are excluded, and with them also goes the thesis of a genuine long-term spiritual growth, to which they are essential.

Materialism likewise shuts out the notion of a progressive spiritual evolution of beings, but more simply and directly, by explicitly denying the basic presupposition of such a notion. The will's claim to freedom is here rejected, its autonomy usurped by the irresistible pressure of the determinative influences at its base. Consciousness becomes a mere by-product of material processes; the individual life-stream leaves no impact on any continuous current of experience enduring beyond the grave. Both conscious action and evolution in the biotic sphere proceed in the grip of the same play of cosmic forces—blind, brute, and insentient in their fundamental mode of operation.

Buddhism also offers an explanation for the diversity of the sentient order, an explanation which bridges the gap between volition and the diversity and thus opens up the prospect for long-term spiritual development. According to

Buddhism, the explanation for the variegation of sentient beings—in their kinds, faculties, and fortunes—lies in their kamma, that is, their volitional action. Beings are, in the words of the Buddha, "heirs of their action." They spring forth from their store of accumulated action as a matrix out of which they are fashioned, inheriting the results proper to their deeds even across the gulf of lifetimes. Through the succession of life-terms, kamma holds sway over the individual evolutionary current. Acts of will, once completed, recede into the forward moving mental stream out of which they emerged, and remaining in the form of psychic potencies, pilot the future course of evolution to be taken by that particular current of experience called an "individual being." Just as the kamma rises up out of the stream of consciousness, so does the stream of consciousness again flow forth from the germinative kamma, which thus serves to link into a single chain the series of separated lives. The kammic force drives the current of consciousness onward into new modes of existence conformable to its nature; it determines the specific form of life in which the individual will take remanifestation, the set of faculties with which the new being will be endowed, and a substantial portion of the happiness and suffering that being will meet during the course of its life.

It is, therefore, not God or chance in the Buddhist picture, but the differentiation in volitional action, functioning across the succession of lives, that accounts for the differentiation in the animate order, and the differentiation in action again that divides beings into the high and low, the happy and the miserable, the gifted and the deprived. As the Buddha declares: "Beings are the owners of their actions, heirs of their actions. Their action is the source from which they spring, their kinsman and their refuge. Action divides beings into the inferior and the superior."

Since the effective determinant of destiny is kamma, and kamma is essentially volition, this means that the operative factor in the formation of future becoming is lodged in the individual will. The will, from the Buddhist perspective, is no accidental offshoot of the machinery of nature, compelled to its course by the conspiracy of cosmic forces; it is, rather, in the deepest sense the artisan behind the entire process of animate evolution. Here will is primary and the material factors secondary, the plastic substance with which the will works and by which it gives tangible expression to its store of dispositional tendencies. The varied landscape of sentient existence, for Buddhism, represents but an outward register of the inward transactions of the will, and the hierarchy of living forms—the "great chain of being"—but a congelation of its functional modalities in the world of spatio-temporal extension.

Differentiation in the biological sphere is thus preceded and paralleled by a set of transformations in the mental sphere, which finds in animate nature the channel for actualizing its own potentialities throughout the series of successive becomings comprising the individual continuum. Through the exercise of our will, therefore, we build for ourselves our own world independent of coercion by extrinsic forces and mould the destiny that awaits us in time to come, whether for happiness or misery, for bondage or liberation.

For the spiritual aspirant, however, it is not sufficient merely to understand the theoretical ground for the differentiation of living beings. For us it is of the utmost importance to know what we can do to further our own progress along the scale of spiritual evolution—to advance to higher levels of attainment during the course of our earthly life, to secure a rebirth conducive to spiritual growth in the life to come, and ultimately to transcend this repetitive cycle of birth and death and attain Nibbāna, the supreme and irreversible deliverance.

The answer to this problem begins with the fact that kamma divides itself, according to its moral quality, into two types—the unwholesome (*akusala*) and the wholesome (*kusala*). Unwholesome kamma is action—physical, verbal or mental—that springs from the three unwholesome roots of action: greed (*lobha*), hatred (*dosa*) and delusion (*moha*). Any action grounded in these roots is spiritually detrimental and morally defective. It destroys the higher faculties, entails suffering as its consequence, and causes a plunge into lower states of existence; in short, it brings decline along the scale of spiritual evolution and deeper immersion in the mire of phenomenal existence. Wholesome kamma, on the other hand, is action springing from the three contrary wholesome roots—non-greed (*alobha*), non-hatred (*adosa*) and non-delusion (*amoha*), finding positive expression in the qualities of charity, loving-kindness and wisdom, respectively. Wholesome action functions in a way diametrically opposite to its dark counterpart. It is spiritually beneficial and morally commendable, stimulates the unfolding of the higher faculties, and entails happiness both in the present and in time to come. Consistently practised, it promotes progress along the evolutionary scale, leading to higher states of existence in successive life-spans, and finally to the realization of deliverance.

On ultimate analysis, life is a self-regenerating sequence of occasions of experience, comprising occasions of action and occasions of reception. Action is volition, and volition inevitably involves decision or choice—a selection from the welter of possibilities open to the will of that alternative most, conformable to the individual's purpose, a selection even, at a higher level, of the purposes themselves. Every moment of morally significant action, therefore, confronts us with the call for a decision, with the necessity for choice. Choice must work within the gamut of options open to the will, and these options, despite their great differences of qualitative character, necessarily fall into one of two classes according to their ethical nature—into the wholesome or the unwholesome. The one leads to progress, the other to decline.

Thence progress or decline depends entirely upon our choice, and not upon any external agency whether conceived in spiritualistic or materialistic garb. Through our fleeting, momentary decisions, accumulated over long periods, we model our fortune and chisel out of the unshaped block of futurity the destiny that will befall us in the span of time to come. Each call for a decision may be depicted as a ladder, one end leading upward to unknown heights, and the other extending downward into forbidding depths, while our successive decisions may be taken as the steps that lead us up or down the ladder's graded rungs. Or again, each moment of action may be compared to a crossroad at which we stand, a forked road one side of which leads to a city of bliss and the other to a swampland of misery and despair. The two roads stand, fixed and silent, awaiting our choice, and only our decision determines whether we shall reach the one destination or the other.

In sum, then, it is our kamma that precipitates our destiny, for it is kamma that brings about manifestation of all the destinations *(gati)* or realms of sentient existence, and kamma ultimately that fashions the entire variegated landscape of sentient existence itself, according to the ethical tone of its associated moral roots. As the Exalted One explains, speaking not through speculation but through his own direct penetration of the paths leading to all destinations:

"It is not celestial beings *(deva)*, or humans, or any other creatures belonging to happy forms of existence, that appear through action *(kamma)* born of greed, born of hate, born of delusion; it is rather beings of the hells, of the animal kingdom, of the ghostly realm, or any other others of miserable form of existence that make their appearance through action born of greed, hate and delusion...

"It is not creatures of the hells, of the animal kingdom, of the ghostly realm, or any others of a miserable form of existence, that appear through action born of non-greed, born of non-hate, born of non-delusion; it is rather celestial beings, humans, or any other creatures belonging to a happy form of existence that make their appearance through action born of non-greed, non-hate, and non-delusion."

Aṅguttara Nikāya 6:39

From Nourishing the Roots: Essays on Buddhist Ethics, *Wheel Publications No. 259–260, first published in 1978.*

4. Merit and Spiritual Growth

The performance of deeds of merit forms one of the most essential elements of Buddhist practice. Its various modes provide in their totality a compendium of applied Buddhism, showing Buddhism not as a system of ideas but as a complete way of life. Buddhist popular belief has often emphasized merit as a productive source of worldly blessings—of health, wealth, long life, beauty and friends. As a result of this emphasis, meritorious activity has come to be conceived rather in terms of a financial investment, as a religious business venture yielding returns to the satisfaction of the agent's mundane desires. While such a conception no doubt contains an element of truth, its popularization has tended to eclipse the more important function merit plays in the context of Buddhist practice. Seen in correct perspective, merit is an essential ingredient in the harmony and completeness of the spiritual life, a means of self-cultivation, and an indispensable stepping-stone to spiritual progress.

The accumulation of a 'stock of merit' is a primary requisite for acquiring all the fruits of the Buddhist religious life, from a pleasant abiding here and now to a favourable rebirth in the life to come, from the initial stages of meditative progress to the realization of the states of sanctity that come as the fruits of entering upon the noble path. The highest fruition of merit is identical with the culmination of the Buddhist holy life itself—that is, emancipation from the shackles of saṃsāric existence and the realization of Nibbāna, the unconditioned state beyond the insubstantial phenomena of the world. The mere piling up of merit, to be sure, is not in itself sufficient to guarantee the attainment of this goal. Merit is only one requisite, and it must be balanced by its counterpart to secure the breakthrough from bondage to final freedom. The counterpart of merit is knowledge (ñāṇa), the direct confrontation with the basic truths of existence through the eye of intuitive wisdom.

Merit and knowledge together constitute the two sets of equipment the spiritual aspirant requires in the quest for deliverance, the equipment of merit (puññasambhāra) and the equipment of knowledge (ñāṇasambhāra), respectively. Each set of equipment has its own contribution to make to the fulfilment of the spiritual life. The equipment of merit facilitates progress in the course of saṃsāric wandering: it brings a favourable rebirth, the encounter with good friends to guide one's footsteps along the path, the meeting with opportunities for spiritual growth, the flowering of the lofty qualities of character, and the maturation of the spiritual faculties required for the higher attainments. The equipment of knowledge brings the factor directly necessary for cutting the bonds of saṃsāric existence: the penetration of truth, enlightenment, the undistorted comprehension of the nature of actuality.

Either set of equipment, functioning in isolation, is insufficient to the attainment of the goal; either pursued alone leads to a deviant, one-sided development that departs from the straight path to deliverance taught by the Buddha. Merit without knowledge produces pleasant fruit and a blissful rebirth, but cannot issue in the transcendence of the mundane order and entrance upon the supramundane path. And knowledge without the factors of merit deteriorates into dry intellectualism, mere erudition or scholasticism, impotent when confronted with the task of grasping a truth outside the pale of intellection. But when they function together in unison in the life of the aspirant, the two sets of equipment acquire a potency capable of propelling him to the heights of realization. When each set of equipment complements the other, polishes the other, and perfects the other, then they undergo a graduated course of mutual purification culminating at the crest in the twin endowments of the Emancipated One—in that clear knowledge (*vijjā*) and flawless conduct (*caraṇa*) which make him, in the words of the Buddha, "supreme among gods and humans."

But while merit and knowledge thus occupy coordinate positions, it is merit that claims priority from the standpoint of spiritual dynamics. The reason is that works of merit come first in the process of inner growth. If knowledge be the flower that gives birth to the fruit of liberation, and faith (*saddhā*) the seed out of which the flower unfolds, then merit is the soil, water and fertilizer all in one—the indispensable nutriment for every stage of growth. Merit paves the way for knowledge, and finds in knowledge the sanction for its own claim to a place in the system of Buddhist training.

The reason for this particular sequential structure is closely linked to the Buddhist conception of noetic realization. From the Buddhist standpoint the comprehension of spiritual truth is not a matter of mere intellectual cogitation but of existential actualization. That is, it is a matter of grasping with our whole being the truth towards which we aspire, and of inwardly appropriating that truth in a manner so total and complete that our being becomes transformed into a very reflex and effusion of the truth upon which we stand. The understanding of truth in the context of the spiritual life, in other words, is no affair of accumulating bits and pieces of information publicly accessible and subjectively indifferent; it is, rather, a process of uncovering the deepest truths about ourselves and about the world, and of working the understanding that emerges into the entire complex of the inner life. Hence the use of the words 'actualization' and 'realization,' which bring into the open the ontological backdrop underlying the noetic process.

In order to grasp truth in this totalistic manner at any particular stage of spiritual development, the tenor of our inner being must be raised to a pitch where it is fit for the reception of some new disclosure of the truth. Wisdom and character, though not identical, are at any rate parallel terms, which in most cases mature in a delicately balanced ratio. We can grasp only what we are fit to grasp, and our fitness is largely a function of our character. The existential comprehension of truth thus becomes a matter of inward worth, of deservingness, or of merit. The way to effect this inward worthiness is by the performance of works of merit, not merely outwardly, but backed by the proper attitudes and disposition of mind. For the capacity to comprehend truths pertaining to the spiritual order is always proportional to the store and quality of accumulated merit. The greater and finer the merit, the larger and deeper the capacity for understanding. This principle holds at each level of maturation in the ascent towards full realization, and applies with special force to the comprehension of ultimate truth.

Ultimate truth, in the Buddha's Teaching, is Nibbāna, the unconditioned element *(asaṅkhata-dhātu),* and realization of ultimate truth the realization of Nibbāna. Nibbāna is the perfection of purity: the destruction of all passions, the eradication of clinging, the abolition of every impulse towards self-affirmation. The final thrust to the realization of Nibbāna is the special province of wisdom, since wisdom alone is adequate to the task of comprehending all conditioned phenomena in their essential nature as impermanent, suffering and not-self, and of turning away from them to penetrate the unconditioned, where alone permanent freedom from suffering is to be found. But that this penetration may take place, our interior must be made commensurate in purity with the truth it would grasp, and this requires in the first instance that it be purged of all those elements obstructive to the florescence of a higher light and knowledge. The apprehension of Nibbāna, this perfect purity secluded from the dust of passion, is only possible when a corresponding purity has been set up within ourselves. For only a pure mind can discern, through the dark mist of ignorance and defilement, the spotless purity of Nibbāna, abiding in absolute solitude beyond the turmoil of the phenomenal procession.

The achievement of such a purification of our inward being is the work of merit. Merit scours the mind of the coarser defilements, attenuates the grip of the unwholesome roots, and fortifies the productive power of the wholesome, beneficial states. Through its cumulative force it provides the foundation for wisdom's final breakthrough to the unconditioned. It is the fuel, so to speak, for the ascent of wisdom from the mundane to the supramundane. Just as the initial stages of a lunar rocket work up the momentum that enables the uppermost stage to break the gravitational pull of the earth and reach the moon, so does merit give to the spiritual life that forward thrust that will propel the wisdom-faculty past the gravitational pull of the mundane order and permit it to penetrate the transcendental truth.

The classical Buddhist commentators underscore this preparatory purgative function of merit when they define merit *(puñña)* etymologically as "that which purges and purifies the mental continuum" *(santānaṃ punāti visodheti)*. Merit performs its purgative function in the context of a complex process involving an agent and object of purification, and a mode of operation by which the purification takes place. The agent of purification is the mind itself, in its creative, formative role as the source and matrix of action. Deeds of merit are, as we have already seen, instances of wholesome kamma, and kamma ultimately reduces to volition. Therefore, at the fundamental level of analysis, a deed of merit consists in a volition, a determinative act of will belonging to the righteous order *(puññābhisaṅkhāra)*. Since volition is a mode of mental activity, this means that merit turns out, under scrutiny, to be a mode of mental activity. It is, at the core of the behaviour-pattern which serves as its vehicle, a particular application of thought by which the mind marshals its components for the achievement of a chosen end.

This discovery cautions us against misconstruing the Buddhist stress on the practice of merit as a call for blind subjection to rules and rites. The primary instrument behind any act of merit, from the Buddhist point of view, is the mind. The deed itself in its physical or vocal dimension serves mainly as an expression of a corresponding state of consciousness, and without a keen awareness of the nature and significance of the meritorious deed, the bare outward act is devoid of purgative value. Even when rules of conduct are observed, or rituals and worship performed with a view to the acquisition of merit, the spiritual potency of these structures derives not from any intrinsic sanctity they might possess in themselves, but from their effectiveness in channelizing the current of mental activity in a spiritual beneficial direction. They function, in effect, as skilful means or expedient devices for inducing wholesome states of consciousness.

Mechanical conformity to moral rules, or the performance of religious duties through unquestioning obedience to established forms, far from serving as a means to salvation, in the Buddhist outlook actually constitute obstacles. They are instances of "clinging to rules and rituals" *(sīlabbataparāmāsa)*, the third of the fetters *(saṃyojana)* binding beings to the wheel of becoming, which must be abandoned in order to enter upon the path to final deliverance. Even in such relatively external forms of merit-making as the undertaking of moral precepts and ceremonial worship, mindfulness and clear comprehension are essential; much more, then, are they necessary to the predominantly internal modes of meritorious activity, such as meditation or the study of the Dhamma.

The object of the purifying process of merit is again the mind, only here considered not from the standpoint of its immediacy, as a creative source of action, but from the standpoint of its duration, as a continuum *(cittasantāna)*. For, looked at from the temporal point of view, the mind is no stable entity enduring self-identical through its changing activities; it is, rather, a serial continuity composed of discrete acts of mentation bound to one another by exact laws of causal interconnection. Each thought-unit flashes into being, persists for an extremely brief moment, and then perishes, passing on to its immediate successor its storage of recorded impressions. Each individual member of the series inherits, preserves and transmits, along with its own novel modifications, the entire content of the series as a whole, which thus underlies every one of its components. Thence the series maintains, despite its discontinuous composition, an element of uniformity that gives to the flow of separate thought-moments the character of a continuum.

This sequential current of mentation has been going on, according to Buddhism, without discernible beginning. Driven forward from life to life by ignorance and craving, it appears now in one mode of manifestation, now in another. Embedded in the mental continuum throughout its beginningless journey is a host of particularly afflictive and disruptive mental forces known as *kilesas,* 'defilements.' Foremost among them are the three unwholesome roots—greed, hatred and delusion; from this triad spring the remaining members of the set, such as pride, opinion, selfishness, envy, sloth and restlessness. During moments of passivity the defilements lie dormant at the base of the mental continuum, as *anusaya* or latent tendencies. But when, either through the impact of outer sensory stimuli or their own subliminal process of growth, they acquire sufficient force, they surge to the surface of consciousness in the form of obsessions *(pariyuṭṭhāna).* The obsessions pollute the mind with their toxic flow and rebound upon the deeper levels of consciousness, reinforcing their roots at the base of the continuum. If they should gather still additional charge, the defilements may reach the even more dangerous stage of transgression *(vītikkama),* when they erupt as bodily or verbal actions that violate the fundamental laws of morality and lead to pain and suffering as their retributive consequence.

When merit is said to "purge and purify the mental continuum," it is so described in reference to its capacity to arrest the surging tide of the defilements which threatens to sweep the mind towards the perilous deep of transgressional action. Only wisdom—the supramundane wisdom of the noble paths—can eradicate the defilements at the level of latency, which is necessary if the bonds of existence are to be broken and deliverance attained. But the practice of merit can contribute much towards attenuating their obsessive force and establishing a foothold for wisdom to exercise its liberating function. Wisdom can operate only upon the base of a purified mind; the accumulation of merit purifies the mind; hence merit provides the supporting condition for wisdom.

When the mind is allowed to flow according to its own momentum, without restraint or control, like a turbulent river it casts up to the surface—i.e., to the level of active consciousness—the store of pollutants it harbours at its base: lust, hatred, delusion, and their derivative defilements. If the defilements are then given further scope to grow by indulging them, they will wither the potential for good, darken the beam of awareness, and strangle the faculty of wisdom until it is reduced to a mere vestige. The performance of meritorious deeds serves as a means of resisting the upsurge of defiling states, of replacing them with their wholesome opposites, and of thereby purifying the mental continuum to an extent sufficient to supply wisdom with the storage of strength it requires in the work of abolishing the defilements.

The effectiveness of merit in purifying the mental continuum stems from the concordance of a number of psychological laws. These laws, which can only be indicated briefly here, together function as the silent groundwork for the efficacy of the entire corpus of Buddhist spiritual practice.

The first is the law that only one state of consciousness can occur at a time; though seemingly trivial, this law leads to important consequences when taken in conjunction with the rest. The second holds that states of consciousness with mutually opposed ethical qualities cannot coexist. The third stipulates that all the factors of consciousness—feeling, perception, volition and the remaining states included in the "aggregate of mental formations"—must partake of the same ethical quality as the consciousness itself.

A kammically active state of consciousness is either entirely wholesome, or entirely unwholesome; it cannot (by the second law) be both. Therefore, if a wholesome state is occurring, no unwholesome state can simultaneously occur. A wholesome, spiritually beneficial state of consciousness necessarily shuts out every unwholesome, detrimental state, as well as (by the third law) all unwholesome concomitant factors of consciousness. So at the moment one is performing an act of merit, the consciousness and volition behind that meritorious deed will automatically preclude an unwholesome consciousness, volition, and the associated defilements. At that moment, at least, the consciousness will be pure. And the frequent performance of meritorious acts will, on every occasion, bar out the opportunity for the defilements to arise at the time of their performance.

Thus the performance of deeds of merit always induces a momentary purification, while the frequent performance of such deeds induces many occasions of momentary purification. But that some more durable result might be achieved an additional principle is necessary. This principle is supplied by the fourth law.

The fourth law holds that repetition confers strength. Just as the exercise of a particular muscle can transform that muscle from a frail, ineffectual strip of flesh into a dynamo of power and strength, so the repeated exercise of individual mental qualities can remodel them from sleeping soldiers into invincible warriors in the spiritual quest.

Repetition is the key to the entire process of self-transformation which constitutes the essence of the spiritual life. It is the very grounding that makes self-transformation possible. By force of repetition the fragile, tender shoots of the pure and wholesome qualities—faith, energy, mindfulness, concentration and wisdom—can blossom into sovereign faculties (*indriya*) in the struggle for enlightenment, or into indomitable powers (*bala*) in the battle against the defilements. By repeated resistance to the upsurge of evil and repeated application to the cultivation of the good, the demon can become a god and the criminal a saint.

If repetition provides the key to self-transformation, then volition provides the instrument through which repetition works. Volition acts as a vector force upon the mental continuum out of which it emerges, reorienting the continuum according to its own moral tone. Each act of will recedes with its passing into the onward rushing current of mentation and drives the current in its own direction. Wholesome volitions direct the continuum towards the good—towards purity, wisdom and ultimate liberation; unwholesome volitions drive it towards the evil—towards defilement, ignorance and inevitable bondage.

Every occasion of volition modifies the mental life in some way and to some degree, however slight, so that the overall character of an individual at any one time stands as a reflex and revelation of the volitions accumulated in the continuum.

Since the will propels the entire current of mental life in its own direction, it is the will which must be strengthened by force of repetition. The restructuring of mental life can only take place through the reformation of the will by leading it unto wholesome channels. The effective channel for re-orientation of the will is the practice of merit.

When the will is directed towards the cultivation of merit, it will spontaneously hamper the stream of defilements and bolster the company of noble qualities in the storage of the continuum. Under its gentle tutelage the factors of purity will awaken from their dormant condition and take their place as regular propensities in the personality. A will devoted to the practice of charity will generate kindness and compassion; a will devoted to the observance of the precepts will generate harmlessness, honesty, restraint, truthfulness and sobriety; a will devoted to mental culture will generate calm and insight. Faith, reverence, humility, sympathy, courage and equanimity will come to growth. Consciousness will gain in tranquillity, buoyancy, pliancy, agility and proficiency. And a consciousness made pure by these factors will advance without hindrance through the higher attainments in meditation and wisdom to the realization of Nibbāna, the consummation of spiritual endeavour.

From Nourishing the Roots: Essays on Buddhist Ethics, *Wheel Publications No. 259–260, first published in 1978.*

5. THE PATH OF UNDERSTANDING

Prince Siddhattha renounced the life of the palace and entered the forest as a hermit seeking a solution to the problem of suffering. Six years after entering he came out a Buddha, ready to show others the path he had found so that they too could work out their deliverance. It was the experience of being bound to the perishable and unsatisfying that gave the impetus to the Buddha's original quest, and it was the certainty of having found the unperishing and perfectly complete that inspired the execution of his mission. Thence the Buddha could sum up his Teaching in the single phrase: "I teach only suffering and the cessation of suffering." But though the Buddha's Teaching might be simple in its statement, the meaning behind the verbal formulation is profound and precise.

The Buddha envisages suffering in its full range and essence rather than in its mere manifest forms. It is not just physical or mental pain that he means by suffering, but the recurrent revolution of the wheel of becoming, with its spokes of birth, aging and death. Taking our immersion in a condition intrinsically inadequate as the starting point of his doctrine, he devotes the remainder to showing the way out of this condition. The solution the Buddha offers to the problem of suffering draws its cogency from the strict logic of causality. Suffering is neither an accident nor an imposition from without, but a contingent phenomenon arising through the force of conditions. It hangs upon a specific set of supports, and is therefore susceptible to treatment by tackling the genetic structure which maintains it in being. By removing the conditions out of which it arises, it is possible to bring the whole phenomenon of suffering to an end.

In order to reach the state of emancipation, it is of the first importance that the causal chain which originates suffering be snapped in the right place. Any proposed solution which does not remedy the problem of suffering at its source will eventually prove to be only a palliative, not a final cure. That the chain be broken in the right place requires an accurate determination of the interconnection of its links. The chain must be traced back to its most fundamental factor and cut off at that very point. Then suffering will no longer be able to arise.

According to the Buddha's Teaching, the primary link in the sequence of conditions generating suffering is ignorance (*avijjā*). Ignorance is a primordial blindness to the true nature of phenomena; it is a lack of understanding of things as they really are. It functions as a mental obscuration cloaking our normal process of cognition and permeating our thought patterns with distortion and error.

Among the various misconceptions produced by ignorance, the most basic is the apprehension of phenomena through the category of substantial existence. Phenomena are not isolated units locked up in themselves, but participants in an interconnected field of events. Their being derives from the entire system of relata to which they belong, not from some immutable core of identity intrinsic to themselves. Thence they are devoid of an abiding essence; their mode of being is insubstantial, relational and interdependent. However, under the influence of ignorance, this essenceless nature of phenomena is not understood. It is blotted out by the basic unawareness, and as a consequence, phenomena present themselves to cognition in a mode different from their actual mode of being. They appear substantial, self-subsistent, and exclusivistic.

The sphere where this illusion is most immediately felt is the sphere where it is most accessible to us—namely, our own experience. The experiential domain is reflectively divisible into two sectors—a cognizing or subjective sector made up of consciousness and its adjuncts, and a cognized or objective sector made up of the cognitive data. Though the two sectors are interlocking and mutually dependent, through the operation of ignorance they are conceptually bifurcated and reduced to an adventitious subject-object confrontation. On the one side the cognizing sector is split off from the experiential complex and conceived as a subject distinct from the cognitive act itself; the objective sector in turn congeals into a world of external things pointing to the subject as its field of action and concern. Consciousness awakens to itself as a persisting ego standing up against the world as an "other" perpetually estranged from itself. Thence it commences its long career of conquest, control and domination in order to justify its own suspect claim to a self-subsistent mode of being.

This cognitive error with its consequent solidification of the ego is the source of the afflictions (*kilesa*) which hold us in subjection to suffering. The lurking suspicion that the mode of being we credit to ourselves may be unfounded arouses an inner disquietude, a chronic anxiety compelling a drive to fortify the sense of egoity and give it solid ground on which to stand. We need to establish our existence to ourselves, to give inner confirmation to our conception of personal substantiality, and this need occasions the ordering of the psychic life around the focal point of ego.

The bid for self-confirmation makes its impact felt on both the emotional and intellectual fronts. The dominion of the ego in the emotional sphere appears most conspicuously in the weight of the unwholesome roots—greed, hatred and delusion—as determinants of conduct. Because the ego is essentially a vacuum, the illusion of egohood generates a nagging sense of insufficiency. We feel oppressed by an aching incompleteness, an inner lack requiring constantly to be filled. The result is greed, a relentless drive to reach out and devour whatever we can—of pleasure, wealth, power and fame—in a never successful attempt to bring the discomfort fully to an end. When our drive to satisfaction meets with frustration we react with hatred, the urge to destroy the obstacle between our desire and its satisfaction. If the obstructions to our satisfaction prove too powerful for the tactics of aggression, a third strategy will be used: dullness or delusion, an attitude of deliberate unawareness adopted as a shell to hide our vulnerability to pain.

On the intellectual front the ego-illusion engenders a move by reason to establish on logical grounds the existence of a substantial self. The idea "I am" is a spontaneous notion born of ignorance, the basic unawareness of the egoless nature of phenomena. By accepting this idea at its face value, as pointing to a real "I," and by attempting to fill in the reference, we develop a "view of self," a belief confirming the existence of a self and giving it an identity in the framework of our psycho-physical constitution.

The theories which emerge invariably fall into one or another of the two metaphysical extremes—either eternalism when we assume the self to enjoy eternal existence after death, or annihilationism, when we assume the self to be extinguished at death. Neither doctrine can be established on absolutely compelling grounds, for both are rounded on a common error: the assumption of a self as an enduring, substantial entity.

Because the pivot of our cognitive adherences and their emotional ramifications is the notion of an ego, a powerful current of psychic energy comes to be invested in our interpretive schemes. And because the notion of an ego is in actuality groundless, the product of a fundamental misconception, this investment of energy brings only disappointment in the end. We cling to things in the hope that they will be permanent, satisfying and substantial, and they turn out to be impermanent, unsatisfying and insubstantial. We seek to impose our will upon the order of events, and we find that events obey a law of their own, insubordinate to our urge towards control.

The result of our clinging is eventual suffering. Yet this suffering which arises from the breakdown of our egocentric attempts at dominance and manipulation is not entirely negative in value. It contains a tremendous positive value, a vast potential, for by shattering our presumptions it serves to awaken our basic intelligence and set us on the quest for liberation. It forces us to discover the ultimate futility of our drive to structure the world from the standpoint of the ego, and makes us recognize the need to acquire a new perspective free from the compulsive patterns which keep us tied to suffering.

Since the most fundamental factor in the bondage of the ego is ignorance, to reach this new perspective ignorance must be eliminated. To eliminate ignorance it is not sufficient merely to observe rules of conduct, to generate faith, devotion and virtue, or even to develop a calm and concentrated mind. All these are requisites to be sure, essential and powerful aids along the path, but even in unison they are not enough. Something more is required, some other element that alone can ensure the complete severing of the conditional nexus sustaining the round of saṃsāric suffering. That something more is *understanding*.

The path to liberation is essentially a path of understanding. Its core is the knowledge and vision of things as they really are: "It is for one who knows and sees that the destruction of the defilements takes place, not for one who does not know and does not see." The objective domain where understanding is to be aroused is our own experience. Since our distorted interpretations of our experience provide the food which nourishes the process of ego, it is here, in experience, that the ego-illusion must be dispelled. Our own experience is, of all things, that which is "closest to ourselves," for it is through this that everything else is registered and known. And yet, though so close, our own experience is at the same time shrouded in darkness, its true characteristics hidden from our awareness by the screen of ignorance. The Buddha's Teaching is the key which helps us to correct our understanding, enabling us to see things as they are. It is the light which dispels the darkness of ignorance, so that we can understand our own understanding of things "just as a man with eyes might see forms illuminated by a lamp."

The correct understanding of experience takes place in the context of meditation. It requires the development of insight (*vipassanā*) based on a foundation of meditative calm (*samatha*). No amount of merely intellectual knowledge can replace the need for personal realization. Because our tendency to misconceive phenomena persists through a blindness to their true nature, only the elimination of this blindness through direct vision can rectify our erroneous patterns of cognition. The practice of Buddhist meditation is not a way of dissolving our sense of individual identity in some undifferentiated absolute or of withdrawing into the bliss of a self-contained interiority. It is, rather, a way of understanding the nature of things through the portal where that nature is most accessible to ourselves, namely, our own processes of body and of mind. The practice of meditation has profound effects upon our sense of identity; the alterations it produces, however, do not come about by subordinating the intelligence to some uncritically accepted generalization, but through a detached, sober and exhaustive scrutiny of the experiential field that provides the locus for our sense of identity.

The focal method of the practice of meditation is reflective awareness, a bending back of the beam of awareness upon itself in order to illuminate the true characteristics of existence implicated in each occasion of cognition. The path of understanding unfolds in three successive stages called "the three full understandings." In the first stage, the "full understanding of the known" (*ñātapariññā*), the domain of experience is broken down by meditative analysis into its constituting factors, which are then carefully defined in terms of their salient qualities and functions. The categories employed in this operation are the key terms in the Buddhist analysis of personality—the aggregates (*khandha*), sense bases (*āyatana*), and elements (*dhātu*). The purpose of this dissection is to dispel the illusion of substantiality that hovers over our gross perception of our experience. By revealing that what common sense takes to be a solid monolithic whole is in reality a conglomeration of discrete factors, the contemplation deprives the sense of self-identification of its chief support, the notion of the ego as a simple unity. The factors which emerge from this analytical investigation are then correlated with their causes and conditions, disclosing their contingency and lack of independence.

The second stage of understanding is the "full understanding of scrutiniza-tion" (*tīraṇapariññā*). At this stage the experiential field is examined, not as before in terms of its individuating features, but by way of its universal marks. These universal marks are three: impermanence (*anicca*), suffering (*dukkha*) and non-self (*anattā*). Under the limitations of ordinary cognition, phenomena are apprehended as permanent, pleasurable and self. In the contemplative situa-tion these assumptions must be corrected, replaced by the perception of phe-nomena as impermanent, unpleasurable and non-self. The task of the meditative process, at this level, is to ascribe these qualities to the material and mental processes, and to attempt to view all phenomena in their light.

When the second stage is fully mature, it gives way gradually to the third type of comprehension, the "full understanding of abandonment" (*pahānapari-ññā*). Here the momentary insights achieved at the previous level blossom into full penetrations. Impermanence, suffering and selflessness are no longer merely understood as qualities of phenomena, but are seen with complete clar-ity as the nature of phenomena themselves. These realizations bring about the final abandonment of the deluded perceptions as well as the destruction of the ego-tainted emotions which cluster around them.

To walk the path of understanding is to begin to see through the deceptions which have held our imaginations captive through the long stretch of beginningless time. It is to outgrow our passions and prejudices, and to cast off the mask of false identities we are accustomed to assume, the vast array of identities that constitute our wandering in saṃsāric existence. The path is not an easy one, but calls for great effort and personal integrity. Its reward lies in the happiness of growing freedom which accompanies each courageous step, and the ultimate emancipation which lies at the end.

From Nourishing the Roots: Essays on Buddhist Ethics, *Wheel Publications No. 259–260, first published in 1978.*

6. Two Faces of the Dhamma

O n first encounter, Buddhism confronts us as a paradox. Intellectually, it appears a freethinker's delight—sober, realistic, undogmatic, almost scientific in its outlook and method. But if we come into contact with the living Dhamma from within, we soon discover that it has another side which seems the antithesis of all our rationalistic presuppositions. While we still do not meet rigid creeds or random speculation, we do come upon religious ideals of renunciation, contemplation and devotion; a body of doctrines dealing with matters transcending sense perception and thought; and—perhaps most disconcerting—a program of training in which faith figures as a cardinal virtue, and doubt as a hindrance, barrier and fetter.

When we try to determine our own relationship with the Dhamma, eventually we find ourselves challenged to make sense out of its two seemingly irreconcilable faces: the empiricist face turned to the world, telling us to investigate and verify things for ourselves, and the religious face turned to the Beyond, advising us to dispel our doubts and place trust in the Teacher and his Teaching.

One way we can resolve this dilemma is by accepting only one face of the Dhamma as authentic and rejecting the other as spurious or superfluous. Thus, with traditional Buddhist pietism, we can embrace the religious side of faith and devotion, but shy off from the hard-headed world-view and the task of critical inquiry; or alternatively, along with modern Buddhist apologetics, we can extol the Dhamma's empiricism and resemblance to science, but stumble embarrassingly over the religious side. Yet reflection on what a genuine Buddhist spirituality truly requires makes it clear that both faces of the Dhamma are equally authentic and that both must be taken into account. If we fail to do so, not only do we risk adopting a lopsided view of the teaching, but our own involvement with the Dhamma is likely to be hampered by partiality and conflicting attitudes.

The problem remains, however, of bringing together the two faces of the Dhamma without sliding into self-contradiction. The key, we suggest, to achieving this reconciliation, and thus to securing the internal consistency of our own perspective and practice, lies in considering two fundamental points: first, the guiding *purpose* of the Dhamma; and second, the *strategy* it employs to achieve that purpose. The *purpose* is the attainment of deliverance from suffering. The Dhamma does not aim at providing us with factual information about the world, and thus, despite a compatibility with science, its goals and concerns are necessarily different from those of the latter. Primarily and essentially, the Dhamma is a path to spiritual emancipation, to liberation from the round of repeated birth, death and suffering. Offered to us as the irreplaceable means of deliverance, the Dhamma does not seek mere intellectual assent, but commands a response that is bound to be fully religious. It addresses us at the bedrock of our being, and there it awakens the faith, devotion and commitment appropriate when the final goal of our existence is at stake. But for Buddhism faith and devotion are only spurs which impel us to enter and persevere along the path; by themselves they cannot ensure deliverance.

The primary cause of bondage and suffering, the Buddha teaches, is ignorance regarding the true nature of existence; hence in the Buddhist *strategy* of liberation the primary instrument must be wisdom, the knowledge and vision of things as they really are. Investigation and critical inquiry, cool and uncommitted, constitute the first step toward wisdom, enabling us to resolve our doubts and gain a conceptual grasp of the truths upon which our deliverance depends. But doubt and questioning cannot continue indefinitely. Once we have decided that the Dhamma is to be our vehicle to spiritual freedom, we have to step on board: we must leave our hesitancy behind and enter the course of training which will lead us from faith to liberating vision.

For those who approach the Dhamma in quest of intellectual or emotional gratification, inevitably it will show two faces, and one will always remain a puzzle. But if we are prepared to approach the Dhamma on its own terms, as the way to release from suffering, there will not be two faces at all. Instead we will see what was there from the start: the single face of Dhamma which, like any other face, presents two complementary sides.

From BPS Newsletter No. 2, Autumn 1985.

7. Vision and Routine

All human activity can be viewed as an interplay between two contrary but equally essential factors—vision and repetitive routine. Vision is the creative element in activity, whose presence ensures that over and above the settled conditions pressing down upon us from the past we still enjoy a margin of openness to the future, a freedom to discern more meaningful ends and to discover more efficient ways to achieve them. Repetitive routine, in contrast, provides the conservative element in activity. It is the principle that accounts for the persistence of the past in the present, and that enables the successful achievements of the present to be preserved intact and faithfully transmitted to the future.

Though pulling in opposite directions—the one toward change, the other toward stability—vision and routine intermesh in a variety of ways and every course of action can be found to participate to some extent in both. For any particular action to be both meaningful and effective the attainment of a healthy balance between the two is necessary. When one factor prevails at the expense of the other, the consequences are invariably undesirable. If we are bound to a repetitive cycle of work that deprives us of our freedom to inquire and understand, we soon bog down, crippled by the chains of routine. If we are spurred to act by elevating ideals but lack the discipline to implement them, eventually we find ourselves wallowing in dreams or exhausting our energies on frivolous pursuits. It is only when accustomed routines are infused from within by vision that they become springboards to discovery rather than deadening ruts. And it is only when inspired vision gives birth to a course of repeatable actions that we can bring our ideals down from the ethereal sphere of imagination to the sombre realm of fact. It took a flash of genius for Michelangelo to behold the figure of David invisible in a shapeless block of stone; but it required years of prior training, and countless blows with hammer and chisel, to work the miracle that would leave us a masterpiece of art.

These reflections concerning the relationship between vision and routine apply with equal validity to the practice of the Buddhist path. Like all other human activities, the treading of the way to the cessation of suffering requires that the intelligent grasp of new disclosures of truth be fused with the patient and stabilizing discipline of repetition. The factor of vision enters the path under the heading of right view—as the understanding of the undistorted truths concerning our existence and as the continued penetration of those same truths through deepening contemplation and reflection. The factor of repetition enters the path as the onerous task imposed by the practice itself: the need to undertake specific modes of training and to cultivate them diligently in the prescribed sequence until they yield their fruit. The course of spiritual growth along the Buddhist path might in fact be conceived as an alternating succession of stages in which, during one phase, the element of vision is dominant, during the next, the element of routine. It is a flash of vision that opens our inner eye to the essential meaning of the Dhamma, gradual training that makes our insight secure, and again the urge for still more vision that propels the practice forward to its culmination in final knowledge.

Though the emphasis may alternate from phase to phase, ultimate success in the development of the path always hinges upon balancing vision with routine in such a way that each can make its maximal contribution. However, because our minds are keyed to fix upon the new and distinctive, in our practice we are prone to place a one-sided emphasis on vision at the expense of repetitive routine. Thus we are elated by expectations concerning the stages of the path far beyond our reach, while at the same time we tend to neglect the lower stages—dull and drab, but far more urgent and immediate—lying just beneath our feet. To adopt this attitude, however, is to forget the crucial fact that vision always operates upon a groundwork of previously established routine and must in turn give rise to new patterns of routine adequate to the attainment of its intended aim. Thus if we are to close the gap between ideal and actuality, between the envisaged aim of striving and the lived experience of our everyday lives, it is necessary for us to pay greater heed to the task of repetition. Every wholesome thought, every pure intention, every effort to train the mind represents a *potential* for growth along the Noble Eightfold Path. But to be converted from a mere potential into an active power leading to the end of suffering, the fleeting wholesome thought-formations must be repeated, fostered and cultivated, made into enduring qualities of our being. Feeble in their individuality, when their forces are consolidated by repetition, they acquire a strength that is invincible.

The key to development along the Buddhist path is repetitive routine guided by inspirational vision. It is the insight into final freedom—the peace and purity of a liberated mind—that uplifts us and impels us to overcome our limits. But it is by repetition—the methodical cultivation of wholesome practices—that we cover the distance separating us from the goal and draw ever closer to deliverance.

From BPS Newsletter No. 3, Winter 1985.

8. PURIFICATION OF MIND

An ancient maxim found in the Dhammapada sums up the practice of the Buddha's teaching in three simple guidelines to training, namely, to abstain from all evil, to cultivate good, and to purify one's mind. These three guidelines form a graded sequence of steps that progress from the outward and preparatory to the inward and essential. Each step leads naturally into the one that follows it, and the culmination of the three, purification of mind, makes it plain that the heart of Buddhist practice is to be found here. Purification of mind as understood in the Buddha's teaching is the sustained endeavour to cleanse the mind of defilements, those dark unwholesome mental forces which run beneath the surface stream of consciousness vitiating our thinking, values, attitudes, and actions. The chief among the defilements are the three that the Buddha has termed the roots of evil—greed, hatred, and delusion; from these emerge their numerous offshoots and variants: anger and cruelty, avarice and envy, conceit and arrogance, hypocrisy and vanity, all the multitude of erroneous views.

Contemporary attitudes do not look favourably upon such notions as defilement and purity, and on first encounter they may strike us as throwbacks to an outdated moralism, valid perhaps in an era when prudery and taboo were dominant, but having no claims upon us emancipated torchbearers of modernity. Admittedly, we do not all wallow in the mire of gross materialism and many among us seek our enlightenments and spiritual highs, but we want them on our own terms, and as heirs of the new freedom we believe they are to be won through an unbridled quest for experience without any special need for introspection, personal change or self-control. However, in the Buddha's teaching the criterion of genuine enlightenment lies precisely in purity of mind. The purpose of all insight and enlightened understanding is to liberate the mind from the defilements, and Nibbâna itself, the goal of the teaching, is defined quite clearly as freedom from greed, hatred, and delusion. From the perspective of the Dhamma, defilement and purity are not mere postulates of a rigid authoritarian moralism but real and solid facts essential to a correct understanding of the human situation in the world.

As facts of lived experience, defilement and purity pose a vital distinction having a crucial significance for those who seek deliverance from suffering. They represent the two points between which the path to liberation unfolds— the former its problematic and starting point, the latter its resolution and end. The defilements, the Buddha declares, lie at the bottom of all human suffering.

Burning within as lust and craving, as rage and resentment, they lay to waste hearts, lives, hopes, and civilisations, and drive us blind and thirsty through the round of birth and death. The Buddha describes the defilements as bonds, fetters, hindrances, and knots; thence the path to unbonding, release and liberation, to untying the knots, is at the same time a discipline aimed at inward cleansing. The work of purification must be undertaken in the same place where the defilements arise, in the mind itself, and the main method the Dhamma offers for purifying the mind is meditation. Meditation, in the Buddhist training, is neither a quest for self-effusive ecstasies nor a technique of home-applied psychotherapy, but a carefully devised method of mental development—theoretically precise and practically efficient—for attaining inner purity and spiritual freedom. The principal tools of Buddhist meditation are the core wholesome mental factors of energy, mindfulness, concentration and understanding. But in the systematic practice of meditation, these are strengthened and yoked together in a program of self-purification which aims at extirpating the defilements root and branch so that not even the subtlest unwholesome stirrings remain.

Since all defiled states of consciousness are born from ignorance—the most deeply embedded defilement, the final and ultimate purification of mind is to be accomplished through the instrumentality of wisdom, the knowledge and vision of things as they really are. Wisdom, however, does not arise through chance or random good intentions, but only in a purified mind. Thus in order for wisdom to come forth and accomplish the ultimate purification through the eradication of defilements, we first have to create a space for it by developing a provisional purification of mind—a purification which, though temporary and vulnerable, is still indispensable as a foundation for the emergence of all liberative insight.

The achievement of this preparatory purification of mind begins with the challenge of self-understanding. To eliminate defilements we must first learn to know them, to detect them at work infiltrating and dominating our everyday thoughts and lives. For countless aeons we have acted on the spur of greed, hatred and delusion, and thus the work of self-purification cannot be executed hastily in obedience to our demand for quick results. The task requires patience, care and persistence—and the Buddha's crystal clear instructions. For every defilement the Buddha in his compassion has given us the antidote, the method to emerge from it and vanquish it. By learning these principles and applying them properly, we can gradually wear away the most stubborn inner stains and reach the end of suffering, the "taintless liberation of the mind."

From BPS Newsletter No. 4, Summer 1986.

9. THE CASE FOR STUDY

The recent upsurge of interest in Buddhism, both East and West, has been marked by a vigorous practical orientation and a drive to discover the peace and freedom to which the practice of Dhamma leads. This zeal for practice, however, has often been accompanied by another trait which may not be so fruitful, namely, a tendency to neglect or even belittle the methodical study of the Buddha's teachings. The arguments offered in defence of this attitude have already become familiar currency among us. It is said, for example, that study is concerned with words and concepts, not with realities; that it leads only to learning, not to wisdom; that it can change only our ideas but fails to touch us at the deeper levels of our lives. To clinch the case the testimony of the Buddha himself is enlisted, with his famous remarks that to learn much without practising is like counting the cows of others or like carrying a raft on one's head instead of using it to cross the stream.

This contention, to be sure, has its aspect of truth, but it also suffers from a one-sided emphasis which may actually thwart rather than aid our progress on the Buddhist path. It is certainly true that learning without practice is fruitless, but the other side of the issue also should be considered. Should a person gather cows if he knows nothing about how to take care of them? Should he try to cross a rough and dangerous river without knowing how to operate a raft? The Buddha himself insisted that his followers learn and transmit the Dhamma both in the letter and the spirit. But rather than appealing just to traditional formulations, let us inquire ourselves into the value and function of Dhamma study.

The point at issue, it must be stressed, is not study as an academic discipline or the accumulation of a wealth of learning, but the acquisition of a sound and solid working knowledge of the basic Buddhist doctrines. Now to see why this is so essential, we must recall that the entire practice of the proper Buddhist path develops out of the act through which we enter the path—the going for refuge to the Triple Gem. If we have taken this step honestly, with correct motivation, it implies that we have acknowledged our need for spiritual guidance and have entrusted ourselves to the Buddha as our guide and to his teaching as our vehicle of guidance. By taking refuge in the Dhamma we accept not merely a technique of meditation that we can use at liberty for our own self-appointed purposes, but a profound and comprehensive teaching on the true nature of the human condition, a teaching designed to awaken in us a perception of this truth as the means for reaching the full and final end of suffering. The liberation offered by the Dhamma comes not from simply practising meditation in the context of our own preconceptions and desires, but from practising upon the groundwork of the right understanding and right intentions communicated to us by the Buddha.

This cognitive character of the Buddhist path elevates doctrinal study and intellectual inquiry to a position of great importance. Though the knowledge that frees the mind from bondage emerges only from intuitive insight and not from a mass of doctrinal facts, genuine insight always develops on the basis of a preliminary conceptual grasp of the basic principles essential to right understanding, in the absence of which its growth will inevitably be obstructed. The study and systematic reflection through which we arrive at this preparatory right view necessarily involve concepts and ideas. But before we hasten to dismiss Dhamma study as being therefore only a worthless tangle of verbiage, let us consider that concepts and ideas are our indispensable tools of understanding and communication. Concepts, however, can be valid and invalid tools of understanding; ideas can be fruitful or useless, capable of bringing immense benefit or of entailing enormous harm. The object of studying the Dhamma as part of our spiritual quest is to learn to comprehend our experience correctly: to be able to distinguish the valid from the invalid, the true from the false, the wholesome from the unwholesome.

It is only by making a thorough and careful investigation that we will be in a position to reject what is detrimental to our growth and to apply ourselves with confidence to cultivating what is truly beneficial. Without having reached this preliminary conceptual clarification, without having succeeded in 'straightening out our views,' there can indeed be the earnest practice of Buddhist meditation techniques, but there will not be the practice of the meditation pertaining to the integral Noble Eightfold Path. And while such free-based meditation may bring its practitioners the mundane benefits of greater calm, awareness and equanimity, lacking the guidance of right view and the driving power of right motivation, it is questionable whether it can lead to the penetrative realisation of the Dhamma, or to its final goal, the complete cessation of suffering.

It is almost impossible to give a single word of counsel on the subject of study applicable to all followers of the Dhamma. Needs and interests vary so greatly from one person to another that each will have to strike the balance between study and practice that suits his or her own disposition. But without hesitation it can be said that all who earnestly endeavour to live by the Buddha's teaching will find their practice strengthened by the methodical study of his Dhamma. Such an undertaking, of course, will not be easy, but it is just through facing and surmounting the challenges we meet that our understanding will ripen and mature in the higher wisdom.

From BPS Newsletter No. 5, Winter 1986.

10. Dhamma Without Rebirth?

I n line with the present-day stress on the need for religious teachings to be personally relevant and directly verifiable, in certain Dhamma circles the time-honoured Buddhist doctrine of rebirth has come up for severe re-examination. Although only a few contemporary Buddhist thinkers still go so far as to suggest that this doctrine be scrapped as "unscientific," another opinion has been gaining ground to the effect that whether or not rebirth itself be a fact, the doctrine of rebirth has no essential bearings on the practice of Dhamma and thence no claim to an assured place in the Buddhist teachings. The Dhamma, it is said, is concerned solely with the here and now, with helping us to resolve our personal hang-ups through increased self-awareness and inner honesty. All the rest of Buddhism we can now let go as the religious trappings of an ancient culture utterly inappropriate for the Dhamma of our technological age.

If we suspend our own predilections for the moment and instead go directly to our sources, we come upon the indisputable fact that the Buddha himself taught rebirth and taught it as a basic tenet of his teaching. Viewed in their totality, the Buddha's discourses show us that far from being a mere concession to the outlook prevalent in his time or an Asiatic cultural contrivance, the doctrine of rebirth has tremendous implications for the entire course of Dhamma practice, affecting both the aim with which the practice is taken up and the motivation with which it is followed through to completion. The aim of the Buddhist path is liberation from suffering, and the Buddha makes it abundantly clear that the suffering from which liberation is needed is the suffering of bondage to *saṃsāra*, the round of repeated birth and death. To be sure, the Dhamma does have an aspect which is directly visible and personally verifiable. By direct inspection of our own experience we can see that sorrow, tension, fear and grief always arise from our greed, aversion and ignorance, and thus can be eliminated with the removal of those defilements. The importance of this directly visible side of Dhamma practice cannot be underestimated, as it serves to confirm our confidence in the liberating efficacy of the Buddhist path. However, to downplay the doctrine of rebirth and explain the entire import of the Dhamma as the amelioration of mental suffering through enhanced self-awareness is to deprive the Dhamma of those wider perspectives from which it derives its full breadth and profundity. By doing so one seriously risks reducing it in the end to little more than a sophisticated ancient system of humanistic psychotherapy.

The Buddha himself has clearly indicated that the root problem of human existence is not simply the fact that we are vulnerable to sorrow, grief and fear, but that we tie ourselves through our egoistic clinging to a constantly self-regenerating pattern of birth, ageing, sickness and death within which we undergo the more specific forms of mental affliction. He has also shown that the primary danger in the defilements is their causal role in sustaining the round of rebirths. As long as they remain unabandoned in the deep strata of the mind, they drag us through the round of becoming in which we shed a flood of tears "greater than the waters of the ocean." When these points are carefully considered, we then see that the practice of Dhamma does not aim at providing us with a comfortable reconciliation with our present personalities and our situation in the world, but at initiating a far-reaching inner transformation which will issue in our deliverance from the cycle of worldly existence in its entirety.

Admittedly, for most of us the primary motivation for entering upon the path of Dhamma has been a gnawing sense of dissatisfaction with the routine course of our unenlightened lives rather than a keen perception of the dangers in the round of rebirths. However, if we are going to follow the Dhamma through to its end and tap its full potential for conferring peace and higher wisdom, it is necessary for the motivation of our practice to mature beyond that which originally induced us to enter the path. Our underlying motivation must grow towards those essential truths disclosed to us by the Buddha and, encompassing those truths, must use them to nourish its own capacity to lead us towards the realisation of the goal.

Our motivation acquires the requisite maturity by the cultivation of right view, the first factor of the Noble Eightfold Path, which as explained by the Buddha includes an understanding of the principles of kamma and rebirth as fundamental to the structure of our existence. Though contemplating the moment is the key to the development of insight meditation, it would be an erroneous extreme to hold that the practice of Dhamma consists wholly in maintaining mindfulness of the present. The Buddhist path stresses the role of wisdom as the instrument of deliverance, and wisdom must comprise not only a penetration of the moment in its vertical depths, but a comprehension of the past and future horizons within which our present existence unfolds. To take full cognisance of the principle of rebirth will give us that panoramic perspective from which we can survey our lives in their broader context and total network of relationships. This will spur us on in our own pursuit of the path and will reveal the profound significance of the goal towards which our practice points, the end of the cycle of rebirths as mind's final liberation from suffering.

From BPS Newsletter No. 6, Spring 1987.

11. TAKING STOCK OF ONESELF

Though in principle the Buddhist path leads straight and unerringly from bondage to freedom, when we apply it to ourselves it often seems to take a tortuous route as imposed by the twists and turns of our own contorted mental topography. Unless we have exceptionally mature wholesome roots, we cannot expect to approach the goal "as the crow flies," soaring unhindered through the quick and blissful skyways of the jhānas and higher insights. Instead we must be prepared to tread the path at ground level, moving slowly, steadily and cautiously through the winding mountain roads of our own minds. We begin at the inevitable point of departure—with the unique constellation of personal qualities, habits and potentials that we bring with us into the practice. Our ingrained defilements and obstinate delusions, as well as our hidden reserves of goodness, inner strength and wisdom—these are at once the material out of which the practice is forged, the terrain to be passed through, and the vehicle that takes us to our destination.

Confidence in the Buddhist path is a prerequisite for persisting on this journey. Yet it often happens that though we may be fully convinced of the liberating efficacy of the Dhamma, we stumble along perplexed as to how we can apply the Dhamma fruitfully to ourselves. One major step towards reaping the benefits of Dhamma practice consists in making an honest assessment of one's own character. If we are to utilise effectively the methods the Buddha has taught for overcoming the mind's defilements, we first must take stock of those particular defilements that are prevalent in our individual makeup. It will not suffice for us to sit back and console ourselves with the thought that the path leads infallibly to the end of greed, hate and delusion. For the path to be effective in our own practice, we have to become familiar with our own persistent greeds, hates and delusions as they crop up in the round of daily life. Without this honest confrontation with ourselves, all our other pursuits of Dhamma may be to no avail and can actually lead us astray. Though we may gain extensive knowledge of the Buddhist scriptures, clarify our view and sharpen our powers of thought, invest so many hours on the meditation cushion and walkway, if we do not attend to the blemishes in our characters, these other achievements, far from extricating the defilements, may instead only go to reinforce them.

Yet, though honest self-assessment is one of the most vital steps in Dhamma practice, it is also one of the most difficult. What makes it so difficult is the radically new perspective that must be adopted to undertake an investigation of oneself and the dense barriers that must be penetrated to arrive at truthful self-understanding. In attempting to assess ourselves we are no longer observing an external entity which we can treat as an adventitious object to be evaluated in terms of our subjective purposes. We are observing instead the seat of observation itself, that most elusive centre from which we gaze out upon the world, and we are doing so in a mode which casts all its motives and projects in a critical light. To enter this domain of inquiry is to run smack up against our very sense of personal identity, and thus to have to pierce the thick screens of delusion and blind emotion which keep that sense of identity intact.

Normally, in subservience to our need to confirm to ourselves our uniqueness and irreplaceable importance, we proceed to construct mental pictures—indeed a picture gallery—of what we imagine ourselves to be. The self-image that emerges from these pictures becomes simultaneously a mainstay which we cling to in order to maintain our self-esteem and a standpoint from which we orient ourselves towards others and launch our projects in the world. To secure its tenuous status the mind employs a variety of tactics 'behind the back' of our conscious awareness. It throws up blinders which keep out disturbing information, it flatters us with fantasied projections, it drives us to manipulate people and situations in ways that will seem to validate our tacit assumptions about our virtues and identity.

All these projects born of the quest to substantiate our sense of identity only increase our suffering. The more we lock ourselves into the images we form of ourselves, the more we alienate ourselves from others and close off our access to liberating truth. Thence release from suffering requires that we gradually discard our delusive self-images through rigorous examination of our minds.

The venerable Sāriputta, in the 'Discourse on No Blemishes' (Majjhima Nikāya 5), stresses the role of honest self-assessment as a prerequisite of spiritual growth. He points out that just as a dirty bronze bowl, deposited in a dusty place and utterly neglected, becomes only dirtier and dustier, so if we fail to recognise the blemishes of our minds we will not make any effort to eliminate them, but will continue to harbour greed, hate and delusion and will die with a corrupted mind. And just as a dirty bronze bowl which is cleaned and polished will in time become bright and radiant, so if we recognise the blemishes of our minds we will arouse our energy to purify them, and having purged ourselves of blemishes we will die with an undefiled mind. The task of self-knowledge is always a difficult one, but it is only by knowing our minds that we will be able to shape them, and it is only by shaping our minds that we can liberate them.

From BPS Newsletter No. 7, Summer-Autumn 1987.

12. THE BALANCED WAY

L ike a bird in flight borne by its two wings, the practice of Dhamma is sustained by two contrasting qualities whose balanced development is essential to straight and steady progress. These two qualities are renunciation and compassion. As a doctrine of renunciation, the Dhamma points out that the path to liberation is a personal course of training that centres on the gradual control and mastery of desire, the root cause of suffering. As a teaching of compassion, the Dhamma bids us to avoid harming others, to act for their welfare and to help realise the Buddha's own great resolve to offer the world the way to the Deathless. Considered in isolation, renunciation and compassion have inverse logics that at times seem to point us in opposite directions. The one steers us to greater solitude aimed at personal purification, the other to increased involvement with others issuing in beneficent action.

Yet, despite their differences, renunciation and compassion nurture each other in dynamic interplay throughout the practice of the path, from its elementary steps of moral discipline to its culmination in liberating wisdom. The synthesis of the two, their balanced fusion, is expressed most perfectly in the figure of the Fully Enlightened One, who is at once the embodiment of complete renunciation and of all-embracing compassion. Both renunciation and compassion share a common root in the encounter with suffering. The one represents our response to suffering confronted in our own individual experience, the other our response to suffering witnessed in the lives of others. Our spontaneous reactions, however, are only the seeds of these higher qualities, not their substance. To acquire the capacity to sustain our practice of Dhamma, renunciation and compassion must be methodically cultivated, and this requires an ongoing process of reflection which transmutes our initial stirrings into full-fledged spiritual virtues.

The framework within which this reflection is to be exercised is the teaching of the Four Noble Truths, which thus provides the common doctrinal matrix for both renunciation and compassion. Renunciation develops out of our innate urge to avoid suffering and pain. But whereas this urge, prior to reflection, leads to an anxious withdrawal from particular situations perceived as personally threatening, reflection reveals the basic danger to lie in our existential situation itself—in being bound by ignorance and craving to a world which is inherently fearsome, deceptive and unreliable. Thence the governing motive behind the act of renunciation is the longing for spiritual freedom, coupled with the recognition that self-purification is an inward task most easily accomplished when we distance ourselves from the outer circumstances that nourish our unwholesome tendencies.

Compassion develops out of our spontaneous feelings of sympathy with others. However, as a spiritual virtue, compassion cannot be equated with a sentimental effusion of emotion, nor does it necessarily imply a dictum to lose oneself in altruistic activity. Though compassion surely includes emotional empathy and often does express itself in action, it comes to full maturity only when guided by wisdom and tempered by detachment. Wisdom enables us to see beyond the adventitious misfortunes with which living beings may be temporarily afflicted to the deep and hidden dimensions of suffering inseparable from conditioned existence. As a profound and comprehensive understanding of the Four Noble Truths, wisdom discloses to us the wide range, diverse gradations, and subtle roots of the suffering to which our fellow beings are enmeshed, as well as the means to lead them to irreversible release from suffering. Thence the directives of spontaneous sympathy and mature compassion are often contradictory, and only the latter are fully trustworthy as guides to beneficent action effective in the highest degree. Though often the judicious exercise of compassion will require us to act or speak up, sometimes it may well enjoin us to retreat into silence and solitude as the course most conducive to the long-range good of others as well as of ourselves.

In our attempt to follow the Dhamma, one or the other of these twin cardinal virtues will have to be given prominence, depending on our temperament and circumstances. However, for monk and householder alike, success in developing the path requires that both receive due attention and that deficiencies in either gradually be remedied. Over time we will find that the two, though tending in different directions, eventually are mutually reinforcing. Compassion impels us towards greater renunciation, as we see how our own greed and attachment make us a danger to others. And renunciation impels us towards greater compassion, since the relinquishing of craving enables us to exchange the narrow perspectives of the ego for the wider perspectives of a mind of boundless sympathy. Held together in this mutually strengthening tension, renunciation and compassion contribute to the wholesome balance of the Buddhist path and to the completeness of its final fruit.

From BPS Newsletter No. 8, Winter 1987.

13. A LOOK AT THE KĀLĀMA SUTTA

I n this issue of the newsletter we take a fresh look at an often quoted discourse of the Buddha, the Kālāma Sutta. The discourse, found in translation in Wheel No. 8, has been described as 'the Buddha's Charter of Free Inquiry,' and though the discourse certainly does counter the decrees of dogmatism and blind faith with a vigorous call for free investigation, it is problematic whether the sutta can support all the positions that have been ascribed to it. On the basis of a single passage quoted out of context, the Buddha has been made out to be a pragmatic empiricist who dismisses all doctrine and faith, and whose Dhamma is simply a freethinker's kit to truth that invites each one to accept and reject whatever he likes.

But does the Kālāma Sutta really justify such views? Or do we meet in these claims only another set of variations on that egregious old tendency to interpret the Dhamma according to whatever notions are congenial to oneself—or to those to whom one is preaching? Let us take as careful a look at the Kālāma Sutta as the limited space allotted to this essay will allow, remembering that in order to understand the Buddha's utterances correctly it is essential to take account of his own intentions in making them.

The passage that has been cited so often runs as follows: "Come, Kālāmas. Do not go upon what has been acquired by repeated hearing, nor upon tradition, nor upon rumour, nor upon scripture, nor upon surmise, nor upon axiom, nor upon specious reasoning, nor upon bias towards a notion pondered over, nor upon another's seeming ability, nor upon the consideration 'The monk is our teacher.' When you yourselves know: 'These things are bad, blameable, censured by the wise; undertaken and observed, these things lead to harm and ill,' abandon them...: When you yourselves know: 'These things are good, blameless, praised by the wise; undertaken and observed, these things lead to benefit and happiness,' enter on and abide in them."

Now this passage, like everything else spoken by the Buddha, has been stated in a specific context—with a particular audience and situation in view—and thus must be understood in relation to that context. The Kālāmas, citizens of the town of Kesaputta, had been visited by religious teachers of divergent views, each of whom would propound his own doctrines and tear down the doctrines of his predecessors. This left the Kālāmas perplexed, and thus when "the recluse Gotama," reputed to be an Awakened One, arrived in their township, they approached him in the hope that he might be able to dispel their confusion. From the subsequent development of the Sutta, it is clear that the issues that perplexed them were the reality of rebirth and kammic retribution for good and evil deeds.

The Buddha begins by assuring the Kālāmas that under such circumstances it is proper for them to doubt, an assurance which encourages free inquiry. He next speaks the passage quoted above, advising the Kālāmas to abandon those things they know for themselves to be bad and to undertake those things they know for themselves to be good. This advice can be dangerous if given to those whose ethical sense is undeveloped, and we can thus assume that the Buddha regarded the Kālāmas as people of refined moral sensitivity. In any case he did not leave them wholly to their own resources, but by questioning them led them to see that greed, hate and delusion, being conducive to harm and suffering for oneself and others, are to be abandoned, and their opposites, being beneficial to all, are to be developed.

The Buddha next explains that a "noble disciple, devoid of covetousness and ill-will, undeluded" dwells pervading the world with boundless loving-kindness, compassion, appreciative joy and equanimity. Thus purified of hate and malice, he enjoys here and now four "solaces". If there is an afterlife and kammic result, then he will undergo a pleasant rebirth, while if there is none he still lives happily here and now; if evil results befall an evil-doer, then no evil will befall him, and if evil results do not befall an evil-doer, then he is purified anyway. With this the Kālāmas express their appreciation of the Buddha's discourse and go for refuge to the Triple Gem.

Now does the Kālāma Sutta suggest, as is often held, that a follower of the Buddhist path can dispense with all faith and doctrine, that he should make his own personal experience the criterion for judging the Buddha's utterances and for rejecting what cannot be squared with it? It is true the Buddha does not ask the Kālāmas to accept anything he says out of confidence in himself, but let us note one important point: the Kālāmas, at the start of the discourse, were not the Buddha's disciples. They approached him merely as a counsellor who might help dispel their doubts, but they did not come to him as the Tathāgata, the Truth-finder, who might show them the way to spiritual progress and to final liberation.

Thus, because the Kālāmas had not yet come to accept the Buddha in terms of his unique mission as the discloser of the liberating truth, it would not have been in place for him to expound to them the Dhamma unique to his own Dispensation—such teachings as the Four Noble Truths, the three characteristics, and the methods of contemplation based upon them. These teachings are specifically intended for those who have accepted the Buddha as their guide to deliverance, and in the suttas he expounds them only to those who have gained faith in the Tathāgata" and who possess the perspective necessary to grasp them and apply them.

The Kālāmas, however, at the start of the discourse are not yet fertile soil for him to sow the seeds of his liberating message. Still confused by the conflicting claims to which they have been exposed, they are not yet clear even about the groundwork of morality.

Nevertheless, after advising the Kālāmas not to rely upon established tradition, abstract reasoning or charismatic gurus, the Buddha proposes to them a teaching that is immediately verifiable and capable of laying a firm foundation for a life of moral discipline and mental purification. He shows that whether or not there be another life after death, a life of moral restraint and of love and compassion for all beings brings its own intrinsic rewards here and now, a happiness and sense of inward security far superior to the fragile pleasures that can be won by violating moral principles and indulging the mind's desires. For those who are not concerned to look further, who are not prepared to adopt any convictions about a future life and worlds beyond the present one, such a teaching will ensure their present welfare and their safe passage to a pleasant rebirth—provided they do not fall into the wrong view of denying an after-life and kammic causation.

However, for those whose vision is capable of widening to encompass the broader horizons of our existence, this teaching given to the Kālāmas points beyond its immediate implications to the very core of the Dhamma. For the three states brought forth for examination by the Buddha—greed, hate and delusion—are not merely grounds of wrong conduct or moral stains upon the mind. Within his teaching's own framework they are the root defilements, the primary causes of all bondage and suffering, and the entire practice of the Dhamma can be viewed as the task of eradicating these evil roots by developing to perfection their antidotes—dispassion, kindness and wisdom.

Thus the discourse to the Kālāmas offers an acid test for gaining confidence in the Dhamma as a viable doctrine of deliverance. We begin with an immediately verifiable teaching whose validity can be attested by anyone with the moral integrity to follow it through to its conclusions, namely, that the defilements cause harm and suffering both personal and social, that their removal brings peace and happiness, and that the practices taught by the Buddha are effective means for achieving their removal. By putting this teaching to a personal test, with only a provisional trust in the Buddha as one's collateral, one eventually arrives at a firmer, experientially-grounded confidence in the liberating and purifying power of the Dhamma. This increased confidence in the teaching brings along a deepened faith in the Buddha as teacher, and thus disposes one to accept on trust those principles he enunciates that are relevant to the quest for awakening, even when they lie beyond one's own capacity for verification. This, in fact, marks the acquisition of right view, in its preliminary role as the forerunner of the entire Noble Eightfold Path.

Partly in reaction to dogmatic religion, partly in subservience to the reigning paradigm of objective scientific knowledge, it has become fashionable to hold, by appeal to the Kālāma Sutta, that the Buddha's teaching dispenses with faith and formulated doctrine and asks us to accept only what we can personally verify. This interpretation of the Sutta, however, forgets that the advice the Buddha gave the Kālāmas was contingent upon the understanding that they were not yet prepared to place faith in him and his doctrine; it also forgets that the Sutta omits, for that very reason, all mention of right view and of the entire perspective that opens up when right view is acquired. It offers instead the most reasonable counsel on wholesome living possible when the issue of ultimate beliefs has been put into brackets.

What can be justly maintained is that those aspects of the Buddha's teaching that come within the purview of our ordinary experience can be personally confirmed within experience, and that this confirmation provides a sound basis for placing faith in those aspects of the teaching that necessarily transcend ordinary experience. Faith in the Buddha's teaching is never regarded as an end in itself nor as a sufficient guarantee of liberation, but only as the starting point for an evolving process of inner transformation that comes to fulfilment in personal insight. But in order for this insight to exercise a truly liberative function, it must unfold in the context of an accurate grasp of the essential truths concerning our situation in the world and the domain where deliverance is to be sought. These truths have been imparted to us by the Buddha out of his own profound comprehension of the human condition. To accept them in trust after careful consideration is to set foot on a journey which transforms faith into wisdom, confidence into certainty, and culminates in liberation from suffering.

From BPS Newsletter No. 9, Spring 1988.

14. A STATEMENT OF CONSCIENCE

"All beings tremble at the rod" says the Buddha, yet today the ominous rod of terrorism has become one of the gravest problems that we face. No longer is the terrorist threat reserved for the vulnerable public figure or the outspoken adversary. With their lightning speed and global reach, our modern media of communication have given the terrorist cadres a tremendous new power to intimidate whole populations. Far too often the victims of their hits are the helpless and innocent, struck down in a symbolic show of hate.

This appalling increase in terrorist violence pierces the moral consciousness at its core, leaving behind painful and persisting wounds. For those of us who reside in Sri Lanka the problem becomes ever more acute as we witness the tide of terrorism sweep across this traditional homeland of the Dhamma. It is no longer possible for us to immerse ourselves in the comfortable routines of our familiar world. Instead we must struggle in anguish and hope to deal with this frightful menace in our midst-to understand it and to confront it in a manner worthy of our Buddhist heritage. It cannot be disputed that the world-wide rise of terrorism springs from complex causes of a political, economic and social character, which must be tackled by any adequate solution to the problem. At the same time, however, we have to insist that terrorism also has a deeper underlying human dimension that can only be ignored at our peril. If we probe beneath the burning issues of political ideology and ethnic grievances around which the terrorist forces rally, we will discover at its epicentre those same malignant drives that, in less virulent form, motivate so much ordinary human conduct.

As the vital dynamism from which terrorism springs we will find greed, a rapacious lust for power and domination. We will find hate, smouldering within as cold resentment or whipped up into a frenzy of destruction. And we will find delusion, a collective paranoia instilled by inflammatory ideologies or the blind submergence of the individual in the group. These are the hidden human roots of terrorism; fed by personal frustration and social discontent, they yield as their fruits the violence that surrounds us.

As we grapple with the problem of terrorism, asking ourselves what we can contribute to stem its rising tide, we may find an answer closer to home than we imagine. Let us first note that the spread of terrorism is not so much a macabre deviation from prevailing norms as an extreme manifestation of a wholesale decline in human fellow feeling. This lack of empathy and sensitivity to others can already be discerned in the everyday functioning of society in the spreading disease of corruption, apathy and selfishness infecting the social organism. Add to this a frantic search for a sense of belonging through the rediscovery of ethnic roots, and the result is a potentially very explosive mixture.

If this much is recognised, we may then see that one of the most effective countermeasures we can apply in our individual capacity against the growth of terrorism lies very much within our reach. Simply put, it consists in reaffirming to ourselves, and teaching by precept and example those fundamental ethical values upon which a harmonious and peaceful society is founded. This reaffirmation of genuine moral values of compassion, honesty, truthfulness, tolerance and respect for others will sound a thunderous statement of conscience. Whether made audibly or privately to oneself, it will raise a note of protest against the moral negligence from which terrorism draws its sustenance, acclaiming our confidence in the power of the good. While we should not cherish unrealistic expectations about our ability to reshape the world, we also should not lose sight of our responsibility to counter prevalent trends. Nor should we discount our ability to make an impact. The clear and decisive commitment to ethical values has a quiet potency that can effect important changes both outwardly and inwardly. While subtly altering the interpersonal aspects of our lives, within our hearts it will fortify those two mental factors that the Buddha called the guardians of the world-shame and moral dread-the former the innate repugnance towards evil, the latter the fear of its consequences. Above all, we must reaffirm the need to rise above the limiting perspectives of the self-centred point of view in which so many today have become entrenched. Recognising that every community, and the world as a whole, is ultimately harmed by the struggle of each faction to secure its individual ends, we must stand up for the development of a sense of humane responsibility that will transcend divisive loyalties. The lesson that we must learn and teach is that embedded in the ancient maxim taught by the Buddha: "Considering others as oneself, do not hurt them or cause them harm." To recognise others as being essentially the same as oneself and to feel their wish for happiness as one's own, this is the only effective means we can propose to build the peaceful society for which we yearn.

From BPS Newsletter No. 10, Summer-Fall 1988.

15. The Vital Link

At the same time that Buddhism has begun to gain a firm foothold in the West, its fate in its traditional Asian homelands has been moving, sadly, in the opposite direction, towards atrophy and decline. Already in several Asian Buddhist countries Buddhism has been forcibly suppressed, while even in those countries which have preserved their political integrity the Dhamma no longer occupies the same sovereign place in people's hearts that it held in an earlier era. Although devotional piety and a sense of Buddhist personal identity still remain strong, throughout the breadth of Buddhist Asia cultural and ideological forces of great power have been unleashed which daily challenge the hegemony of the Dhamma as the key to meaning and value for those who profess it as their refuge.

Among the changes taking place in current patterns of thinking, perhaps the most detrimental to the Dhamma has been the rise to prominence of a materialistic world view which focuses upon the present life as the only field for all human endeavour. This world view need not be assented to intellectually, with full awareness of its implications, for it to become a major determinant of our attitudes and conduct. Often a curious ambivalence prevails in our minds, where with one part of the mind we profess our confidence in the lofty principles of the Dhamma, while with the other we think and act as if the present life were the sole occasion for human happiness and the achievement of worldly success were the true mark of the accomplished individual.

The rapid spread of the materialistic world view has in turn brought about a far-ranging secularisation of values that invades every nook and cranny of our lives. This transformation of values gives precedence to goals and attitudes diametrically opposed to those advocated by the Dhamma, and under its impact the scales have tipped far away even from a reasonable balance between material and spiritual goods. Now we see acquisitiveness replacing contentment as the reigning ideal, competition taking the place of co-operation, fast efficiency the place of compassionate concern, and selfish indulgence the place of abstinence and self-control.

The attempt to live simultaneously by two conflicting sets of principles—those being ushered in by secular materialism and those grounded in the Dhamma—generates a tension that contains within it a seed of very destructive potential. Often the tension is only dimly felt by those in the older generation, who accept the new outlook and values without clearly perceiving the challenge they pose to traditional Buddhist ideals.

It is when the contradiction is pushed down to the next generation, to the Buddhist youth of today, that the inherent incompatibility of the two perspectives comes into the open as a clear-cut choice between two alternative philosophies of life, one proposing a hierarchy of values which culminates in the spiritual and sanctions restraint and renunciation, the other holding up the indulgence and gratification of personal desire as the highest conceivable goal. Since the latter appeals to strong and deep-seated human drives, it is hardly puzzling that so many young people today have turned away from the guidance of the Dhamma to pursue the new paths to instant pleasure opened up by the consumer society or, in their frustration at missed opportunities, to take to the path of violence.

Since it is the younger generation that forms the vital link in the continuity of Buddhism, connecting its past with its future, it is of paramount importance that the Buddhist youth of today should retain their fidelity to the Dhamma. The Dhamma should be for them not merely a symbol of cultural and ethnic identity, not merely a focus point of sentimental piety, but above all a path to be taken to heart, personally applied, and adhered to in those critical choices between present expediency and long-range spiritual gain. The problem, however, is precisely how to inspire the young to look to the Dhamma as their guide and infallible refuge.

It must be stressed that our present dilemma goes far deeper than a breakdown of moral standards, and thus that it cannot be easily rectified by pious preaching and moral exhortation. If conduct deviating from the Dhamma has become widespread among today's youth, this is because the Buddhist vision has ceased to be meaningful to them, and it has ceased to be meaningful not because it has lost its relevance but because it is not being presented in ways which highlight its timeless and ever-immediate relevance. The most urgent task facing those concerned with the preservation of Buddhism must be the attempt to communicate to the young the central vision at the heart of the Dhamma, the vision from which all the specific doctrines and practices of Buddhism issue forth. This does not require a mastery of the technical details of the Dhamma, but it does require that we ourselves understand the Dhamma's essence and are actively striving to make that understanding the foundation of our lives. Both by precept and example we must show that true freedom is to be found not in uncontrolled licence, but in the control and mastery of desire; that true happiness lies not in a proliferation of goods, but in peace and contentment; that our relations with others are most rewarding when they are governed not by conflict and competition, but by kindness and compassion; and that true security is to be achieved not by the acquisition of wealth and power, but by the conquest of self with all its ambitions and conceits.

From BPS Newsletter No. 11, Winter 1989.

16. A REMEDY FOR DESPAIR

Most of us live in the cramped cold cages of our private projects, frantically struggling to stake out our own little comfortable place in the sun. Driven in circles by anxious yearnings and beckoning desires, we rarely ever glance aside to see how our neighbour is faring, and when we do, it is usually only to assure ourselves that he is not trying to encroach upon our own domain or to find some means by which we might extend our dominion over his.

Occasionally, however, it somehow happens that we manage to detach ourselves from our obsessive pursuits long enough to arrive at a wider clearing. Here our focus of concern undergoes a remarkable shift. Lifted above our habitual fixation on myopic goals, we are brought to realise that we share our journey from birth to death with countless other beings who, like ourselves, are each intent on a quest for the good. This realisation, which often topples our egocentric notions of the good, broadens and deepens our capacity for empathy. By breaking down the walls of self-concern it allows us to experience, with a particularly inward intimacy, the desire all beings cherish to be free from harm and to find an inviolable happiness and security. Nevertheless, to the extent that this flowering of empathy is not a mere emotional effusion but is accompanied by a facility for accurate observation, it can easily turn into a chute plunging us down from our new-found freedom into a chasm of anguish and despair.

For when, with eyes unhindered by emotively-tinged blinkers, we turn to contemplate the wide expanse of the world, we find ourselves gazing into a mass of suffering that is vertiginous in its volume and ghastly in its intensity. The guarantor of our complacency is the dumb thoughtless glee with which we acquiesce in our daily ration of sensual excitation and ego-enhancing kudos. Let us raise our heads a little higher and cast our eyes about, and we behold a world steeped in pain where the ills inherent in the normal life-cycle are compounded still more by the harshness of nature, the grim irony of accident, and the cruelty of human beings. As we grope about for a handle to prevent ourselves from plummeting down into the pits of despondency, we may find the support we need in a theme taught for frequent recollection by the Buddha: "Beings are the owners of their kamma, the heirs of their kamma; they are moulded, formed and upheld by their kamma, and they inherit the results of their own good and bad deeds." Often enough this reflection has been proposed as a means to help us adjust to the vicissitudes in our personal fortunes: to accept gain and loss, success and failure, pleasure and pain, with a mind that remains unperturbed. This same theme, however, can also serve a wider purpose, offering us succour when we contemplate the immeasurably greater suffering in which the multitudes of our fellow beings are embroiled.

Confronted with a world that is ridden with conflict, violence, exploitation and destruction, we feel compelled to find some way to make sense out of their evil consequences, to be able to see in calamity and devastation something more than regrettable but senseless quirks of fate. The Buddha's teaching on kamma and its fruit gives us the key to decipher the otherwise unintelligible stream of events. It instructs us to recognise in the diverse fortunes of living beings, not caprice or accident, but the operation of a principle of moral equilibrium which ensures that ultimately a perfect balance obtains between the happiness and suffering beings undergo and the ethical quality of their intentional actions.

Contemplation on the operation of kamma is not a cold and calculated expedient for justifying a stoical resignation to the status quo. The pathways of kamma are labyrinthine in their complexity, and acceptance of this causal order does not preclude a battle against human avarice, brutality and stupidity, or stifle beneficent action intended to prevent unwholesome deeds from finding the opportunity to ripen. Deep reflection on kammic retribution does, however, brace us against the shocks of calamity and disappointment by opening up to our vision the stubborn unwieldiness of a world ruled by greed, hate and delusion, and the deep hidden lawfulness connecting its turbulent undercurrents with the back-and-forth swing of surface events. While on the one hand this contemplation awakens a sense of urgency, a drive to escape the repetitive round of deed and result, on the other it issues in equanimity, an unruffled inner poise founded upon a realistic grasp of our existential plight. Genuine equanimity, which is far from callous indifference, sustains us in our journey through the rapids of *saṃsāra*. Bestowing upon us courage and endurance, it enables us to meet the fluctuations of fortune without being shaken by them, and to look into the face of the world's sufferings without being shattered by them.

From BPS Newsletter No. 12, Spring 1989.

17. THE PROBLEM OF CONFLICT

I
t is one of the bitterest ironies of human life that although virtually all human beings cherish a desire to live in peace, we continually find ourselves embroiled in conflict, pitted against others in relationships marred by tension, distrust or open hostility. This irony is particularly poignant because it is immediately evident to us that cordial, harmonious relations with others are a necessary condition for our own genuine happiness. Not only do such relations allow us to pursue undisturbed the goals we consider essential to our personal fulfilment, but they bring us the deeper joy of meaningful communion with our fellow human beings. Contentious living, in contrast, is always intrinsically painful, involving a hardening of our subjective armour, a tightening of the knots of anger and hate. Indeed, whatever the outcome of conflict may be, whether victory or defeat, the result itself is ultimately detrimental for both victor and victim alike.

Nevertheless, although harmonious living promises such rich blessings and discordant relations entail so much harm and misery, for the most part our lives and the lives of those around us are entangled in a ravelled net of quarrels and disputes. Conflict may simmer within as silent suspicion and resentment or it may explode into violent rage and devastation. It may implicate us at the level of personal relationships, or as members of an ethnic group, a political party, a social class or a nation. But in one or another of its many manifestations, the presence of conflict in our lives seems inescapable. Peace and harmony hover in the distance as beautiful dreams for a summer's night or noble ideals to which we pledge formal allegiance. But when reality knocks and dreams are dispelled, we find ourselves drawn, usually against our better judgment, into an arena where the pleasures that we seek exact as their price the hard cash of struggle and contention.

The teachings of the Buddha, while framed around the goal of individual deliverance from suffering, are also expounded for the purpose of instructing us in how we can live in harmony with others. Such harmony is desirable not only as a source of satisfaction in itself, but also because it is a prerequisite for treading the path to the higher freedom. The final peace of enlightenment can arise only in a mind that is at peace with others, and the mind can only be at peace with others when we are actively committed to a course of training that enables us to extricate the roots of conflict that lie buried deep within our hearts.

Once, in ancient India, Sakka the ruler of the gods came to the Buddha and asked: "By what bonds are people bound whereby, though they wish to live in peace without hate and hostility, they yet live in conflict with hate and hostility." The Master replied: "It is the bonds of envy and avarice that so bind people that, though they wish to live in peace, they live in conflict with hate and hostility." If we trace external conflicts back to their source, we will find that they originate not in wealth, position or possessions, but in the mind itself. They spring up because we envy others for the qualities they possess which we desire for ourselves, and because we are driven by an unquenchable avarice to extend the boundaries of what we can label 'mine'.

Envy and avarice in turn are grounded in two more fundamental psychological conditions. Envy arises because we identify things as 'I', because we perpetually seek to establish a personal identity for ourselves internally and to project that identity outward for others to recognize and accept. Avarice arises because we appropriate: we attempt to carve out a territory for ourselves and to furnish that territory with possessions that will titillate our greed and sense of self-importance. Conflict being thus rooted in envy and avarice, it follows that the path to non-conflict must be a course of relinquishment, of removing the constrictive thoughts and desires that pivot around the notions of 'I' and 'mine', the drives to identify and to possess. This course reaches consummation with the full maturity of wisdom, with insight into the empty, egoless nature of all phenomena; for it is this insight which exposes the hollowness of the notions of 'I' and 'mine' that underlie envy and avarice. However, although the final liberation from clinging may lie far away, the path leading to it is a gradual one, growing out of simpler, more basic steps that lie very close to our feet.

Two such necessary steps are changes in attitude with the power to transmute envy and avarice. One is altruistic joy (*muditā*), the ability to view the success of others with the same gladness we experience at our own success. The other is generosity (*cāga*), the readiness to give and to relinquish. The former is the specific antidote for envy, the latter the antidote for avarice. What is common to both is a lifting of the sense of identity from its narrow fixation on the self, and a broadening of it to encompass others who share our desire to be happy and free from suffering.

As private individuals we cannot hope to resolve by our will the larger patterns of conflict that engulf the societies and nations to which we belong. We live in a world that thrives on conflict, and in which the forces that nurture conflict are pervasive, obstinate and terribly powerful. But as followers of the Enlightened One, what we can do and must do is to testify by our conduct to the supremacy of peace: to avoid words and actions that engender animosity, to heal divisions, to demonstrate the value of harmony and concord. The model we must emulate is that provided by the Master in his description of the true disciple: "He is one who unites the divided, who promotes friendships, enjoys concord, rejoices in concord, delights in concord, and who speaks words that promote concord."

From BPS Newsletter No. 13, Summer–Autumn 1989.

18. THE QUEST FOR MEANING

However much the modern world may pride itself on its triumphs over the follies and foibles of the past, it appears that the progress we credit ourselves with has been bought at a price so steep as to throw into question the worth of our achievements. This price has been nothing less than the shared conviction that our lives are endowed with ultimate meaning. Though in earlier ages men and women lived in a space populated largely by figments of the collective imagination, they could still claim a precious asset that we sorely lack: a firm and buoyant belief that their everyday lives were encompassed by a penumbra of enduring significance stemming from their relation to a transcendent goal. Present-day attitudes, however, moulded by scientific reductionism and technocratic audacity, have combined forces to sweep away from our minds even the faint suspicion that our lives may possess any deeper meaning than material prosperity and technological innovation. For an increasing number of people today the consequence of this militancy has been a pervasive sense of meaninglessness. Cut loose from our moorings in a living spiritual tradition, we find ourselves adrift on a sea of confusion where all values seem arbitrary and relative. We float aimlessly along the waves of caprice, without any supreme purpose to serve as the polestar for our ideals, as the wellspring for inspired thought and action.

But just as little as nature can tolerate a vacuum, so humankind can little tolerate a complete loss of meaning. Thence, to escape the plunge into the abyss of meaninglessness, we grasp after flotsam, attempting to immerse ourselves in distractions. We pursue pleasure and power, seek to augment our wealth and status, surround ourselves with contraptions, invest our hopes in personal relationships that only conceal our own inner poverty. At the same time, however, that our absorption in distractions helps us to cope with the psychological void, it also stifles in us a deeper and still more insistent need—the longing for a peace and freedom that does not depend upon external contingencies. One of the great blessings of the Buddha's teaching is the remedy it can offer for the problem of meaninglessness so widespread in human life today. The Dhamma can serve as a source of meaning primarily because it provides us with the two requisites of a meaningful life: an ultimate goal for which to live, and a clear-cut but flexible set of instructions by which we can advance towards that goal from whatever station in life we start from.

In the Buddha's teaching the quest for ultimate meaning does not begin, as in the theistic religions, with propositions about a supernatural scheme of salvation to be assented to in faith. It begins, rather, by focusing upon an experiential problem right at the crux of human existence. The problem, of course, is the problem of suffering, the boundaries of which are shown to extend beyond our immediate subjection to pain, misery and sorrow, and to encompass all that is conditioned precisely because of its impermanence, its vulnerability, its lack of abiding substance.

The goal of the teaching, the unconditioned element which is Nibbāna, then comes to have a decisive bearing upon our vital concerns because it is apprehended as the cessation of suffering. Though in its own nature it defies all the limiting categories of conceptual thought, as the cessation of suffering Nibbāna provides the final answer to our innermost yearnings for an imperishable peace, for complete freedom from sorrow, anxiety and distress. The way that the quest for this goal intersects with the course of our everyday life is made plain by the Buddha's analysis of the cause of suffering. The cause of suffering, the Buddha holds, lies within ourselves, in our selfish craving conjoined with blinding ignorance, in the three evil roots that taint our normal engagement with the world: greed, hate and delusion. Thence the freedom from suffering that we seek lies in the eradication of these three roots.

To orient our life towards the goal of deliverance from suffering requires that we tread the path that leads to and merges with the goal. This path is the Noble Eightfold Path, which brings an end to suffering and bondage by enabling us to extricate the causes of suffering embedded in our hearts. We begin the path exactly where we are, in the midst of error and defilement, and by clarifying our views, transforming our attitudes and purifying our minds, we advance by stages towards the direct realisation of the ultimate good.

If the goal towards which the path points lies beyond the pale of conditioned existence, to walk the eightfold path is to discover within the confines of conditioned existence dimensions of meaning previously unknown. This richness of meaning stems from a twofold source. One is the recognition that the following of the path brings a diminishment of suffering for ourselves as well as others, and at the same time an enhancement of joy, mental equipoise and peace. The other source of meaning is the conviction that the values we are pursuing are not merely subjective and arbitrary, but are grounded in an absolutely objective order, in the very nature of things.

As we embark on the way to the end of suffering, the final goal no longer appears merely as a distant shore but becomes refracted in our experience as the challenge of overcoming the unwholesome roots, and of assisting our fellow beings to do the same. This challenge, the task of actualising our own good and the good of others, becomes at the same time life's inner core of meaning: to transmute greed into generosity and relinquishment, to replace hate with love and compassion, and to dispel delusion with the light of liberative wisdom.

From BPS Newsletter No. 14, Winter 1990.

19. The Search for Security

It may be a truism of psychology that the desire for happiness is the most fundamental human drive, but it is important to note that this desire generally operates within the bounds set by another drive just as deep and pervasive. This other drive is the need for security. However insistent the raw itch for pleasure and gain may be, it is usually held in check by a cautious concern for our personal safety. We only feel at ease when we are sealed off from manifest danger, comfortably at home with ourselves and with our world, snugly tucked into familiar territory where everything seems friendly and dependable.

When we come across the Buddha's teaching and begin to take that teaching seriously, we often find that it provokes in us disturbing waves of disquietude. This feeling arises from a clash, a sensed incompatibility, between the picture of the world that we hold to as the essential basis for our normal sense of security and the new perspectives on existence opened up to us by the Dhamma. We may try to shun the vistas that trouble us, we may pick and choose from the Dhamma what we like, but to the extent that we are prepared to take the teaching in earnest—on its own terms rather than on ours—we may discover that the insights which the Buddha wants to impart to us can be quite unsettling in their impact.

The first noble truth was never intended to be a comfortable truth; indeed, it is the discomforting quality of this truth that makes it noble. It tells us frankly that the routinely placid and predictable surface of our everyday lives is extremely fragile—a shared delusion with which we lull ourselves and each other into a false sense of security. Just beneath the surface, hidden from view, turbulent currents are stirring which at any time can break the surface calm. From the moment we are born we are sliding towards old age and death, susceptible to various diseases and accidents that may hasten our arrival at the appointed end. Driven by our desires we wander from life to life across the sand dunes of *saṃsāra*, elated by our rises, shaken by our falls. The very stuff of our lives consists of nothing more than a conglomeration of five 'heaps' of psychophysical processes, without any permanence or substance.

Perhaps the Buddha's most poignant statement on the human condition is his image of a man being swept along by a mountain torrent: he grasps for safety at the grasses along the banks only to find that they break off just as he takes hold of them. However, though the Buddha begins by drawing our attention to the uncertainty that encompasses us even in the midst of comfort and enjoyment, he by no means ends there. The discourse on suffering is expounded, not to lead us to despair, but to awaken us from our complacent slumbers and to set us moving in the direction where our ultimate welfare can be found. Far from undercutting our need to feel secure, the Buddha's teaching unfolds from that very same need, turning it into a sustained inquiry into what genuine security actually means. Ordinarily, our benighted attempts to achieve security are governed by a myopic but imperious self-interest oriented around the standpoint of self. We assume that we possess a solid core of individual being, an inherently existent ego, and thus our varied plans and projects take shape as so many manoeuvres to ward off threats to the self and promote its dominance in the overall scheme of things.

The Buddha turns this whole point of view on its head by pointing out that anxiety is the dark twin of ego. He declares that all attempts to secure the interests of the ego necessarily arise out of clinging, and that the very act of clinging paves the way for our downfall when the object to which we hold perishes, as it must by its very nature. The Buddha maintains that the way to true security lies precisely in the abolition of clinging. When all clinging has been uprooted, when all notions of 'I' and 'mine' have lost their obsessive sting, we will have no more fear, no more worry, no more anxious concern. Touched by the fluctuations of worldly events the mind remains stable, "sorrowless, stainless and secure" (Sn 268). While ultimate security lies only in the unconditioned, in Nibbāna "the supreme security from bondage" (*anuttara yogakkhema*), as we wend our way through the rough terrain of our mundane lives we have available a provisional source of security that will help us deal effectively with the dangers and difficulties that beset us. This provisional security lies in firmly committing ourselves to the Dhamma as our source of solace and guidance, as our incomparable refuge. The word '*dhamma*' itself means that which upholds and supports. The Buddha's teaching is called the Dhamma because it upholds those who live by it—it wards off the dangers to which we would be exposed if we were to flout it; it sustains us in our endeavour for the final good if we revere it and make it the foundation of our lives.

The Dhamma provides protection, not by any mystical blessing or downpour of saving grace, but by indicating the sure and certain guidelines that enable us to protect ourselves. Beneath the apparent randomness of visible events there runs an invisible but indomitable law which ensures that all goodness finds its due recompense. To act counter to this law is to invite disaster. To act in harmony with it is to tap its reserves of energy, to yoke them to one's spiritual growth, and to make oneself a channel of help for others who likewise roam in search of a refuge.

The essential counsel that the Buddha gives us to secure our self-protection is to shun all evil, to practise the good, and to purify our minds. By the pursuit of non-violence, honesty, righteousness and truth, we weave around ourselves an impenetrable net of virtue that ensures our well-being even in the midst of violence and commotion. By cultivating the good we sow the seeds of wholesome qualities that will come to maturity as we continue on our path throughout the saṃsāric journey. And by purifying our minds of greed, hatred and delusion by mindfulness and diligent effort, we will find for ourselves an island that no flood can overwhelm, the island of the Deathless.

From BPS Newsletter No. 15, Spring 1990.

20. SELF-TRANSFORMATION

I t is perhaps symptomatic of the 'fallen' nature of the ordinary human condition that few of us pass the full extent of our lives comfortably reconciled to our natural selves. Even in the midst of prosperity and success, grinding notes of discontent trouble our days and disturbing dreams come to haunt our sleep. As long as our eyes remain coated with dust we incline to locate the cause of our discontent outside ourselves—in spouse, neighbour or job, in implacable fate or fluky chance. But when the dust drops off and our eyes open, we soon find that the real cause lies within.

When we discover how deeply the cause of our unhappiness is lodged in the mind, the realization dawns that cosmetic changes will not be anywhere near enough, that a fundamental internal transformation is required. This desire for a transformed personality, for the emergence of a new man from the ashes of the old, is one of the perennial lures of the human heart. From ancient times it has been a potent wellspring of the spiritual quest, and even in the secular, life-affirming culture of our own cosmopolitan age this longing has not totally disappeared.

While such concepts as redemption, salvation and deliverance may no longer characterize the transformation that is sought, the urge for a radical reshaping of the personality persists as strong as ever, appearing in guises that are compatible with the secular worldview. Where previously this urge sought fulfilment in the temple, ashram and monastery, it now resorts to new venues: the office of the psychoanalyst, the weekend workshop, the panoply of newly spawned therapies and cults. However, despite the change of scene and conceptual framework, the basic pattern remains the same. Disgruntled with the ruts of our ingrained habits, we long to exchange all that is dense and constrictive in our personalities for a new, lighter, freer mode of being.

Self-transformation is also a fundamental goal of the Buddha's teaching, an essential part of his program for liberation from suffering. The Dhamma was never intended for those who are already perfect saints. It is addressed to fallible human beings beset with all the shortcomings typical of unpolished human nature: conduct that is fickle and impulsive, minds that are tainted by greed, anger and selfishness, views that are distorted and habits that lead to harm for oneself and others. The purpose of the teaching is to transform such people—ourselves—into 'accomplished ones', into those whose every action is pure, whose minds are calm and composed, whose wisdom has fathomed the deepest truths and whose conduct is always marked by a compassionate concern for others and for the welfare of the world.

Between these two poles of the teaching—the flawed and knotted personality that we bring with us as raw material into the training; and the fully liberated personality that emerges in the end—there lies a gradual process of self-transformation governed by highly specific guidelines. This transformation is effected by the twin aspects of the path: abandoning (*pahāna*)—the removal from the mind of all that is harmful and unwholesome; and development (*bhāvanā*)—the cultivation of qualities that are wholesome, pure and purifying.

What distinguishes the Buddha's program for self-transformation from the multitude of other systems proposing a similar end is the contribution made by another principle with which it is invariably conjoined. This is the principle of self-transcendence, the endeavour to relinquish all attempts to establish a sense of solid personal identity. In the Buddhist training the aim of transforming the personality must be complemented by a parallel effort to overcome all identification with the elements that constitute our phenomenal being. The teaching of *anatta* or not-self is not so much a philosophical thesis calling for intellectual assent as a prescription for self-transcendence. It maintains that our on-going attempt to establish a sense of identity by taking our personalities to be 'I' and 'mine' is in actuality a project born out of clinging, a project that at the same time lies at the root of our suffering. If, therefore, we seek to be free from suffering, we cannot stop with the transformation of the personality into some sublime and elevated mode as the final goal. What is needed, rather, is a transformation that brings about the removal of clinging, and with it, the removal of all tendencies to self-affirmation.

It is important to stress this transcendent aspect of the Dhamma because in our own time when 'immanent' secular values are ascendant, the temptation is great to let this aspect drop out of sight. If we assume that the worth of a practice consists solely in its ability to yield concrete this-worldly results, we may incline to view the Dhamma simply as a means of refining and healing the divided personality, leading in the end to a renewed affirmation of our mundane selves and our situation in the world. Such an approach, however, would ignore the Buddha's insistence that all the elements of our personal existence are impermanent, unsatisfactory and not self, and his counsel that we should learn to distance ourselves from such things and ultimately to discard them. In the proper practice of the Dhamma both principles, that of self-transformation and that of self-transcendence, are equally crucial. The principle of self-transformation alone is blind, leading at best to an ennobled personality but not to a liberated one. The principle of self-transcendence alone is barren, leading to a cold ascetic withdrawal devoid of the potential for enlightenment. It is only when these two complementary principles work in harmony, blended and balanced in the course of training, that they can bridge the gap between the actual and ideal and bring to a fruitful conclusion the quest for the end of suffering.

Of the two principles, that of self-transcendence claims primacy both at the beginning of the path and at the end, for it is this principle that gives direction to the process of self-transformation, revealing the goal towards which a transformation of the personality should lead and the nature of the changes required to bring the goal within our reach. However, the Buddhist path is not a perpendicular ascent to be scaled with picks, ropes and studded boots, but a step-by-step training which unfolds in a natural progression. Thus the abrupt challenge of self-transcendence—the relinquishing of all points of attachment—is met and mastered by the gradual process of self-transformation. By moral discipline, mental purification and the development of insight, we advance by stages from our original condition of bondage to the domain of untrammelled freedom.

From BPS Newsletter No. 16, Summer–Autumn 1990.

21. Laying Down the Rod

The textbooks of history come into our hands bound in decorative covers and set in crisp clear types. To the discerning reader, however, their glossy pages are stained with blood and wet with streams of tears. The story of man's sojourn on this planet has generally not been a very pretty one. For sure, deeds of virtue and flashes of the sublime light up the tale like meteorites shooting across the night-time sky. But the pageant of events that the records spell out for us unfolds according to a repeated pattern in which the dominant motifs are greed and ambition, deceit and distrust, aggression, destruction and revenge.

Each age, when the dust of its own battles clears, tends to see itself as standing at the threshold of a new era in which peace and harmony will at last prevail. This appears to be particularly true of our own time, with its high ideals and great expectations aroused by dramatic shifts in international relations. It would be ingenuous, however, to think that a package solution to the tensions inherent in human coexistence can be devised as easily as a solution to a problem in data management. To cherish the dream that we have arrived at the brink of a new world order in which all conflict, in obedience to our good intentions, will be relegated to the past is to lose sight of the grim obstinacy of those deep dark drives that stir in the human heart: the defilements of greed, hatred and delusion. It is these drives that have brought us into this world of strife and suffering, and it is these same drives that keep the wheel of history turning, erupting periodically in orgies of senseless violence.

Like any other stream, the stream of mundane existence inevitably flows in the direction of least resistance: downwards. The task the Buddha sets before us is not the impossible one of reversing the direction of the flow, but the feasible one of crossing the stream, of arriving safely at the far shore where we will be free from the dangers that beset us as we are swept along by the stream. To cross the stream requires a struggle, not against the current itself, but against the forces that carry us down the current, a struggle against the defilements lodged in the depths of our own minds.

Though violence, either overt or subtle, may hold sway over the world in which we are afloat, the Buddha's path to freedom requires of us that we make a total break with prevailing norms. Thus one of the essential steps in our endeavour to reach the abode of safety is to "lay down the rod," to put away violence, aggression and harmfulness towards all living beings. In the Buddha's teaching, the "laying down of the rod" is not merely an ethical principle, a prescription for right action. It is a comprehensive strategy of self-training that spans all stages of the Buddhist path, enabling us to subdue our inclinations towards ill will, animosity and cruelty.

The key to developing a mind of harmlessness is found in the ancient maxim stated in the Dhammapada: "Putting oneself in the place of another, one should not slay, or incite others to slay." The reason we should avoid harming others is because all living beings, in their innermost nature, share the same essential concern for their own wellbeing and happiness. When we look into our own minds, we can immediately see with intuitive certainty that the fundamental desire at the root of our being is the desire to be well and happy, to be free from all harm, danger and distress. We see at once that we wish to live, not to die; that we wish to be happy, not to suffer; that we wish to pursue our goals freely, without hindrance and obstruction by others. When we see that this wish for wellbeing and happiness is the most basic desire at the root of our own being, by a simple imaginative projection we can then recognise, again with intuitive certainty, that the same fundamental desire also animates the minds of all other living beings. Just as we wish to be well, so every other being wishes to be well; just as we wish to be happy, so every other being wishes to be happy; just as we wish to pursue our goals freely, so all other beings wish to pursue their goals freely, without hindrance and obstruction.

This fundamental identity of aim that we share with all other beings has implications for each stage of the threefold Buddhist training in morality, mental purification and wisdom. Since all other beings, like ourselves, are intent on their welfare and happiness, by putting ourselves in their place we can recognise the need to regulate our conduct by principles of restraint that hold in check all harmful bodily and verbal deeds. Because afflictive deeds originate from the mind, from thoughts of animosity and cruelty, it becomes necessary for us to purify our minds of these taints through the practice of concentration, developing as their specific antidotes the "divine abodes" of loving kindness and compassion. And because all defiled thoughts tending towards harm for others arise from roots lodged deep in the recesses of the mind, we need to undertake the development of wisdom which alone can extricate the hidden roots of evil.

Since the state of the world is a manifestation and reflection of the minds of its inhabitants, the achievement of a permanent universal peace would require nothing short of a radical and widespread transformation in the minds of these inhabitants—a beautiful but unrealistic fantasy. What lies within the scope of real possibility is the attainment of a lasting individual peace within ourselves, a peace that comes with the fulfilment of the Buddha's threefold training. This internal peace, however, will not remain locked up in our hearts. Overflowing its source, it will radiate outwards, exercising a gentle and uplifting influence upon the lives of those who come within its range. As the old Indian adage says, one can never make the earth safe for one's feet by sweeping away all thorns and gravel, but if one wears a pair of shoes, one's feet will be comfortable everywhere. One can never be free from enmity by eliminating all one's foes, but if one strikes down one thing—the thought of hate—then one will see no enemies anywhere.

From BPS Newsletter No. 18, Spring 1991.

22. THE NOBILITY OF THE TRUTHS

The most common and widely known formulation of the Buddha's teaching is that which the Buddha himself announced in the First Sermon at Benares, the formula of the Four Noble Truths. The Buddha declares that these truths convey in a nutshell all the essential information that we need to set out on the path to liberation. He says that just as the elephant's footprint, by reason of its great size, contains the footprints of all other animals, so the Four Noble Truths, by reason of their comprehensiveness, contain within themselves all wholesome and beneficial teachings. However, while many expositors of Buddhism have devoted attention to explaining the actual content of the four truths, only rarely is any consideration given to the reason why they are designated *noble* truths. Yet it is just this descriptive word 'noble' that reveals to us why the Buddha chose to cast his teaching into this specific format, and it is this same term that allows us to experience, even from afar, the unique flavour that pervades the entire doctrine and discipline of the Enlightened One.

The word 'noble'—*ariya*—is used by the Buddha to designate a particular type of person, the type of person which it is the aim of his teaching to create. In the discourses, the Buddha classifies human beings into two broad categories. On one side there are the *puthujjanas*, the worldlings, those belonging to the multitude, whose eyes are still covered with the dust of defilements and delusion. On the other side, there are the ariyans, the noble ones, the spiritual elite, who obtain this status not from birth, social station or ecclesiastical authority but from their inward nobility of character.

These two general types are not separated from each other by an impassable chasm, each confined to a tightly sealed compartment. A series of gradations can be discerned rising up from the darkest level of the blind worldling trapped in the dungeon of egotism and self-assertion, through the stage of the virtuous worldling in whom the seeds of wisdom are beginning to sprout, and further through the intermediate stages of noble disciples to the perfected individual at the apex of the entire scale of human development. This is the arahant, the liberated one, who has absorbed the purifying vision of truth so deeply that all his defilements have been extinguished, and with them, all liability to suffering.

While the path from bondage to deliverance, from worldliness to spiritual nobility, is a graded path involving gradual practice and gradual progress, it is not a uniform continuum. Progress occurs in discrete steps, and at a certain point—the point separating the status of a worldling from that of a noble one—a break is reached which must be crossed, not by simply taking another step forward, but by making a leap, by jumping across from the near side to the farther shore. This decisive event in the inner development of the practitioner, this radical leap that propels the disciple from the domain and lineage of the worldling to the domain and lineage of the noble ones, occurs precisely through the penetration of the Four Noble Truths. This discloses to us the critical reason why the four truths revealed by the Buddha are called noble truths. They are noble truths because when we have penetrated them through to the core, when we have grasped their real import and implications, we cast off the status of the worldling and acquire the status of a noble one, drawn out from the faceless crowd into the community of the Blessed One's disciples united by a unique and unshakeable vision.

Prior to the penetration of the truths, however well-endowed we may be with spiritual virtues, we are not yet on secure ground. We are not immune from regression, not yet assured of deliverance, not invincible in our striving on the path. The virtues of a worldling are tenuous virtues. They may wax or they may wane, they may flourish or decline, and in correspondence with their degree of strength we may rise or fall in our movement through the cycle of becoming. When our virtues are replete, we may rise upwards and dwell in bliss among the gods. When our virtues decline or our merit is exhausted, we may sink again to miserable depths.

But with the penetration of the truths, we leap across the gulf that separates us from the ranks of the noble ones. The eye of Dhamma has been opened, the vision of truth stands revealed, and though the decisive victory has not yet been won, the path to the final goal lies at our feet and the supreme security from bondage hovers on the horizon. One who has comprehended the truths has changed lineage, crossed over from the domain of the worldlings to the domain of the noble ones. Such a disciple is incapable of regression to the ranks of the worldling, incapable of losing the vision of truth that has flashed before his inner eye. Progress towards the final goal, the complete eradication of ignorance and craving, may be slow or rapid; it may occur easily or result from an uphill battle. But however long it may take, with whatever degree of facility one may advance, one thing is certain: such a disciple who has seen with immaculate clarity the Four Noble Truths can never slide backwards, can never lose the status of a noble one, and is bound to reach the final fruit of arahantship in a maximum of seven lives. The reason why the penetration of the Four Noble Truths can confer this immutable nobility of spirit is implied by the four tasks the noble truths impose on us. By taking these tasks as our challenge in life—our challenge as followers of the Enlightened One—from whatever station of development we find ourselves beginning at, we can gradually advance towards the infallible penetration of the noble ones.

The first noble truth, the truth of suffering, is to be fully understood: the task it assigns us is that of full understanding. A hallmark of the noble ones is that they do not flow along thoughtlessly in the stream of life, but endeavour to comprehend existence from within as honestly and thoroughly as possible. For us, too, it is necessary to reflect upon the nature of our life. We must attempt to fathom the deep significance of an existence bounded on one side by birth and on the other by death, and subject in between to all the types of suffering detailed by the Buddha in his discourses.

The second noble truth, of the origin or cause of suffering, implies the task of abandonment. A noble one is such because he has initiated the process of eliminating the defilements at the root of suffering, and we too, if we aspire to reach the plane of the noble ones, must be prepared to withstand the seductive lure of the defilements. While the eradication of craving can come only with the supramundane realisations, even in the mundane course of our daily life we can learn to restrain the coarser manifestation of defilements, and by keen self-observation can gradually loosen their grip upon our hearts.

The third noble truth, the cessation of suffering, implies the task of realisation. Although Nibbāna, the extinction of suffering, can only be personally realised by the noble ones, the confidence we place in the Dhamma as our guideline to life shows us what we should select as our final aspiration, as our ultimate ground of value. Once we have grasped the fact that all conditioned things in the world, being impermanent and insubstantial, can never give us total satisfaction, we can then lift our aim to the unconditioned element, Nibbāna, the Deathless, and make that aspiration the pole around which we order our everyday choices and concerns.

Finally, the fourth noble truth, the Noble Eightfold Path, assigns us the task of development. The noble ones have reached their status by developing the eightfold path, and while only the noble ones are assured of never deviating from the path, the Buddha's teaching gives us the meticulous instructions that we need to tread the path culminating in the plane of the noble ones. This is the path that gives birth to vision, that gives birth to knowledge, that leads to higher comprehension, enlightenment and Nibbāna, the crowning attainment of nobility.

From BPS Newsletter No. 20, First Mailing 1992.

23. Refuge in the Buddha

The first step in entering the Buddhist path is going for refuge to the Triple Gem, and the first of the three gems that we approach as refuge is the Buddha, the Enlightened One. Because the act of going for refuge to the Buddha marks the beginning of a new chapter in our life, it is worth our while to repeatedly pause and reflect upon the significance of this momentous step. Too often we are prone to take our first steps for granted. Yet it is only if we review these steps from time to time in a deepening awareness of their implications that we can be sure the following steps we take will bring us closer to our desired destination.

The going for refuge to the Buddha is not a single action which occurs only once and is then completed with absolute finality. It is, or should be, a continually evolving process which matures in tandem with our practice and understanding of the Dhamma. To go for refuge does not imply that at the outset we already possess a clear grasp of the dangers that make a refuge necessary or of the goal towards which we aspire. Comprehension of these matters grows gradually over time. But to the extent that we have actually gone for refuge with sincere intent, we should make an earnest effort to sharpen and deepen our understanding of the objects to which we have turned as the basis for our deliverance.

In going for refuge to the Buddha it is most essential at the outset to clarify our conception of what a Buddha is and how he functions as a refuge. If such clarification is lacking, our sense of refuge can easily become tainted by erroneous views. We may ascribe to the Buddha a status he never claimed for himself, as when we regard him as the incarnation of a god, as the emanation of the Absolute, or as a personal saviour. On the other hand, we may detract from the exalted status to which the Buddha is properly entitled, as when we regard him simply as a benevolent sage, as an unusually astute Asiatic philosopher, or as a genius of meditative technology.

A correct view of the Buddha's nature would see him in terms of the title he assigned to himself: as a Fully Self-Enlightened One (*sammā sambuddha*). He is self-enlightened because he has awakened to the essential truths of existence entirely on his own, without a teacher or guide. He is fully enlightened because he has comprehended these truths completely, in all their ramifications and implications. And as a Buddha, he has not only fathomed these truths himself, but has also taught them to the world so that others may awaken from the long sleep of ignorance and attain the fruits of liberation.

Taking refuge in the Buddha is an act anchored in a particular historical individual, the recluse Gotama, the scion of the Sakyan clan, who lived and taught in the Ganges valley in the fifth century BC. When we take refuge in the Buddha, we rely upon this historical individual and the body of instruction that stems from him. It is important to stress this point in view of the fashionable notion that taking refuge in the Buddha means that we take refuge in 'the Buddha-mind within ourselves' or in 'the universal principle of enlightenment.' Such ideas, allowed to go unchecked, can lead to the belief that anything we contrive in the flights of our imagination can qualify as true Dhamma. To the contrary, the Buddhist tradition insists that when we go for refuge to the Buddha, we place ourselves under the guidance of one who is distinctly different from ourselves, one who has scaled heights that we have barely begun to glimpse.

But when we rely upon the recluse Gotama as our refuge, we do not apprehend him merely as a particular individual, a wise and sensible sage. We apprehend him rather as a Buddha. It is his Buddhahood—his possession of the full range of excellent qualities that come with perfect enlightenment—that makes the recluse Gotama a refuge. In any cosmic epoch, a Buddha is that being who first breaks through the dark mass of ignorance encompassing the world and rediscovers the lost path to Nibbāna, the cessation of suffering. He is the pioneer, the trail-blazer, who discovers the path and proclaims the path so that others, by following his tracks, may extinguish their ignorance, arrive at true wisdom, and break the fetters that tie them to the round of repeated birth and death.

For the refuge in the Buddha to be genuine, it must be accompanied by a commitment to the Buddha as an incomparable teacher, as unexcelled and unsurpassed. Strictly speaking, the historical Buddha is not unique since there have been earlier Fully Enlightened Ones who have arisen in past epochs and there will be others who will arise in future epochs as well. But in any one world system it is impossible for a second Buddha to arise while the teaching of another Buddha is still extant, and thus in terms of human history we are justified in regarding the Buddha as a unique teacher, unequalled by any other spiritual teacher known to humanity. It is this readiness to recognise the Buddha as "the unsurpassed trainer of persons to be tamed, the teacher of gods and humans" that is the hallmark of an authentic act of taking refuge in the Buddha.

The Buddha serves as a refuge by teaching the Dhamma. The actual and final refuge, embedded within the Dhamma as refuge, is Nibbāna, "the deathless element free from clinging, the sorrowless state that is void of stain" (It 51). The Dhamma as refuge comprises the final goal, the path that leads to that goal, and the body of teachings that explain the practice of the path. The

Buddha as refuge has no capacity to grant us liberation by an act of will. He proclaims the path to be travelled and the principles to be understood. The actual work of walking the path is then left to us, his disciples.

The proper response to the Buddha as refuge is trust and confidence. Trust is required because the doctrine taught by the Buddha runs counter to our innate understanding of ourselves and our natural orientation towards the world. To accept this teaching thus tends to arouse an inner resistance, even to provoke a rebellion against the changes it requires us to make in the way we lead our lives. But when we place trust in the Buddha we open ourselves to his guidance. By going to him for refuge we show that we are prepared to recognise that our inherent tendencies to self-affirmation and grasping are in truth the cause of our suffering. And we are ready to accept his counsel that to become free from suffering, these tendencies must be controlled and eliminated.

Confidence in the Buddha as our refuge is initially awakened when we contemplate his sublime virtues and his excellent teaching. It grows through our undertaking of the training. At first our confidence in the Buddha may be hesitant, punctured by doubts and perplexity. But as we apply ourselves to the practice of his path, we find that our defilements gradually lessen, that wholesome qualities increase, and with this comes a growing sense of freedom, peace and joy. This experience confirms our initial trust, disposing us to advance a few steps further. When at last we see the truth of the Dhamma for ourselves, the refuge in the Buddha becomes inviolable. Confidence then becomes conviction, the conviction that the Blessed One is "the speaker, the proclaimer, the bringer of the good, the giver of the Deathless, the lord of the Dhamma, the Tathāgata."

From BPS Newsletter No. 21, Spring 1992.

24. THE FIVE SPIRITUAL FACULTIES

The practice of the Buddha's teaching is most commonly depicted by the image of a journey, the eight factors of the Noble Eightfold Path constituting the royal roadway along which the disciple must travel. The Buddhist scriptures, however, illustrate the quest for liberation in a variety of other ways, each of which throws a different spotlight on the nature of the practice. Although the alternative formulations inevitably draw upon the same basic set of mental factors as those that enter into the eightfold path, they structure these factors around a different 'root metaphor'—an image which evokes its own particular range of associations and highlights different aspects of the endeavour to reach the cessation of suffering. One of the groups of factors given special prominence in the suttas and included by the Buddha among the thirty-seven requisites of enlightenment is the five spiritual faculties: the faculties of faith, energy, mindfulness, concentration and wisdom.

The term *indriya*, faculties, applied to this group as a whole is derived from the name of the ancient Vedic god Indra, ruler of the devas, and the term accordingly suggests the divine-like quality of control and domination. The five faculties are so designated because they exercise control in their own specific compartments of the spiritual life. As the god Indra vanquished the demons and attained supremacy among the gods, so each of the five faculties is called upon to subdue a particular mental disability and to marshal the corresponding potency of mind towards the breakthrough to final enlightenment.

The notion of 'faculty' is partly akin to the ancient Greek conception of the virtues. Like the virtues, the faculties are active powers which coordinate and canalise our natural energies, directing them towards the achievement of an inward harmony and balance essential to our true happiness and peace. Since the faculties are to serve as agents of inward control, this implies that, apart from their restraining influence, our nature is not under our own control. Left to itself, without the guidance of a superior source of instruction, the mind is prey to forces that swell up from within itself, dark forces which hold us in subjection and prevent us from attaining our own highest welfare and genuine good. These forces are the defilements (*kilesa*). As long as we live and act under their dominion, we are not our own masters but passive pawns, driven by our blind desires into courses of conduct that promise fulfilment but in the end lead only to misery and bondage. True freedom necessarily involves the attainment of inner autonomy, the strength to withstand the pushes and pulls of our appetites, and this is accomplished precisely by the development of the five spiritual faculties.

The qualities that exercise the function of faculties are of humble origin, appearing initially in mundane roles in the course of our everyday lives. In these humble guises they manifest as trustful confidence in higher values, as vigorous effort towards the good, as attentive awareness, as focused concentration, and as intelligent understanding. The Buddha's teaching does not implant these dispositions into the mind from scratch, but harnesses those pre-existent capacities of our nature towards a supramundane goal—towards the realisation of the Unconditioned—thereby conferring upon them a transcendental significance. By assigning them a task that reveals their immense potential, and by guiding them along a track that can bring that potential to fulfilment, the Dhamma transforms these commonplace mental factors into spiritual faculties, mighty instruments in the quest for liberation that can fathom the profoundest laws of existence and unlock the doors to the Deathless.

In the practice of the Dhamma each of these faculties has simultaneously to perform its own specific function and to harmonise with the other faculties to establish the balance needed for clear comprehension. The five come to fullest maturity in the contemplative development of insight, the direct road to awakening. In this process the faculty of faith provides the element of inspiration and aspiration which steers the mind away from the quagmire of doubt and settles it with serene trust in the Triple Gem as the supreme basis of deliverance. The faculty of energy kindles the fire of sustained endeavour that burns up obstructions and brings to maturity the factors that ripen in awakening. The faculty of mindfulness contributes clear awareness, the antidote to carelessness and the prerequisite of penetration. The faculty of concentration holds the beam of attention steadily focused on the rise and fall of bodily and mental events, calm and composed. And the faculty of wisdom, which the Buddha calls the crowning virtue among all the requisites of enlightenment, drives away the darkness of ignorance and lights up the true characteristics of phenomena.

Just as much as the five faculties, considered individually, each perform their own unique tasks in their respective domains, as a group they accomplish the collective task of establishing inner balance and harmony. To achieve this balanced striving, four of the faculties are divided into two pairs in each of which each member must counter the undesirable tendency inherent in the other, thus enabling it to actualise its fullest potential. The faculties of faith and wisdom form one pair, aimed at balancing the capacities for devotion and comprehension; the faculties of energy and concentration form a second pair, aimed at balancing the capacities for active exertion and calm recollection. Above the complementary pairs stands the faculty of mindfulness, which protects the mind from extremes and ensures that the members of each pair hold one another in a mutually restraining, mutually enriching tension.

Born of humble origins in everyday functions of the mind, through the Dhamma the five faculties acquire a transcendent destiny. When they are developed and regularly cultivated, says the Master, "they lead to the Deathless, are bound for the Deathless, culminate in the Deathless."

From BPS Newsletter No. 22, Winter 1992.

25. The Guardians of the World

L ike the Roman god Janus, every person faces simultaneously in two opposite directions. With one face of our consciousness we gaze. in upon ourselves and become aware of ourselves as individuals motivated by a deep urge to avoid suffering and to secure our own well-being and happiness. With the other face we gaze out upon the world and discover that our lives are thoroughly relational, that we exist as nodes in a vast net of relationships with other beings whose fate is tied up with our own. Because of the relational structure of our existence, we are engaged in a perpetual two-way interaction with the world: the influence of the world presses in upon ourselves, shaping and altering our own attitudes and dispositions, while our own attitudes and dispositions flow out into the world, a force that affects the lives of others for better or for worse.

This seamless interconnection between the inner and outer domains acquires a particular urgency for us today owing to the rampant deterioration in ethical standards that sweeps across the globe. Such moral decline is as widespread in those societies which enjoy a comfortable measure of stability and prosperity as it is in those countries where poverty and desperation make moral infringements an integral aspect of the struggle for survival. Of course we should not indulge in pastel-coloured fantasies about the past, imagining that we lived in a Garden of Eden until the invention of the steam engine. The driving forces of the human heart have remained fairly constant through the ages, and the toll they have taken in human misery surpasses calculation. But what we find today is a strange paradox that would be interesting if it were not sinister: while there appears to be a much wider verbal acknowledgement of the primacy of moral and human values, there is at the same time more blatant disregard for the lines of conduct such values imply.

This undermining of traditional ethical values is in part a result of the inter-nationalisation of commerce and the global penetration of virtually all media of communication. Vested interests, in quest of wider loops of power and expand-ing profits, mount a sustained campaign aimed at exploiting our moral vulnera-bility. This campaign proceeds at full pace, invading every nook and corner of our lives, with little regard for the long-term consequences for the individual and society. The results are evident in the problems that we face, problems that respect no national boundaries: rising crime rates, spreading drug addiction, eco-logical devastation, child labour and prostitution, smuggling and pornography, the decline of the family as the unit of loving trust and moral education.

The Buddha's teaching at its core is a doctrine of liberation that provides us with the tools for cutting through the fetters that keep us bound to this world of suffering, the round of repeated births. Although the quest for liberation by practice of the Dhamma depends on individual effort, this quest necessarily takes place within a social environment and is thus subject to all the influences, helpful or harmful, imposed upon us by that environment. The Buddhist training unfolds in the three stages of morality, concentration and wisdom, each the foundation for the other: purified moral conduct facilitates the attainment of purified concentration, and the concentrated mind facilitates the attainment of liberating wisdom. The basis of the entire Buddhist training is thus purified conduct, and the necessary means for safeguarding the purity of one's conduct is the firm adherence to the code of training rules one has undertaken—the Five Precepts in the case of a lay Buddhist. Living as we do in an era when we are provoked through every available channel to deviate from the norms of rectitude, and when social unrest, economic hardships and political conflict further fuel volatile emotions, the need for extra protection becomes especially imperative: protection for oneself, protection for the world.

The Buddha points to two mental qualities as the underlying safeguards of morality and thus as the protectors of both the individual and society as a whole. These two qualities are called in Pali *hiri* and *ottappa*. *Hiri* is an innate sense of shame over moral transgression; *ottappa* is moral dread, fear of the results of wrongdoing. The Buddha calls these two states "the bright guardians of the world" (*sukka lokapālā*). He gives them this designation because as long as these two states prevail in people's hearts the moral standards of the world remain intact, while when their influence wanes the human world falls into unabashed promiscuity and violence, becoming almost indistinguishable from the animal realm (It 42).

While moral shame and fear of wrongdoing are united in the common task of protecting the mind from moral defilement, they differ in their individual characteristics and modes of operation. *Hiri*, the sense of shame, has an internal reference; it is rooted in self-respect and induces us to shrink from wrongdoing out of a feeling of personal honour. *Ottappa*, fear of wrongdoing, has an external orientation. It is the voice of conscience that warns us of the dire consequences of moral transgression: blame and punishment by others, the painful kammic results of evil deeds, the impediment to our desire for liberation from suffering. Ācariya Buddhaghosa illustrates the difference between the two with the simile of an iron rod smeared with excrement at one end and heated to a glow at the other end: *hiri* is like one's disgust at grabbing the rod in the place where it is smeared with excrement, *ottappa* is like one's fear of grabbing it in the place where it is red hot.

In the present-day world, with its secularisation of all values, such notions as shame and fear of wrong are bound to appear antiquated, relics from a puritanical past when superstition and dogma manacled our rights to uninhibited self-expression. Yet the Buddha's stress on the importance of *hiri* and *ottappa* was based on a deep insight into the different potentialities of human nature. He saw that the path to deliverance is a struggle against the current, and that if we are to unfold the mind's capacities for wisdom, purity and peace, then we need to keep the powder keg of the defilements under the watchful eyes of diligent sentinels.

The project of self-cultivation, which the Buddha proclaims as the means to liberation from suffering, requires that we keep a critical watch over the movements of our minds, both on occasions when they motivate bodily and verbal deeds and when they remain inwardly absorbed with their own preoccupations. To exercise such self-scrutiny is an aspect of heedfulness (*appamāda*), which the Buddha states is the path to the Deathless. In the practice of self-examination, the sense of shame and fear of wrongdoing play a crucial role. The sense of shame spurs us to overcome unwholesome mental states because we recognise that such states are blemishes on our character. They detract from the inward loftiness of character to be fashioned by the practice of the Dhamma, the stature of the ariyans or noble ones who shine resplendent like lotus flowers upon the lake of the world. Fear of wrongdoing bids us to retreat from morally risky thoughts and actions because we recognise that such deeds are seeds with the potency to yield fruits, fruits that inevitably will be bitter.

The Buddha asserts that whatever evil arises springs from a lack of shame and fear of wrong, while all virtuous deeds spring from the sense of shame and fear of wrong. By cultivating within ourselves the qualities of moral shame and fear of wrongdoing we not only accelerate our own progress along the path to deliverance, but also contribute our share towards the protection of the world. Given the intricate interconnections that hold between all living forms, to make the sense of shame and fear of wrong the guardians of our own minds is to make ourselves guardians of the world. As the roots of morality, these two qualities sustain the entire efficacy of the Buddha's liberating path; as the safeguards of personal decency, they at the same time preserve the dignity of the human race.

From BPS Newsletter No. 23, Spring 1993.

26. TOLERANCE & DIVERSITY

T oday all the major religions of the world must respond to a double challenge. On one side is the challenge of secularism, a trend which has swept across the globe, battering against the most ancient strongholds of the sacred and turning all man's movements towards the Beyond into a forlorn gesture, poignant but devoid of sense. On the other side is the meeting of the great religions with each other. As the most far-flung nations and cultures merge into a single global community, the representatives of humankind's spiritual quest have been brought together in an encounter of unprecedented intimacy, an encounter so close that it leaves no room for retreat. Thus at one and the same time each major religion faces, in the amphitheatre of world opinion, all the other religions of the earth, as well as the vast numbers of people who regard all claims to possess the Great Answer with a skeptical frown or an indifferent yawn.

In this situation, any religion which is to emerge as more than a relic from humanity's adolescence must be able to deal, in a convincing and meaningful manner, with both sides of the challenge. On the one hand it must contain the swelling tide of secularism, by keeping alive the intuition that no amount of technological mastery over external nature, no degree of proficiency in providing for humanity's mundane needs, can bring complete repose to the human spirit; can still the thirst for a truth and value that transcends the boundaries of contingency. On the other hand, each religion must find some way of disentangling the conflicting claims that all religions make to understand our place in the grand scheme of things and to hold the key to our salvation. While remaining faithful to its own most fundamental principles, a religion must be able to address the striking differences between its own tenets and those of other creeds, doing so in a manner that is at once honest yet humble, perspicacious yet unimposing.

In this brief essay I wish to sketch the outline of an appropriate Buddhist response to the second challenge. Since Buddhism has always professed to offer a "middle way" in resolving the intellectual and ethical dilemmas of the spiritual life, we may find that the key to our present problematic also lies in discovering the response that best exemplifies the middle way. As has often been noted, the middle way is not a compromise between the extremes but a way that rises above them, avoiding the pitfalls into which they lead. Therefore, in seeking the proper Buddhist approach to the problem of the diversity of creeds, we might begin by pinpointing the extremes which the middle way must avoid.

The first extreme is a retreat into fundamentalism, the adoption of an aggressive affirmation of one's own beliefs coupled with a proselytizing zeal towards those who still stand outside the chosen circle of one's coreligionists. While this response to the challenge of diversity has assumed alarming proportions in the folds of the great monotheistic religions, Christianity and Islam, it is not one towards which Buddhism has a ready affinity, for the ethical guidelines of the Dhamma naturally tend to foster an attitude of benign tolerance towards other religions and their followers. Though there is no guarantee against the rise of a militant fundamentalism from within Buddhism's own ranks, the Buddha's teachings can offer no sanctification, not even a remote one, for which a malignant development.

For Buddhists the more alluring alternative is the second extreme: This extreme, which purchases tolerance at the price of integrity, might be called the thesis of spiritual universalism: the view that all the great religions, at their core, espouse essentially the same truth, clothed merely in different modes of expression. Such a thesis could not, of course, be maintained in regard to the formal creeds of the major religions, which differ so widely that it would require a strenuous exercise in word-twisting to bring them into accord. The universalist position is arrived at instead by an indirect route. Its advocates argue that we must distinguish between the outward face of a religion—its explicit beliefs and exoteric practices—and its inner nucleus of experiential realization. On the basis of this distinction, they then insist, we will find that beneath the markedly different outward faces of the great religions, at their heart—in respect of the spiritual experiences from which they emerge and the ultimate goal to which they lead—they are substantially identical. Thus the major religions differ simply in so far as they are different means, different expedients, to the same liberative experience, which may be indiscriminately designated "enlightenment," or "redemption," or "God-realization," since these different terms merely, highlight different aspects of the same goal. As the famous maxim puts it: the roads up the mountain are many, but the moonlight at the top is one. From this point of view, the Buddha Dhamma is only one more variant on the "perennial philosophy" underlying all the mature expressions of man's spiritual quest. It may stand out by its elegant simplicity, its clarity and directness; but a unique and unrepeated revelation of truth it harbours not.

On first consideration the adoption of such a view may seem to be an indispensable stepping-stone to religious tolerance, and to insist that doctrinal difference are not merely verbal but real and important may appear to border on bigotry. Thus those who embrace Buddhism in reaction against the doctrinaire narrowness of the monotheistic religions may find in such a view— so soft and accommodating—a welcome respite from the insistence on privileged access to truth typical of those religions. However, an unbiased study of the Buddha's own discourses would show quite plainly that the universalist thesis does not have the endorsement of the Awakened One himself. To the contrary, the Buddha repeatedly proclaims that the path to the supreme goal of the holy life is made known only in his own teaching, and therefore that the attainment of that goal—final deliverance from suffering—can be achieved only from within his own dispensation. The best known instance of this claim is the Buddha's assertion, on the eve of his Parinibbāna, that only in his dispensation are the four grades of enlightened persons to be found, that the other sects are devoid of true ascetics, those who have reached the planes of liberation.

The Buddha's restriction of final emancipation to his own dispensation does not spring from a narrow dogmatism or a lack of good will, but rests upon an utterly precise determination of the nature of the final goal and of the means that must be implemented to reach it. This goal is neither an everlasting afterlife in a heaven nor some nebulously conceived state of spiritual illumination, but the Nibbāna element with no residue remaining, release from the cycle of repeated birth and death. This goal is effected by the utter destruction of the mind's defilements—greed, aversion and delusion—all the way down to their subtlest levels of latency. The eradication of the defilements can be achieved only by insight into the true nature of phenomena, which means that the attainment of Nibbāna depends upon the direct experiential insight into all conditioned phenomena, internal and external, as stamped with the "three characteristics of existence": impermanence, suffering, and non-selfness. What the Buddha maintains, as the ground for his assertion that his teaching offers the sole means to final release from suffering, is that the knowledge of the true nature of phenomena, in its exactitude and completeness, is accessible only in his teaching. This is so because, theoretically, the principles that define this knowledge are unique to his teaching and contradictory in vital respects to the basic tenets of other creeds; and because, practically, this teaching alone reveals, in its perfection and purity, the means of generating this liberative knowledge as a matter of immediate personal experience. This means is the Noble Eightfold Path which, as an integrated system of spiritual training, cannot be found outside the dispensation of a Fully Enlightened One. Surprisingly, this exclusivistic stance of Buddhism in regard to the prospects for final emancipation has never engendered a policy of intolerance on the part of Buddhists towards the adherents of other religions. To the contrary, throughout its long history, Buddhism has displayed a thoroughgoing tolerance and genial good will towards the many religions with which it has come into contact. It has maintained this tolerance simultaneously with its deep conviction that the doctrine of the Buddha offers the unique and unsurpassable way to release from the ills inherent in conditioned existence. For Buddhism, religious tolerance is not achieved by reducing all religions to a common denominator, nor by explaining away formidable differences in thought and practice as accidents of historical development. From the Buddhist point of view, to make tolerance contingent upon whitewashing discrepancies would not be to exercise genuine tolerance at all; for such an approach can "tolerate" differences only by diluting them so completely that they no longer make a difference. True tolerance in religion involves the capacity to admit differences as real and fundamental, even as profound and unbridgeable, yet at the same time to respect the rights of those who follow a religion different from one's own (or no religion at all) to continue to do so without resentment, disadvantage or hindrance.

Buddhist tolerance springs from the recognition that the dispositions and spiritual needs of human beings are too vastly diverse to be encompassed by any single teaching, and thus that these needs will naturally find expression in a wide variety of religious forms. The non-Buddhist systems will not be able to lead their adherents to the final goal of the Buddha's Dhamma, but that they never proposed to do in the first place. For Buddhism, acceptance of the idea of the beginningless round of rebirths implies that it would be utterly unrealistic to expect more than a small number of people to be drawn towards a spiritual path aimed at complete liberation. The overwhelming majority, even of those who seek deliverance from earthly woes, will aim at securing a favourable mode of existence within the round, even while misconceiving this to be the ultimate goal of the religious quest.

To the extent that a religion proposes sound ethical principles and can promote to some degree the development of wholesome qualities such as love, generosity, detachment and compassion, it will merit in this respect the approbation of Buddhists. These principles advocated by outside religious systems will also conduce to rebirth in the realms of bliss—the heavens and the divine abodes. Buddhism by no means claims to have unique access to these realms, but holds that the paths that lead to them have been articulated, with varying degrees of clarity, in many of the great spiritual traditions of humanity. While the Buddhist will disagree with the belief structures of other religions to the extent that they deviate from the Buddha's Dhamma, he will respect them to the extent that they enjoin virtues and standards of conduct that promote spiritual development and the harmonious integration of human beings with each other and with the world.

From BPS Newsletter No. 24, Summer–Autumn 1993.

27. FROM VIEWS TO VISION

The Buddha's teaching repeatedly cautions us about the dangers in clinging—in clinging to possessions, clinging to pleasures, clinging to people, clinging to views. The Buddha sounds such words of warning because he discerns in clinging a potent cause of suffering, and he thus advises us that the price we must pay to arrive at the 'far shore' of liberation is the relinquishment of every type of clinging. In a move that at first glance may even seem self-destructive on the part of a religious founder, the Buddha says that we should not cling even to his teachings, that even the wholesome principles of the Dhamma have to be treated like the makeshift raft used to carry us across the stream.

Such astringent words of advice can easily be misconstrued, and if misconstrued the consequences may be even more bitter than if we simply disregard them. One particular misinterpretation into which newcomers to the Dhamma (and some veterans too!) are especially prone to fall is to hold that the Buddha's counsel to transcend all views means that even the doctrines of Buddhism are ultimately of no vital importance. For these doctrines too, it is said, are merely views, intellectual constructs, filaments of thought, which may have been meaningful in the context of ancient Indian cosmology but have no binding claims on us today. After all, aren't the words and phrases of the Buddhist texts simply that—words and phrases—and aren't we admonished to get beyond words and phrases in order to arrive at direct experience, the only thing that really counts? And doesn't the Buddha enjoin us in the Kālāma Sutta to judge things for ourselves and to let our own experience be the criterion for deciding what we will accept?

Such an approach to the Dhamma may be sweet to chew upon and easy to digest, but we also need to beware of its effect upon our total spiritual organism. Too often this kind of slippery reasoning provides simply a convenient excuse for adhering, at a subtle level of the mind, to ideas which are fundamentally antithetical to the Dhamma. We hang on to such ideas, not because they are truly edifying, but in order to protect ourselves from the radical challenge with which the Buddha's message confronts us. In effect, such claims, though apparently aimed at safeguarding living experience from the encroachment of stodgy intellectualism, may be in reality a clever intellectual ploy for refusing to examine cherished assumptions—assumptions we cherish primarily because they shield deep-rooted desires we do not want to expose to the tonic influence of the Dhamma.

When we approach the Buddha's teachings, we should bear in mind that its vast array of doctrines has not been devised as elaborate exercises in philosophical sleight of hand. They are propounded because they constitute Right View, and Right View stands at the head of the Noble Eightfold Path, to be used as a chisel to cut away the dross of wrong views and confused thoughts that impede the light of wisdom from illumining our minds. In the present-day world, wrong views have gained widespread currency and assumed more baneful forms than earlier epochs ever could have imagined. Today they are no longer the province of a few eccentric philosophers and their cliques. They have become, rather, a major determinant of cultural and social attitudes, moulding the moral spirit of the age, and are the driving force behind economic empires and international relations. Under such circumstances, Right View is our candle against the dark, our compass in the desert, our isle above the flood. Without a clear understanding of the truths enunciated by Right View, and without a keen awareness of the areas where these truths collide with popular opinion, it is only too easy to stumble in the dark, to get stranded among the sand dunes, to be swept away from one's position above the deluge.

Both Right View and wrong view, though cognitive in character, do not remain locked up in a purely cognitive space of their own. Our views exercise an enormously potent influence upon all areas of our lives, and the Buddha, in his genius, recognised this when he placed Right View and wrong view respectively at the beginning of the good and evil pathways of life. Views flow out and interlock with the practical dimension of our lives at many levels: they determine our values, they give birth to our goals and aspirations, they guide our choices in morally difficult dilemmas. Wrong view promotes wrong intentions, wrong modes of conduct, leads us in pursuit of a deceptive type of freedom. It draws us towards the freedom of licence, by which we feel justified in casting off moral restraint for the sake of satisfying transient but harmful impulses. Though we may then pride ourselves on our spontaneity and creativity, may convince ourselves that we have discovered our true individuality, one with clear sight will see that this freedom is only a more subtle bondage to the chains of craving and delusion.

Right View, even in its elementary form as a recognition of the moral law of *kamma*, the capacity of our deeds to bring results, becomes our gentle guide towards true freedom. And when it matures into an accurate grasp of the three signs of existence, of dependent arising and of the Four Noble Truths, it then becomes our navigator up the mountain slope of final deliverance. It will lead us to Right Intentions, to virtuous conduct, to mental purification, and to the cloudless peak of unobstructed vision. Although we must eventually learn to let go of this guide in order to stand confidently on our own feet, without its astute eye and willing hand we would only meander in the foothills oblivious to the peak.

The attainment of Right View is not simply a matter of assenting to a particular roster of doctrinal formulas or of skill in juggling an impressive array of cryptic Pali terms. The attainment of Right View is, at its core, essentially a matter of understanding—of understanding, in a deeply personal way, the vital truths of existence upon which our lives devolve. Right View aims at the big picture. It seeks to comprehend our place in the total scheme of things and to discern the laws that govern the unfolding of our lives for better or for worse. The ground of Right View is the Perfect Enlightenment of the Buddha, and by striving to rectify our view we seek nothing less than to align our own understanding of the nature of existence with that of the Buddha's Enlightenment. Right View may begin with concepts and propositional knowledge but it does not end with them. Through study, deep reflection and meditative development it gradually becomes transmuted into wisdom, the wisdom of insight that can cut asunder the beginningless fetters of the mind.

From BPS Newsletter No. 25, Winter 1993.

28. The Living Message of the Dhammapada

The Dhammapada is a work familiar to every devout Buddhist and to every serious student of Buddhism. This small collection of 423 verses on the Buddha's doctrine is so rich in insights that it might be considered the perfect compendium of the Dhamma in its practical dimensions. In the countries of Theravada Buddhism the Dhammapada is regarded as an inexhaustible source of guidance and spiritual inspiration, as the wise counsellor to which to turn for help in resolving the difficult moral and personal problems inescapable in daily life. Just as the Buddha is looked upon as the human *kalyāṇamitta* or spiritual friend par excellence, so the Dhammapada is looked upon as the scriptural *kalyāṇamitta* par excellence, a small embodiment in verse of the boundless wisdom and great compassion of the Master.

To draw out the living message of any great spiritual classic, it is not enough for us merely to investigate it in terms of questions that might be posed by scientific scholarship. We have to take a step beyond scholarly examination and seek to make an application of those teachings to ourselves in our present condition. To do this requires that we use our intelligence, imagination and intuition to see through the limiting cultural contexts out of which the work was born, and to see into those universal features of the human condition to which the spiritual classic being studied is specifically addressed. With these stipulations in mind we will examine the Dhammapada in order to discover what this ancient book of wisdom regards as the fundamental and perennial spiritual problems of human life and to learn what solutions it can propose for them that may be relevant to us today. In this way we will uncover the living message of the Dhammapada: the message that rings down through the centuries and speaks to us in our present condition in the fullness of our humanity.

When we set out to make such an investigation, one difficulty that we meet at the outset is the great diversity of teachings contained in the Dhammapada. It is well known that during his teaching career the Buddha always adjusted his discourses to fit the needs and capacities of his disciples. Thus the prose discourses found in the four main Nikāyas display richly variegated presentations of the doctrine, and this diversity becomes even more pronounced in the Dhammapada, a collection of utterances spoken in the intuitive and highly charged medium of verse. We even find in the work apparent inconsistencies, which may perplex the superficial reader and lead to the supposition that the Buddha's teaching is rife with self-contradiction. Thus in many verses the Buddha commends certain practices to his disciples on the ground that they lead to heaven, while in others he discourages disciples from aspiring for heaven and praises the one who takes no delight in celestial joys. Often the Buddha enjoins works of merit, yet elsewhere in the work he enjoins his disciples to go beyond both merit and demerit.

To make sense out of such contrary statements, to find a consistent message running through the Dhammapada's diversified pronouncements, let us begin with a statement the Buddha makes in another small but beautiful book of the Pali Canon, the Udana: "Just as the great ocean has but one taste, the taste of salt, so this doctrine-and-discipline has but one taste, the taste of freedom." Despite their variety in meaning and formulation, the Buddha's teachings all fit together into a perfectly coherent system which gains its unity from its final goal. That goal is freedom (*vimutti*), which here means spiritual freedom: the liberation of the mind from all bonds and fetters, the liberation of our being from the suffering inseparable from wandering in saṃsāra, the cycle of rebirths. But while the Buddha's teachings fit together harmoniously through the unity of their final goal, they are addressed to people standing at different levels of spiritual development and thus must be expressed in different ways determined by the needs of the people to be taught. Here again water provides a fitting analogy. Water has one essence—chemically, it is a union of two hydrogen atoms with one oxygen atom—but it takes on the different shapes of the vessels into which it is poured; similarly, the Dhamma has a single essence—deliverance from suffering—but it assumes varying expressions in accordance with the dispositions of those who are to be instructed and trained. It is because the different expressions lead to a single end, and because the same end can be reached via teachings that are differently expressed, that the Dhamma is said to be *sāttha sabyañjana*, "good in meaning and good in formulation."

To make sense out of the various teachings found in the Dhammapada, to grasp the vision of human spirituality expressed by the work as a whole, I would like to suggest a schematism of four levels of instruction set forth in the Dhammapada. This fourfold schematism develops out of three primary and perennial spiritual needs of man: first, the need to achieve welfare and happiness in the present life, in the immediately visible sphere of human relations; second, the need to attain a favorable future life in accordance with a principle that confirms our highest moral intuitions; and third, the need for transcendence, to overcome all the limits imposed upon us by our finitude and temporality and to attain a freedom that is boundless, timeless, and irreversible. These three needs give rise to four levels of instruction by distinguishing two levels pertaining to the third need: the level of path, when we are on the way to transcendence, and the level of fruit, when we have won through to transcendence.

Now let us examine each of these levels in turn, illustrating them with citations of relevant verses from the Dhammapada

1. The Human Good Here and Now

The first level of instruction in the Dhammapada is addressed to the need to establish human welfare and happiness in the immediately visible domain of personal relation. The aim at this level is to show us the way to live at peace with ourselves and our fellow human beings, to fulfil our family and social responsibilities, and to remove the conflicts which infect human relationships and bring such immense suffering to the individual, society and the world as a whole.

The guidelines appropriate to this level of instruction are largely identical with the basic ethical injunctions proposed by most of the great world religions. However, in the Buddha's teaching these ethical injunctions are not regarded as fiats imposed by an all-powerful God. Rather, they are presented as precepts or training rules grounded upon two directly verifiable foundations: concern for one's own personal integrity and considerations for the welfare of those whom one's actions may affect.

The most general advice the Dhammapada gives is to avoid all evil, to cultivate good, and to cleanse one's own mind; this is said to be the counsel of all the Enlightened Ones (v. 183). More specific directives, however, are also given. To abstain from evil we are advised to avoid irritation in deed, word and thought and to exercise self-control over body, speech and mind (vv. 231–234). One should adhere scrupulously to the five moral precepts: abstinence from destroying life, from stealing, from sexual misconduct, from lying and from intoxicants (vv. 246–247). The disciple should treat all beings with kindness and compassion, live honestly, control his desires, speak the truth, and live a sober upright life. He should fulfil all his duties to parents, to immediate family, to friends, and to recluses and brahmans (vv. 331–333).

A large number of verses pertaining to this first level are concerned with the resolution of conflict and hostility. From other parts of the Sutta Pitaka we learn that the Buddha was a keen and sensitive observer of the social and political developments that were rapidly transforming the Indian states he visited on his preaching rounds. The violence, hatred, cruelty and sustained enmity that he witnessed have persisted right down to the present, and the Buddha's answer to this problem is still the only answer that can work. The Buddha tells us that the key to solving the problem of violence and cruelty is the ancient maxim of using oneself as the standard for deciding how to treat others. I myself tremble at violence, wish to live in peace and do not want to die. Thus, putting myself in the place of others, I should recognize that all other beings tremble at violence, that all wish to live and do not want to die. Recognizing this, I should not intimidate others, harm them, or cause them to be harmed in any way (vv. 129–130).

The Buddha saw that hatred and enmity continue and spread in a self-expanding cycle: responding to hatred by hatred only breeds more hatred, more enmity, more violence, and feed the whole vicious whirlpool of vengeance and retaliation. The Dhammapada teaches us that the true conquest of hatred is achieved by non-hatred, by forbearance, by love (v. 5). When wronged by others we must be patient and forgiving. We must control our anger as a driver controls a chariot; we must bear angry words as the elephant in battle bears the arrows shot into its hide; when spoken to harshly we must remain silent like a broken bell (vv. 222, 320, 134).

According to the Dhammapada, the qualities distinguishing the superior human being (*sapurisa*) are generosity, truthfulness, patience and compassion. By following these ideals we can live at peace with our own conscience and in harmony with our fellows. The scent of virtue, the Buddha declares, is sweeter than the scent of flowers and perfume; the good man or woman shines from afar like the Himalayan mountains; just as the lotus flower rises up in all its beauty above the muck and mire of the roadside refuse heap, so does the disciple of the Buddha rise up in splendour of wisdom above the masses of ignorant worldlings (vv. 54, 304, 59)

2. The Good in Future Lives

The basic emphasis in the first level of teaching in the Dhammapada is ethical, a concern which arises from a desire to promote human well-being here and now. However, the teachings pertaining to this level give rise to a profound religious problem, a dilemma that challenges the mature thinker. The problem is as follows: Our moral intuition, our innate sense of moral justice, tells us that there must be some principle of compensation at work in the world whereby goodness meets with happiness and evil meets with suffering. But everyday experience shows us exactly the opposite. We all know of highly virtuous people beset with every kind of hardship and thoroughly bad people who succeed in everything they do. We feel that there must be some correction to this imbalance, some force that will tilt the scales of justice into the balance that seems right, but our daily experience seems to contradict this intuition totally.

However, in his teachings the Buddha reveals that there is a force at work which can satisfy our demand for moral justice. This force cannot be seen with the eye of the flesh nor can it be registered by any instruments of measurement, but its working becomes visible to the supernormal vision of sages and saints, while all its principles in their full complexity are fathomed by a Perfectly

Enlightened Buddha. This force is called kamma. The law of kamma ensures that our morally determinate actions do not disappear into nothingness, but rather continue on as traces in the deep hidden layers of the mind, where they function in such a way that our good deeds eventually issue in happiness and success, our evil deeds in suffering and misery.

The word kamma, in the Buddha's teaching, means volitional action. Such action may be bodily or verbal, when volition is expressed in deed or speech, or it may be purely mental, when volition remains unexpressed as thoughts, emotions, wishes and desires. The actions may be either wholesome or unwholesome: wholesome when they are rooted in generosity, amity and understanding; unwholesome when they spring from greed, hatred and delusion. According to the principle of kamma, the willed actions we perform in the course of a life have long-term consequences that correspond to the moral quality of the original action. The deeds may utterly fade from our memory, but once performed they leave subtle impressions upon the mind, potencies capable of ripening in the future to our weal or our woe.

According to Buddhism, conscious life is not a chance by-product of molecular configurations or a gift from a divine Creator, but a beginningless process which repeatedly springs up at birth and passes away at death, to be followed by a new birth. There are many spheres besides the human into which rebirth can occur: heavenly realms of great bliss, beauty and power, infernal realms where suffering and misery prevail. The Dhammapada does not give us any systematic teaching on kamma and rebirth. As a book of spiritual counsel it presupposes the theoretical principles explained elsewhere in the Buddhist scriptures and concerns itself with their practical bearings on the conduct of life. The essentials of the law of kamma, however, are made perfectly clear: our willed actions determine the sphere of existence into which we will be reborn after death, the circumstances and endowments of our lives within any given form of rebirth, and our potentials for spiritual progress or decline.

At the second level of instruction found in the Dhammapada the content of the message is basically the same as that of the first level: it is the same set of moral injunctions for abstaining from evil and doing good. The difference lies in the viewpoint from which these precepts are issued and the purpose for which they are taken up. At this level the precepts are prescribed to show us the way to achieve long-range happiness and freedom from sorrow, not only in the visible sphere of the present life, but far beyond into the distant future in our subsequent transmigration in samsara. Despite the apparent discrepancy between action and result, an all-embracing law ensures that ultimately moral justice triumphs. In the short run the good may suffer and the evil may prosper. But all willed actions bring their appropriate results: if one acts or speaks with an evil mind, suffering follows just as the wheel follows the foot of the draft-ox; if one acts or speaks with a pure mind, happiness follows like a shadow that never departs (vv.1–2). The evil-doer grieves here and hereafter; he is tormented by his conscience and destined to planes of misery. The doer of good rejoices here and hereafter, he enjoys a good conscience and is destined to realms of bliss (vv. 15–18). To follow the law of virtue leads upward, to happiness and joy and to higher rebirths; to violate the law leads downward, to suffering and to lower rebirths. The law is inflexible. Nowhere in the world can the evil-doer escape the result of his evil kamma, "neither in the sky nor in mid-ocean nor by entering into mountain clefts" (v. 127). The good person will reap the rewards of his or her good kamma in future lives with the same certainty with which a traveller, returning home after a long journey, can expect to be greeted by his family and friends (v. 220).

3. The Path to the Final Good

The teaching on kamma and rebirth, with its practical corollary that we should perform deeds of merit with the aim of obtaining a higher mode of rebirth, is not by any means the final message of the Buddha or the decisive counsel of the Dhammapada. In its own sphere of application this teaching is perfectly valid as a preparatory measure for those who still require further maturation in their journey through saṃsāra. However, a more searching examination reveals that all states of existence in saṃsāra, even the highest heavens, are lacking in genuine worth; for they are all impermanent, without any lasting substance, incapable of giving complete and final satisfaction. Thus the disciple of mature faculties, who has been prepared sufficiently by previous experience in the world, does not long even for rebirth among the gods (vv. 186–187).

Having understood that all conditioned things are intrinsically unsatisfactory and fraught with danger, the mature disciple aspires instead for deliverance from the ever-repeating round of rebirths. This is the ultimate goal to which the Buddha points, as the immediate aim for those of developed spiritual faculties and also as the long-term ideal for those who still need further maturation: Nibbāna, the Deathless, the unconditioned state where there is no more birth, aging and death, and thus no more suffering.

The third level of instruction found in the Dhammapada sketches the theoretical framework for the aspiration for final liberation and lays down guidelines pertaining to the practical discipline that can bring this aspiration to fulfilment. The theoretical framework is supplied by the teaching of the Four Noble Truths, which the Dhammapada calls the best of all truths (v. 273): suffering, the origin of suffering, the cessation of suffering, and the Noble Eightfold Path leading to the cessation of suffering. The four truths all centre around the problem of *dukkha* or suffering, and the Dhammapada teaches us that *dukkha* is not to be understood only as experienced pain and sorrow but more widely as the pervasive inadequacy and wretchedness of everything conditioned: "There is no ill like the aggregates of existence; all conditioned things are suffering; conditioned things are the worst suffering (vv. 202, 278, 203). The second truth points out that the cause of suffering is craving, the yearning for pleasure, possessions and being which drives us through the round of rebirths, bringing along sorrow, anxiety and despair. The Dhammapada devotes an entire chapter (Ch. 24) to the theme of craving, and the message of this chapter is clear: so long as even the subtlest thread of craving remains in the mind, we are not beyond danger of being swept away by the terrible flood of existence. The third noble truth spells out the goal of the Buddha's teaching: to gain release from suffering, to escape the flood of existence, craving must be destroyed down to its subtlest depths. And the fourth noble truth prescribes the means to gain release, the Noble Eightfold Path, which again is the focus of an entire chapter (Ch. 20).

At the third level of instruction a shift in the practical teaching of the Dhammapada takes place, corresponding to the shift in doctrine from the principles of kamma and rebirth to the Four Noble Truths. The stress now no longer falls on basic morality and purified states of mind as a highway to more favourable planes of rebirth. Instead it falls on the cultivation of the Noble Eightfold Path as the means to destroy craving and thus break free from the entire process of rebirth itself. The Dhammapada declares that the eightfold path is the only way to deliverance from suffering (v. 274). It says this, not as a fixed dogma, but because full release from suffering comes from the purification of wisdom, and this path alone, with its stress on right view and the cultivation of insight, leads to fully purified wisdom, to complete understanding of liberating truth. The Dhammapada states that those who tread the path will come to know the Four Noble Truths, and having gained this wisdom, they will end all suffering. The Buddha assures us that by walking the path we will bewilder Mara, pull out the thorn of lust, and escape from suffering. But he also cautions us about our own responsibility: we ourselves must make the effort, for the Buddhas only point out the way (vv. 275, 276).

In principle the practice of the Noble Eightfold Path is open to people in any walk of life, householders as well as monks and nuns. However, application to the development of the path is most feasible for those who have relinquished all worldly concerns in order to devote themselves fully to living the holy life. For conduct to be completely purified, for the mind to be trained in concentration and insight, the adoption of a different lifestyle becomes advisable, one which minimizes distractions and stimulants to craving and orders all activities around the aim of liberation. Thus the Buddha established the Sangha, the Order of bhikkhus and bhikkhunis, as the field of training for those ready to devote themselves fully to the practice of the path.

In the Dhammapada we find the call to the monastic life resounding throughout. The entry way to the monastic life is an act of radical renunciation spurred on by our confrontation with suffering, particularly by our recognition of our inevitable mortality. The Dhammapada teaches that just as a cowherd drives the cattle to pasture, so old age and death drive living beings from life to life (v. 135). There is no place in the world where one can escape death, for death is stamped into the very substance of our being (v. 128). The body is a painted mirage in which there is nothing lasting or stable; it is a mass of sores, a nest of disease, which breaks up and ends in death; it is a city built of bones containing within itself decay and death; the foolish are attached to it, but the wise, having seen that the body ends as a corpse, lose all delight in mundane joys (vv. 146–150).

Having recognized the transience and hidden misery of mundane life, the thoughtful break the ties of family and social relationships, abandon their homes and sensual pleasures, and enter upon the state of homelessness: "Like swans that abandon the lake, they leave home after home behind... Having gone from home to homelessness, they delight in detachment so difficult to enjoy" (vv. 91, 87). Withdrawn to silent and secluded places, the renunciants seek out the company of wise instructors, who point out their faults, who admonish and instruct them and shield them from wrong, who show them the right path (vv. 76–78, 208). Under their guidance, they live by the rules of the monastic order, content with the simplest material requisites, moderate in eating, practicing patience and forbearance, devoted to meditation (vv. 184–185). Having learned to still the restless waves of thought and to gain one-pointed concentration, they go on to contemplate the arising and falling away of all formations: "The monk who has retired to a solitary abode and calmed the mind, comprehends the Dhamma with insight, and there arises in him a delight that transcends all human delights. Whenever he sees with insight the rise and fall of the aggregates, he is full of joy and happiness (vv. 373, 374).

The life of meditation reaches its peak in the development of insight, and the Dhammapada succinctly enunciates the principles to be seen with the wisdom of insight: "All conditioned things are impermanent... All conditioned things are suffering... All things are not self. When one sees this with wisdom, then one turns away from suffering. This is the path of purification" (vv. 277–279). When these truths are penetrated by direct vision, the fetters of attachment break asunder, and the disciple rises through successive stages of realization to the attainment of full liberation.

4. The Highest Goal

The fourth level of teaching in the Dhammapada does not reveal any new principles of doctrine or approach to practice. This level shows us, rather, the fruit of the third level. The third level exposes the path to the highest goal, the way to break free from all bondage and suffering and to win the supreme peace of Nibbāna. The fourth level is a celebration and acclamation of those who have gained the fruits of the path and won the final goal.

The stages of definite attainment along the way to Nibbāna are enumerated in the Pali Canon as four: stream-entry, when one enters irreversibly upon the path to liberation; once-returning, when one is assured that one will return to the sense sphere of existence only one more time; non-returning, when one will never return to the sense sphere at all but will take a spontaneous birth in a celestial plane and there reach the end of suffering; and arahantship, the stage of full liberation here and now. Although the Dhammapada contains several verses referring to those on the lower stages of attainment, its primary emphasis is on the individual who has reached the fourth and final fruit of liberation, the arahant, and the picture it gives us of the arahant is stirring and inspiring.

The arahant is depicted in two full chapters: in chapter 7 under his own name and in chapter 26, the last chapter, under the name "Brahmana," the holy man. We are told that the arahant is no longer troubled by the fever of the passions; he is sorrowless and wholly set free; he has broken all ties. His taints are destroyed: he is not attached to food; his field is the void and unconditioned freedom. For ordinary worldlings the arahant is incomprehensible: his path cannot be traced, like that of birds in the sky. He has transcended all obstacles, passed beyond sorrow and lamentation, become peaceful and fearless. He is free from anger, devout, virtuous, without craving, self-subdued. He has profound knowledge and wisdom; he is skilled in discriminating the right path and the wrong path; he has reached the highest goal. He is friendly amidst the hostile, peaceful amidst the violent, and unattached amidst the attached.

In this very life the arahant has realized the end of suffering, laying down the burden of the five aggregates. He has transcended the ties of both merit and demerit; he is sorrowless, stainless and pure; he is free from attachment and has plunged into the Deathless. Like the moon he is spotless and pure, serene and clear. He has cast off all human bonds and transcended all celestial bonds; he has gotten rid of the substrata of existence and conquered all worlds. He knows the death and rebirth of beings; he is totally detached, blessed and enlightened. No gods, angels or human beings can find his tracks, for he clings to nothing, has no attachment, holds to nothing. He has reached the end of births, attained the perfection of insight, and reached the summit of spiritual excellence. Bearing his last body, perfectly at peace, the arahant is the living demonstration of the truth of the Dhamma. By his own example he shows that it is possible to free oneself from the stains of greed, hatred and delusion, to rise above suffering, and to win Nibbāna in this very life.

The arahant ideal reaches its optimal exemplification in the first and highest of the arahants, the Buddha, and the Dhammapada makes a number of important pronouncements about the Master. The Buddha is the supreme teacher who depends on no one else for guidance, who has reached perfect enlightenment through his own self-evolved wisdom (v. 353). He is the giver of refuge and is himself the first of the three refuges; those who take refuge in the Buddha, his Doctrine, and his Order are released from all suffering, after seeing with proper wisdom the Four Noble Truths (vv.190–192). The Buddha's attainment of perfect enlightenment elevates him to a level far above that of common humanity: the Enlightened One is trackless, of limitless range, free from worldliness, the conqueror of all, the knower of all, in all things untainted (vv. 179, 180, 353). The sun shines by day, the moon shines by night, the warrior shines in his armour, the brahman shines in meditation, but the Buddha, we are told, shines resplendent all day and all night (v. 387).

This will complete our discussion of the four basic levels of instruction found in the Dhammapada. Interwoven with the verses pertaining to these four main levels, there runs throughout the Dhammapada a large number of verses that cannot be tied down exclusively to any single level but have a wider application. These verses sketch for us the world view of early Buddhism and its distinctive insights into human existence. Fundamental to this world view, as it emerges from the text, is the inescapable duality of human life. Man walks a delicate balance between good and evil, purity and defilement, progress and decline; he seeks happiness, he fears suffering, loss and death. We are free to choose between good and evil, and must bear full responsibility for our decisions. Again and again the Dhammapada sounds this challenge to human freedom: we are the makers and masters of ourselves, the protectors or destroyers of ourselves, we are our own saviours and there is no one else who can save us (vv. 160, 165, 380). Even the Buddha can only indicate the path to deliverance; the work of treading it lies with the disciple (vv. 275–276). In the end we must choose between the way that leads back into the world, to the round of becoming, and the way that leads out of the world, to Nibbāna. And though this last course is extremely difficult, the voice of the Buddha speaks words of assurance confirming that it can be done, that it lies within our power to overcome all barriers and to triumph even over death itself.

The chief role in achieving progress in all spheres, the Dhammapada states, is played by the mind. The Dhammapada opens with a clear assertion that the mind is the forerunner of all that we are, the maker of our character, the creator of our destiny. The entire Buddhist discipline, from basic morality to the attainment of arahantship, hinges upon training the mind. A wrongly directed mind brings greater harm than any enemy; a rightly directed mind brings greater good than any relative or friend (vv. 42–43). The mind is unruly, fickle difficult to subdue, but by effort, mindfulness and self-discipline, one can master the mind, escape the flood of passions, and find "an island which no flood can overwhelm" (v. 25). The person who conquers himself, the victor over his own mind, achieves a conquest that can never be undone, a victory greater than that of the mightiest warriors (vv. 103–105).

What is needed most to train and subdue the mind, according to the Dhammapada, is a quality called heedfulness (*appamāda*). Heedfulness combines critical self-awareness and unremitting energy in a process of constant self-observation in order to detect and expel the defilements whenever they seek an opportunity to come to the surface. In a world where we have no saviour except ourselves, and where the means to deliverance lies in mental purification, heedfulness becomes the crucial factor for ensuring that we keep straight to the path of training without deviating due to the seductive lure of sense pleasures or the stagnating influences of laziness and complacency. The Buddha declares that heedfulness is the path to the Deathless, and heedlessness the path to death. The wise who understand this distinction abide in heedfulness and attain Nibbāna, "the incomparable freedom from bondage" (vv. 21–23).

From Bodhi Leaves No. 129. First published 1993.

29. ASSOCIATION WITH THE WISE

The Mahāmaṅgala Sutta, the Great Discourse on Blessings, is one of the most popular Buddhist suttas, included in all the standard repertories of Pali devotional chants. The Sutta begins when a deity of stunning beauty, having descended to earth in the stillness of the night, approaches the Blessed One in the Jeta Grove and asks about the way to the highest blessings. In the very first stanza of his reply the Buddha states that the highest blessing comes from avoiding fools and associating with the wise (*asevanā ca bālānaṃ, paṇḍitānaṃ ca sevanā*). Since the rest of the Sutta goes on to sketch all the different aspects of human felicity, both mundane and spiritual, the assignment of association with the wise to the opening stanza serves to emphasise a key point: that progress along the path of the Dhamma hinges on making the right choices in our friendships.

Contrary to certain psychological theories, the human mind is not a hermetically sealed chamber enclosing a personality unalterably shaped by biology and infantile experience. Rather, throughout life it remains a highly malleable entity continually remoulding itself in response to its social interactions. Far from coming to our personal relationships with a fixed and immutable character, our regular and repeated social contacts implicate us in a constant process of psychological osmosis that offers precious opportunities for growth and transformation. Like living cells engaged in a chemical dialogue with their colleagues, our minds transmit and receive a steady barrage of messages and suggestions that may work profound changes even at levels below the threshold of awareness.

Particularly critical to our spiritual progress is our selection of friends and companions, who can have the most decisive impact upon our personal destiny. It is because he perceived how susceptible our minds can be to the influence of our companions that the Buddha repeatedly stressed the value of good friendship (*kalyāṇamittatā*) in the spiritual life. The Buddha states that he sees no other thing that is so much responsible for the arising of unwholesome qualities in a person as bad friendship, nothing so helpful for the arising of wholesome qualities as good friendship (AN I.vii, 10; I.viii, 1). Again, he says that he sees no other external factor that leads to so much harm as bad friendship, and no other external factor that leads to so much benefit as good friendship (AN I.x, 13, 14). It is through the influence of a good friend that a disciple is led along the Noble Eightfold Path to the release from all suffering (SN 45:2).

Good friendship, in Buddhism, means considerably more than associating with people that one finds amenable and who share one's interests. It means in effect seeking out wise companions to whom one can look for guidance and instruction. The task of the noble friend is not only to provide companionship in the treading of the way. The truly wise and compassionate friend is one who, with understanding and sympathy of heart, is ready to criticise and admonish, to point out one's faults, to exhort and encourage, perceiving that the final end of such friendship is growth in the Dhamma. The Buddha succinctly expresses the proper response of a disciple to such a good friend in a verse of the Dhammapada: "If one finds a person who points out one's faults and who reproves one, one should follow such a wise and sagacious counsellor as one would a guide to hidden treasure" (Dhp. 76).

Association with the wise becomes so crucial to spiritual development because the example and advice of a noble-minded counsellor is often the decisive factor that awakens and nurtures the unfolding of our own untapped spiritual potential. The uncultivated mind harbours a vast diversity of unrealised possibilities, ranging from the depths of selfishness, egotism and aggression to the heights of wisdom, self-sacrifice and compassion. The task confronting us, as followers of the Dhamma, is to keep the unwholesome tendencies in check and to foster the growth of the wholesome tendencies, the qualities that lead to awakening, to freedom and purification. However, our internal tendencies do not mature and decline in a vacuum. They are subject to the constant impact of the broader environment, and among the most powerful of these influences is the company we keep, the people we look upon as teachers, advisors and friends. Such people silently speak to the hidden potentials of our own being, potentials that will either unfold or wither under their influence.

In our pursuit of the Dhamma it therefore becomes essential for us to choose as our guides and companions those who represent, at least in part, the noble qualities we seek to internalise by the practice of the Dhamma. This is especially necessary in the early stages of our spiritual development when our virtuous aspirations are still fresh and tender, vulnerable to being undermined by inward irresolution or by discouragement from acquaintances who do not share our ideals. In this early phase our mind resembles a chameleon which alters its colour according to its background. Just as this remarkable lizard turns green when in the grass and brown when on bare ground, so we become fools when we associate with fools, and sages when we associate with sages. Internal changes do not generally occur suddenly; but slowly, by increments so slight that we ourselves may not be aware of them, our characters undergo a metamorphosis that in the end may prove to be dramatically significant. If we associate closely with those who are addicted to the pursuit of sense pleasures, power, riches and fame, we should not imagine that we will remain immune from those addictions: in time our own minds will gradually incline to these same ends. If we associate closely with those who, while not given up to moral recklessness, live their lives comfortably adjusted to mundane routines, we too will remain stuck in the ruts of the commonplace. If we aspire for the highest—for the peaks of transcendent wisdom and liberation—then we must enter into association with those who represent the highest. Even if we are not so fortunate as to find companions who have already scaled the heights, we can well count ourselves blessed if we cross paths with a few spiritual friends who share our ideals and who make earnest efforts to nurture the noble qualities of the Dhamma in their hearts.

When we raise the question how to recognise good friends, how to distinguish good advisors from bad advisors, the Buddha offers us crystal-clear advice. In the Shorter Discourse on a Full-Moon Night (MN 110) he explains the difference between the companionship of the bad person and the companionship of the good person. The bad person chooses as friends and companions those who are without faith, whose conduct is marked by an absence of shame and moral dread, who have no knowledge of spiritual teachings, who are lazy and unmindful, and who are devoid of wisdom. As a consequence of choosing such bad friends as his advisors, the bad person plans and acts for his own harm, for the harm of others, and the harm of both, and he meets with sorrow and misery.

In contrast, the Buddha continues, the good person chooses as friends and companions those who have faith, who exhibit a sense of shame and moral dread, who are learned in the Dhamma, energetic in cultivation of the mind, mindful, and possessed of wisdom. Resorting to such good friends, looking to them as mentors and guides, the good person pursues these same qualities as his own ideals and absorbs them into his character. Thus, while drawing ever closer to deliverance himself, he becomes in turn a beacon light for others. Such a one is able to offer those who still wander in the dark an inspiring model to emulate, and a wise friend to turn to for guidance and advice.

From BPS Newsletter No. 26, 1ˢᵗ Mailing 1994.

30. DHAMMA AND NON-DUALITY

One of the most challenging issues facing Theravada Buddhism in recent years has been the encounter between classical Theravada vipassanā meditation and the 'non-dualistic' contemplative traditions best represented by Advaita Vedanta and Mahāyāna Buddhism. Responses to this encounter have spanned the extremes, ranging from vehement confrontation all the way to attempts at synthesis and hybridisation. While the present essay cannot pretend to illuminate all the intricate and subtle problems involved in this sometimes volatile dialogue, I hope it may contribute a few sparks of light from a canonically oriented Theravada perspective.

My first preliminary remark would be to insist that a system of meditative practice does not constitute a self-contained discipline. Any authentic system of spiritual practice is always found embedded within a conceptual matrix that defines the problems the practice is intended to solve and the goal towards which it is directed. Hence the merging of techniques grounded in incompatible conceptual frameworks is fraught with risk. Although such mergers may appease a predilection for experimentation or eclecticism, it seems likely that their long-term effect will be to create a certain 'cognitive dissonance' that will reverberate through the deeper levels of the psyche and stir up even greater confusion.

My second remark would be to point out simply that non-dualistic spiritual traditions are far from consistent with each other, but comprise, rather, a wide variety of views profoundly different and inevitably coloured by the broader conceptual contours of the philosophies which encompass them.

For the Vedanta, non-duality (*advaita*) means the absence of an ultimate distinction between the Atman, the innermost self, and Brahman, the divine reality, the underlying ground of the world. From the standpoint of the highest realisation, only one ultimate reality exists—which is simultaneously Atman and Brahman—and the aim of the spiritual quest is to know that one's own true self, the Atman, is the timeless reality which is Being, Awareness, Bliss. Since all schools of Buddhism reject the idea of the Atman, none can accept the non-dualism of Vedanta. From the perspective of the Theravada tradition, any quest for the discovery of selfhood, whether as a permanent individual self or as an absolute universal self, would have to be dismissed as a delusion, a metaphysical blunder born from a failure to properly comprehend the nature of concrete experience. According to the Pāli suttas, the individual being is merely a complex unity of the five aggregates which are all stamped with the three marks of impermanence, suffering, and selflessness. Any postulation of selfhood in regard to this compound of transient, conditioned phenomena is an instance of 'personality view' (*sakkāyadiṭṭhi*), the most basic fetter that binds beings to the round of rebirths. The attainment of liberation, for Buddhism, does not come to pass by the realisation of a true self or absolute 'I,' but through the dissolution of even the subtlest sense of selfhood in relation to the five aggregates, "the abolition of all I-making, mine-making, and underlying tendencies to conceit."

The Mahāyāna Buddhist schools, despite their great differences, concur in upholding a thesis that, from the Theravada point of view, borders on the outrageous. This is the claim that there is no ultimate difference between saṃsāra and Nirvāna, defilement and purity, ignorance and enlightenment. For the Mahāyāna, the enlightenment which the Buddhist path is designed to awaken consists precisely in the realisation of this non-dualistic perspective. The validity of conventional dualities is denied because the ultimate nature of all phenomena is emptiness, the lack of any substantial or intrinsic reality, and hence in their emptiness all the diverse, apparently opposed phenomena posited by mainstream Buddhist doctrine finally coincide: "All dharmas have one nature, which is no-nature."

The teaching of the Buddha as found in the Pāli Canon does not endorse a philosophy of non-dualism of any variety, nor, I would add, can a non-dualistic perspective be found lying implicit within the Buddha's discourses. At the same time, however, I would not maintain that the Pāli suttas propose dualism, the positing of duality as a metaphysical hypothesis aimed at intellectual assent. I would characterise the Buddha's intent in the Canon as primarily pragmatic rather than speculative, though I would also qualify this by saying that this pragmatism does not operate in a philosophical void but finds its grounding in the nature of actuality as the Buddha penetrated it in his enlightenment. In contrast to the non-dualistic systems, the Buddha's approach does not aim at the discovery of a unifying principle behind or beneath our experience of the world. Instead it takes the concrete fact of living experience, with all its buzzing confusion of contrasts and tensions, as its starting point and framework, within which it attempts to diagnose the central problem at the core of human existence and to offer a way to its solution. Hence the polestar of the Buddhist path is not a final unity but the extinction of suffering, which brings the resolution of the existential dilemma at its most fundamental level.

When we investigate our experience exactly as it presents itself, we find that it is permeated by a number of critically important dualities with profound implications for the spiritual quest. The Buddha's teaching, as recorded in the Pāli suttas, fixes our attention unflinchingly upon these dualities and treats their acknowledgement as the indispensable basis for any honest search for liberating wisdom. It is precisely these antitheses—of good and evil, suffering and happiness, wisdom and ignorance—that make the quest for enlightenment and deliverance such a vitally crucial concern.

At the peak of the pairs of opposites stands the duality of the conditioned and the Unconditioned: saṃsāra as the round of repeated birth and death wherein all is impermanent, subject to change and liable to suffering, and Nibbāna as the state of final deliverance, the unborn, ageless and deathless. Although Nibbāna, even in the early texts, is definitely cast as an ultimate reality and not merely as an ethical or psychological state, there is not the least insinuation that this reality is metaphysically indistinguishable at some profound level from its manifest opposite, saṃsāra. To the contrary, the Buddha's repeated lesson is that saṃsāra is the realm of suffering governed by greed, hatred, and delusion, wherein we have shed tears greater than the waters of the ocean, while Nibbāna is irreversible release from saṃsāra, to be attained by demolishing greed, hatred and delusion, and by relinquishing all conditioned existence.

Thus the Theravada makes the antithesis of saṃsāra and Nibbāna the starting point of the entire quest for deliverance. Even more, it treats this antithesis as determinative of the final goal, which is precisely the transcendence of saṃsāra and the attainment of liberation in Nibbāna. Where Theravada differs significantly from the Mahāyāna schools, which also start with the duality of saṃsāra and Nirvana, is in its refusal to regard this polarity as a mere preparatory lesson tailored for those with blunt faculties, to be eventually superseded by some higher realisation of non-duality. From the standpoint of the Pāli suttas, even for the Buddha and the arahants, suffering and its cessation, saṃsāra and Nibbāna, remain distinct. Spiritual seekers still exploring the different contemplative traditions commonly assume that the highest spiritual teaching must be one which posits a metaphysical unity as the philosophical foundation and final goal of the quest for enlightenment. Taking this assumption to be axiomatic, they may then conclude that the Pāli Buddhist teaching, with its insistence on the sober assessment of dualities, is deficient or provisional, requiring fulfilment by a non-dualistic realisation. For those of such a bent, the dissolution of dualities in a final unity will always appear more profound and complete.

However, it is just this assumption that I would challenge. I would assert, by reference to the Buddha's own original teaching, that profundity and completeness need not be bought at the price of distinctions, that they can be achieved at the highest level while preserving intact the dualities and diversity so strikingly evident to mature reflection on the world. I would add, moreover, that the teaching which insists on recognising real dualities as they are is finally more satisfactory. The reason it is more satisfactory, despite its denial of the mind's yearning for a comprehensive unity, is because it takes account of another factor which overrides in importance the quest for unity. This 'something else' is the need to remain grounded in actuality.

Where I think the teaching of the Buddha, as preserved in the Theravada tradition, surpasses all other attempts to resolve the spiritual dilemmas of humanity is in its persistent refusal to sacrifice actuality for unity. The Buddha's Dhamma does not point us towards an all-embracing absolute in which the tensions of daily existence dissolve in metaphysical oneness or inscrutable emptiness. It points us, rather, towards actuality as the final sphere of comprehension, towards things as they really are (*yathābhūta*). Above all, it points us towards the Four Noble Truths of suffering, its origin, its cessation, and the way to its cessation as the liberating proclamation of things as they really are. These four truths, the Buddha declares, are noble truths, and what makes them noble truths is precisely that they are actual, undeviating, invariable (*tathā, avitatha, anaññata*). It is the failure to face the actuality of these truths that has caused us to wander for so long through the long course of saṃsāra. It is by penetrating these truths exactly as they are that one can reach the true consummation of the spiritual quest: making an end to suffering.

Now I shall address three major areas of difference between the Buddha's Teaching, which we may refer to here as 'the Ariyan Dhamma,' and the philosophies of non-duality. These areas correspond to the three divisions of the Buddhist path—virtue, concentration and wisdom.

In regard to virtue, the distinction between the two teachings is not immediately evident, as both generally affirm the importance of virtuous conduct at the start of training. The essential difference between them emerges, not at the outset, but later, in the way they evaluate the role of morality in the advanced stages of the path. For the non-dual systems, all dualities are finally transcended in the realisation of the non-dual reality, the Absolute or fundamental ground. As the Absolute encompasses and transcends all diversity, for one who has realised it, the distinctions between good and evil, virtue and non-virtue, lose their ultimate validity. Such distinctions, it is said, are valid only at the conventional level, not at the level of final realisation; they are binding on the trainee, not on the adept. Thus we find that in their historical forms (particularly in Hindu and Buddhist Tantra), philosophies of non-duality hold that the conduct of the enlightened sage cannot be circumscribed by moral rules. The sage has transcended all conventional distinctions of good and evil. He acts spontaneously from his intuition of the Ultimate and therefore is no longer bound by the rules of morality valid for those still struggling towards the light. His behaviour is an elusive, incomprehensible outflow of what has been called 'crazy wisdom.'

For the Ariyan Dhamma, the distinction between the two types of conduct, moral and immoral, is sharp and clear, and this distinction persists all the way through to the consummation of the path: "Bodily conduct is twofold, I say, to be cultivated and not to be cultivated, and such conduct is either the one or the other" (MN 114). The conduct of the ideal Buddhist sage, the arahant, necessarily embodies the highest standards of moral rectitude both in the spirit and in the letter, and for him conformity to the letter is spontaneous and natural. The Buddha says that the liberated one lives restrained by the rules of the Vinaya, seeing danger in the slightest faults. He cannot intentionally commit any breach of the moral precepts, nor would he ever pursue any course of action motivated by desire, hatred, delusion or fear.

In the sphere of concentration, or meditation practice, we again find a striking difference in outlook between the non-dual systems and the Ariyan Dhamma. Since, for the non-dual systems, distinctions are ultimately unreal, meditation practice is not explicitly oriented towards the removal of mental defilements and the cultivation of virtuous states of mind. In these systems, it is often said that defilements are mere appearances devoid of intrinsic reality, even manifestations of the Absolute. Hence to engage in a program of practice to overcome them is an exercise in futility, like fleeing from an apparition demon: to seek to eliminate defilements is to reinforce the illusion of duality. The meditative themes that ripple through the non-dual currents of thought declare: "no defilement and no purity"; "the defilements are in essence the same as transcendent wisdom"; "it is by passion that passion is removed."

In the Ariyan Dhamma, the practice of meditation unfolds from start to finish as a process of mental purification. The process begins with the recognition of the dangers in unwholesome states: they are real pollutants of our being that need to be restrained and eliminated. The consummation is reached in the complete destruction of the defilements through the cultivation of their wholesome antidotes. The entire course of practice demands a recognition of the differences between the dark and bright qualities of the mind, and devolves on effort and diligence: "One does not tolerate an arisen unwholesome thought; one abandons it, dispels it, abolishes it, nullifies it" (MN 2). The hindrances are "causes of blindness, causes of ignorance, destructive to wisdom, not conducive to Nibbāna" (SN 46:40). The practice of meditation purges the mind of its corruptions, preparing the way for the destruction of the cankers (*āsavakkhaya*).

Finally, in the domain of wisdom, the Ariyan Dhamma and the non-dual systems once again move in contrary directions. In the non-dual systems the task of wisdom is to break through the diversified appearances (or the appearance of diversity) in order to discover the unifying reality that underlies them. Concrete phenomena, in their distinctions and their plurality, are mere appearance, while true reality is the One: either a substantial Absolute (the Atman, Brahman, the

Godhead, etc.), or a metaphysical zero (Sunyata, the Void Nature of Mind, etc.). For such systems, liberation comes with the arrival at the fundamental unity in which opposites merge and distinctions evaporate like dew.

In the Ariyan Dhamma wisdom aims at seeing and knowing things as they really are (*yathābhūtañāṇadassana*). Hence, to know things as they are, wisdom must respect phenomena in their precise particularity. Wisdom leaves diversity and plurality untouched. It instead seeks to uncover the characteristics of phenomena, to gain insight into their qualities and structures. It moves, not in the direction of an all-embracing identification with the All, but towards disengagement and detachment, release from the All. The cultivation of wisdom in no way 'undermines' concrete phenomena by reducing them to appearances, nor does it treat them as windows opening to some fundamental ground. Instead it investigates and discerns, in order to understand things as they are: "And what does one understand as it really is? One understands: 'Such is form, such its arising and passing away. Such is feeling ... perception ... formations ... consciousness, such its arising and passing away'." "When one sees, 'All formations are impermanent, all are suffering, everything is not self,' one turns away from suffering: this is the path to purity."

Spiritual systems are coloured as much by their favourite similes as by their formulated tenets. For the non-dual systems, two similes stand out as predominant. One is space, which simultaneously encompasses all and permeates all yet is nothing concrete in itself; the other is the ocean, which remains self-identical beneath the changing multitude of its waves. The similes used within the Ariyan Dhamma are highly diverse, but one theme that unites many of them is acuity of vision—vision which discerns the panorama of visible forms clearly and precisely, each in its own individuality: "It is just as if there were a lake in a mountain recess, clear, limpid, undisturbed, so that a man with good sight standing on the bank could see shells, gravel, and pebbles, and also shoals of fish swimming about and resting. He might think: 'There is this lake, clear, limpid, undisturbed, and there are these shells, gravel, and pebbles, and also these shoals of fish swimming about and resting.' So too a monk understands as it actually is: 'This is suffering, this is the origin of suffering, this is the cessation of suffering, this is the way leading to the cessation of suffering.' When he knows and sees thus his mind is liberated from the cankers, and with the mind's liberation he knows that he is liberated" (MN 39).

From BPS Newsletters Nos 27 and 29, 2ⁿᵈ Mailing 1994 and 1ˢᵗ Mailing 1995.

31. Towards a Threshold of Understanding

Pope John Paul II's recent book, *Crossing the Threshold of Hope* is a collection of reflections primarily on issues of Christian faith; but the book also features the Pope's assessment of other religions, including a short chapter on Buddhism. The Pontiff s words in this chapter are far from appreciative. The release of the book in Sri Lanka on the eve of the Pope's visit to this country this past January stirred up waves of indignation in the Buddhist community that spread as far as the Vatican. The Buddhist prelates announced that they would not attend an inter-religious meeting requested by the Pope unless he formally retracted his unfavourable remarks about Buddhism. Although on arrival the Pope tried to appease the feelings of Buddhist leaders by declaring his esteem for their religion, even quoting the Dhammapada, he fell short of proffering a full apology, and this did not satisfy the Sangha elders.

The following essay is intended as a short corrective to the Pope's demeaning characterisation of Buddhism. It addresses the issues solely at the level of ideas, without delving into the question whether ulterior motives lay behind the Pope's pronouncements. The essay is based on an article written for a Polish publisher, Source (Katowice), which is presently compiling a book on the Buddhist response to the Pope's book.

The Pope states that "the Buddhist tradition and the methods deriving from it have an almost exclusively negative soteriology (doctrine of salvation)." Such a view of the Buddhist teachings was widespread among Christian missionaries in Asia during the 19th century, serving to justify their evangelical incursions into the heartlands of Buddhism. Serious scholars of comparative religion have long recognised this view to be a misrepresentation, rooted, in the case of the early missionaries, partly in misunderstanding, partly in deliberate distortion. It is therefore puzzling that the present head of the Catholic Church, otherwise so well informed, should repeat these worn-out lines, particularly at a time when greater mutual understanding is expected from the leaders of different religions.

The Pope does not explain exactly why he regards Buddhist soteriology as negative. Most likely, he takes this view because the Buddhist path of deliverance does not recognise a personal God as the agent and end of salvation. Like beauty, however, what is negative and what is positive lies in the eye of the beholder, and what is negative for one may turn out to be another's supreme ideal. If one seeks an everlasting union between one's eternal soul and a creator God, then a doctrine that denies the existence of an eternal soul and a Divine Creator will inevitably appear negative. If one regards everything conditioned as impermanent and devoid of self, and seeks deliverance in Nibbāna, the Deathless Element, then a doctrine of everlasting union between God and the soul will seem—not negative perhaps—but founded upon wishful thinking and unacceptable articles of faith. For the ordinary reader, however, the word "negative," when applied to Buddhism, will suggest something far different from a philosophically acute way of approaching the Ultimate, conjuring up pictures of a bleak doctrine of escapism aimed at personal annihilation. Behind the Pope's words we can detect echoes of the ancient texts: "There are, monks, some recluses and brahmins who charge me with being an annihilationist, saying that the recluse Gotama teaches the annihilation of an existent being. That is false misrepresentation. What I teach, in the past as also now, is suffering and the cessation of suffering" (MN 22).

Even more worrisome than the Pope's characterisation of the Buddhist doctrine of salvation as negative is his contention that "the Buddhist doctrine of salvation constitutes the central point, or rather the only point, of this system." The conclusion implied by this pronouncement, left hanging silently behind the lines, is that Buddhism is incapable of offering meaningful guidance to people immersed in the problems of everyday life; it is an otherworldly religion of escape suited only for those of an ascetic bent.

While Western scholars in the past have focused upon the Buddhist doctrine of salvation as their main point of interest, the living traditions of Buddhism as practised by its adherents reveal that this attitude, being one-sided to begin with, must yield one-sided results. The Buddhist texts themselves show that Buddhism addresses as wide a range of concerns as any other of humanity's great religions. Nibbāna remains the ultimate goal of Buddhism, and is certainly "the central point" of the Dhamma, but it is by no means "the only point" for which the Buddha proclaimed his Teaching.

According to the Buddhist texts, the Dhamma is intended to promote three types of good, each by way of different but overlapping sets of principles. These three goals, though integrated into the framework of a single internally consistent teaching, enable the Dhamma to address individuals at different stages of spiritual development, with varying capacities for comprehension. The three goods are:

> the good pertaining to the present life (*ditthadhammattha*), i.e. the achievement of happiness and well-being here and now, through ethical living and harmonious relationships based on kindness and compassion;

the good pertaining to the future life (*samparāyikattha*), i.e. a favourable rebirth within the round of existence, by practising generosity, observing the precepts, and cultivating the mind in meditation;

and the ultimate good (*paramattha*), i.e. the attainment of Nibbāna, by following the complete training defined by the Noble Eightfold Path.

For most Buddhists in their day-to-day lives, the pursuit of Nibbāna is a distant rather than an immediate goal, to be approached gradually during the long course of rebirths. Until they are ready for a direct assault on the final good, they expect to walk the path for many lives within *saṃsāra*, pursuing their mundane welfare while aspiring for the Ultimate. To assist them in this endeavour, the Buddha has taught numerous guidelines that pertain to ethically upright living within the confines of the world. In the Sigālovāda Sutta, for example, he enumerates the reciprocal duties of parents and children, husband and wife, friends and friends, employers and employees, teachers and students, religious and laity. He made right livelihood an integral part of the Noble Eightfold Path, and explained what it implies in the life of a busy lay person. During his long ministry he gave advice to merchants on the prudent conduct of business, to young wives on how to behave towards their husbands, to rulers on how to administer their state. All such guidance, issuing from the Buddha's great compassion, is designed to promote the welfare and happiness of the world while at the same time steering his followers towards a pleasant rebirth and gradual progress towards final liberation.

Yet, while the Buddha offers a graduated teaching adjusted to the varying life situations of his disciples, he does not allow any illusion to linger about the ultimate aim of his Doctrine. That aim is Nibbāna, which is not a consoling reconciliation with the world but irreversible deliverance from the world. Such deliverance cannot be gained merely by piety and good works performed in a spirit of social sympathy. It can be won only by renunciation, by "the relinquishment of all acquisitions" (*sabbūpadhipaṭinissagga*), including among such "acquisitions" the bodily and mental processes that we identify as our self. The achievement of this end is necessarily individual. It must be arrived at through personal purification and personal insight, as the fruit of sustained effort in fulfilling the entire course of training. Hence the Buddha did not set out to found a church capable of embracing all humanity within the fold of a single creed. He lays down a path—a path perfect in its ideal formulation—to be trodden by imperfect human beings under the imperfect conditions that life within the world affords. While the quest for the highest goal culminates in deliverance from the world, this same ideal "bends back" towards the world and spells out standards of conduct and a scale of values to guide the unenlightened manyfolk in their daily struggles against the streams of greed, hatred, and delusion. Nibbāna remains the "chief point" and the omega point of the Dhamma. But as this goal is to be experienced as the extinction of greed, hatred, and delusion, it defines the condition for its realisation as a life devoted to overcoming greed through generosity, to overcoming hatred through patience and loving kindness, and to overcoming delusion through wisdom and understanding.

In *Crossing the Threshold of Hope,* Pope John Paul asserts that "the 'enlightenment' experienced by the Buddha comes down to the conviction that the world is bad, that it is the source of evil and suffering for man" (p.85). No doubt the fact that the book consistently encloses the word 'enlightenment' in quotation marks already suggests that the Pope's attitude to Buddhism is not an appreciative one. This suggestion is confirmed by his manner of characterising the content of the enlightenment, which reduces the Buddha's great awakening beneath the Bodhi tree to a caricature.

By way of rejoinder it should first be said that Buddhism does not regard the world in itself as either good or bad, and the Buddha never described the world as 'the source of evil' for man. The Buddhist texts scrupulously use terms with moral connotations, such as 'good' and 'evil,' solely to evaluate intentional actions and the persons and states of mind from which such actions spring. They do not ascribe moral qualities to entities that are incapable of moral initiative. Thus actions are bad (*pāpa, akusala*) when they intend harm and suffering for oneself and others, good (*kalyāṇa, kusala*) when they aim at promoting happiness and well-being. The Buddha's analysis of the roots of good and evil also proceeds entirely within the sphere of psychological ethics without overstepping the bounds of that domain. According to the Buddha the roots of evil are the unwholesome springs of action: greed, hatred, and delusion; the roots of good are non-greed, non-hatred, and non-delusion, i.e. detachment, loving kindness, and understanding. The process of spiritual development in Buddhism can be described, from one angle, as the attenuation and eradication of the unwholesome roots by the cultivation of their wholesome opposites. The entire process centres upon the mind as the sole source of both good and evil, with the world set well in the background of this striving for internal purification.

In his formula of the Four Noble Truths, the Buddha does declare that worldly existence is dukkha, but dukkha does not mean evil. It means, rather, unsatisfactory, inadequate, subject to suffering. To understand why the Buddha states that all worldly existence is dukkha one must view this statement in its wider context. According to the Buddha's teaching, our individual lives unfold within a beginningless cycle of rebirths, saṃsāra, wherein all living beings except the enlightened ones wander on driven by the thirst for continued becoming. Each individual life beginning with birth and ending with death is thus but a 'link' in an infinite chain of lives, a single turn of the wheel of existence. As we move within saṃsāra, again and again we undergo birth, ageing, illness, and death, again and again we experience pain and sorrow. It is for this reason that the Buddha declares that life within the confines of saṃsāra is dukkha.

Buddhism locates the cause of our suffering, not in the world considered as an objective reality, but in our own minds. The root of suffering is ignorance coupled with craving; because we fail to understand the true nature of things, our lives are propelled by blind desires for pleasure, power, and renewed becoming. The Buddha's teaching is concerned, not with the obliteration of the world, but with the obliteration of ignorance and craving. When greed, hatred, and delusion are quenched, one then experiences the perfect peace of Nibbāna throughout the duration of one's life in the world, and with the end of life one is permanently released from the round of rebirths into the Unconditioned.

The Pontiff describes Nibbāna as 'a state of perfect indifference with regard to the world,' adding that in Buddhism salvation means 'above all, to free oneself from evil by becoming indifferent to the world, which is the source of evil' (p.86). By such statements he represents Buddhism to his readers as a quietistic doctrine of withdrawal which can address the momentous problems that face humanity today only by politely turning its back on them. This is hardly a satisfactory depiction of Early Buddhism, in which transcendence of the world is stressed, let alone of Mahayana Buddhism, in which the bodhisattva's compassionate activity on behalf of the world becomes the guiding ideal.

The Pali word that the Pope interprets as 'indifference' is presumably *upekkhā*. The real meaning of this word is equanimity, not indifference in the sense of unconcern for others. As a spiritual virtue, upekkhā means equanimity in the face of the fluctuations of worldly fortune. It is evenness of mind, unshakeable freedom of mind, a state of inner equipoise that cannot be upset by gain and loss, honour and dishonour, praise and blame, pleasure and pain. Upekkhā is freedom from all points of self-reference; it is indifference only to the demands of the ego-self with its craving for pleasure and position, not to the well-being of one's fellow human beings. True equanimity is the pinnacle of the four social attitudes that the Buddhist texts call the 'divine abodes': boundless loving kindness, compassion, altruistic joy, and equanimity. The last does not override and negate the preceding three, but perfects and consummates them.

If Buddhism in practice has not always lived up to the high ideals posited by the original Teaching, this is to be understood as a result of the downward gravitational pull of human nature, not as a consequence of any emphasis on apathy and indifference in the pristine Dhamma. The Buddhist texts provide ample evidence that the attainment of Nibbāna does not issue in a stolid indifference to the world. The Buddha himself, the ideal model for his followers, led an active life of forty-five years after his enlightenment dedicated to the uplift of humanity. Throughout Buddhist history, the great spiritual masters of the Dhamma have emulated the Awakened One's example, heeding his injunction to wander forth 'for the welfare and happiness of many, out of compassion for the world, for the good, welfare, and happiness of devas and humans.'

It is not only enlightened monks and nuns who have displayed this sense of spiritual mission. As a corporate whole, Buddhism has inspired and animated all the Asian cultures in which it has taken root. It spread without violence and bloodshed, without forcible conversions, winning adherents entirely by its lofty teachings and the exemplary lives of its followers. Wherever the Dhamma took root, it has provided hope and encouragement, pointing to lofty ethical and spiritual ideals, spelling out concrete codes of moral guidance for the whole society. It needs only a little reflection to decide whether such a result is possible in a doctrine that advocates total apathy or callous self-absorption as the highest good.

From BPS Newsletters Nos. 30 and 31, 2nd and 3d Mailings 1995.

32. Walking Even Amidst the Uneven

The Buddha often speaks of life in the world as an uneven path that constantly challenges us to walk evenly. Each day countless obstacles threaten to obstruct us, to divert us, to knock us off balance, and steady mindfulness and firm determination are needed to avoid losing our way in the dark side-tracks of greed and anger. To stumble may be inevitable until we reach the great highway of the noble ones, but with a clear vision of the goal and diligent effort we can avoid tumbling into the ditches that line the road.

If the task of practising the Dhamma while living in the world has always been difficult, our modern commercial culture has stretched that difficulty by leaps and bounds. No longer is it the case that the desires to be tamed by Dhamma practice are the simple, relatively innocent urges implanted in us by nature or stimulated by a basic subsistence economy. Like unsuspecting fish caught in a net, we move within the coils of a global social and economic order predicated on the premise that the essential human activity is the production and consumption of commodities. From the standpoint of this system, the final good of human life is to purchase and enjoy goods, and the combined ingenuity of laboratory researchers and business magnates ensures that the goods to be enjoyed pour forth in inexhaustible variety.

The law that governs the global economic order is a simple one: never allow desire to abate. The media of communication, our modern miracle workers, employ every strategy at their disposal to ensure that this calamity will not befall us. Through an uninterrupted series of messages they contrive to inflame our fantasies and titillate our appetites with an intensity that would banish the word "enough" from our vocabulary. But despite its mammoth dimensions and global reach, the entire corporate culture rests upon a pervasive illusion that has become so widespread that it seems almost a self-evident truth. This is the idea that happiness is proportional to the quantity and monetary value of our possessions. We are led to believe that by extending our financial assets, by acquiring ownership over more and more goods, we thereby come closer to the good, to becoming happier, more contented, more deeply fulfilled human beings. Yet this belief, this assumption so rarely questioned, is precisely the magical trick, the sleight-of-hand deception, that creates the prison cage of our misery. For so long as we seek happiness by trying to quench desire, the more we strengthen our bondage to the implacable demands of desire. The Suttas compare this process to the attempt to slake thirst by drinking sea water: far from eliminating thirst, the sea water will only increase it.

At the heart of the consumerist culture we find this puzzling paradox, that when we pursue wealth as an end in itself, instead of arriving at true happiness, we only seem further removed from it. This conclusion is easily confirmed if we examine the lives of those who come closest to fulfilling the consumerist dream. Those who enjoy the most abundant wealth, who exercise the greatest power, who revel in luxuriant pleasures, are rarely models of contentment. To the contrary, they often live on the edge of despair and can avoid slipping over the edge only by kindling again and again the quest for more wealth, more power, and more pleasure in a viciously degrading cycle.

When we reflect on this situation in the light of the Buddha's teaching, the reason for the perpetual failure of consumerism stands forth in clear relief. The reason, as the Buddha tells us so succinctly, is that craving is the cause of suffering. By its own nature craving is insatiable, and thus the more our personal lives are governed by the assumption that the gratification of craving is the way to happiness, the more we are bound to reap disappointment. When an entire society is founded upon the principles of consumerism, upon the drive to produce and sell without concern for genuine human needs, the outcome may well be catastrophic.

According to the Buddha's teaching the way to genuine happiness does not lie in the indulgence of desire but in uncovering and eliminating the cause of suffering, which in practical terms means the control and removal of craving. To adopt such an approach is not a matter of forcing oneself into the mould of a cold puritanical asceticism. The Dhamma is a gradual teaching which instructs us how to order our lives in ways that are immediately rewarding and gratifying. It does not promote personal development by demands for repression and self-affliction, but by gently offering us practical guidelines applicable to our present circumstances, guidelines that help us grow towards genuine happiness and peace.

For those involved in civilian life, seeking to raise a family and to forge their fortune within the world, the Buddha does not enjoin ascetic withdrawal from social and civilian obligations. He recommends, rather, a life regulated by moral values aimed at the cultivation of wholesome qualities of mind. To his lay disciples he does not even decry the accumulation of wealth or extol poverty as a preferred alternative. He recommends only that wealth be acquired by right livelihood and be utilised in meaningful ways to promote the happiness of oneself and others.

In his advice to the village headman Rāsiya (SN 42:12) the Buddha describes three praiseworthy qualities in a householder who enjoys sense pleasures: he acquires wealth righteously; he makes himself happy and comfortable with the wealth thus earned; and he shares his wealth and does meritorious deeds. The practice of meritorious deeds introduces a spiritual dimension to the proper employment of wealth, a dimension based on the recognition that greater happiness comes from giving than from gaining. To give is not only a way to reduce our greed and attachment, not only a way to acquire merit productive of future benefits, but a directly visible source of joy which provides immediate confirmation of the central pillar on which the entire Dhamma rests: that the path to happiness is one of relinquishment rather than one of accumulation.

But while the Buddha praises the virtuous householder who possesses the above three qualities, he does not stop there. He introduces a fourth quality which distinguishes the virtuous lay followers into two groups: on one side, those who enjoy sense pleasures while remaining tied to them, blind to the danger and unaware of an escape; on the other, those who enjoy sense pleasures without being tied to them, seeing the danger and aware of an escape. It is the second of these that the Buddha declares superior. This pronouncement offers us an insight into the Buddha's final solution to the challenge posed by consumerism. The final solution is not a limp compromise between indulgence and virtue, but a bold, decisive step in the direction of detachment, an inner renunciation that enables one to rise above the whole round of production and consumption even while living within its boundaries. The incentive for this movement comes from seeing the danger: from recognising that there is no stable happiness to be gained by the pursuit of sense pleasures, from seeing that sense pleasures "give little satisfaction and are productive of much suffering." Its completion comes from recognising an escape: that the removal of desire and lust brings an unshakeable peace and freedom that is not contingent upon external circumstances.

Although it may be difficult to master desire for material things within the confines of household life, the Buddha, in his wisdom, created a model for the greater Buddhist community to emulate, indeed a model for the world as a whole. This is the Sangha, the order of monks and nuns, pledged to a mode of living in which needs are reduced to the most basic and their satisfaction provided in the simplest ways. While only a few may have the opportunity and capacity to leave behind the household life in order to devote their energies unhindered to the task of self-purification, the ideal Buddhist social order forms a pyramid in which those at the apex, dedicated to the ultimate goal of deliverance, serve as the models and teachers for those still enmeshed in the demands of economic subsistence.

By their purity, peacefulness, and wisdom the monastics demonstrate to the lay community, and to all those who have eyes to see, where true happiness is to be found. They show that happiness is to be found, not in acquisition and self-indulgence, but in freedom from desire, in renunciation and detachment. Whether as lay disciple or as monk, to enter the course of training that culminates in such freedom is to walk evenly within the uneven terrain of the world. It is to recover, even with one's initial steps, a balance of living so sorely needed amidst the loud demands and hollow promises of our rapacious consumerist culture.

From BPS Newsletter No. 33, Second Mailing 1996.

33. MEETING THE DIVINE MESSENGERS

The traditional legend of the Buddha's quest for enlightenment tells us that throughout his youth and early manhood Prince Siddhattha, the Bodhisatta, lived in complete ignorance of the most elementary facts of human life. His father, anxious to protect his sensitive son from exposure to suffering, kept him an unwitting captive of nescience. Incarcerated in the splendour of his palace, amply supplied with sensual pleasures and surrounded by merry friends, the prince did not entertain even the faintest suspicion that life could offer anything other than an endless succession of amusements and festivities. It was only on that fateful day in his twenty-ninth year, when curiosity led him out beyond the palace walls, that he encountered the four 'divine messengers' that were to change his destiny. The first three were the old man, the sick man and the corpse, which taught him the shocking truths of old age, illness, and death; the fourth was a wandering ascetic, who revealed to him the existence of a path whereby all suffering can be fully transcended.

This charming story which has nurtured the faith of Buddhists through the centuries enshrines at its heart a profound psychological truth. In the language of myth it speaks to us, not merely of events that may have taken place centuries ago, but of a process of awakening through which each of us must pass if the Dhamma is to come to life within ourselves. Beneath the symbolic veneer of the ancient legend we can see that Prince Siddhattha's youthful sojourn in the palace was not so different from the way in which most of us today pass our entire lives—often, sadly, until it is too late to strike out in a new direction. Our homes may not be royal palaces and the wealth at our disposal may not approach anywhere near that of a North Indian rajah, but we share with the young Prince Siddhattha a blissful (and often wilful) oblivion to stark realities that are constantly thrusting themselves on our attention. If the Dhamma is to be more than the bland, humdrum background of a comfortable life, if it is to become the inspiring, sometimes harsh voice that steers us on to the great path of awakening, we ourselves must emulate the Bodhisatta in his process of maturation. We must join him on that journey outside the palace walls—the walls of our own self-assuring preconceptions—and see for ourselves the divine messengers we so often miss because our eyes are fixed on 'more important things,' i.e. on our mundane preoccupations and goals.

The Buddha says that there are few who are stirred by things that are truly stirring, compared to those people, far more numerous, who are not so stirred.

The spurs to awakening press in on us from all sides, yet too often, instead of acknowledging them, we respond simply by putting on another layer of clothes to protect ourselves from their sting. This statement is not disproved even by the recent spate of discussion and literature on ageing, life-threatening illnesses and alternative approaches to death and dying, for open and honest awareness is still not sufficient for the 'divine messengers' to get their message across. In order for them to convey their message, the message that can goad us on to the path to liberation, something more is needed. We must confront ageing, illness and death, not simply as inescapable realities with which we must somehow cope at the practical level, but as envoys from the beyond, from the far shore, disclosing new dimensions of meaning.

This disclosure takes place at two levels. First, to become 'divine messengers,' the facts of ageing, illness and death must jolt us into an awareness of the fragile, precarious nature of our normal day-to-day lives. They must impress upon our minds the radical deficiency that runs through all our worldly concerns, extending to conditioned existence in its totality. Thereby they become windows opening upon the first noble truth, the noble truth of suffering, which the Buddha says comprises not only birth, ageing, illness and death, not only sorrow, grief, pain and misery, but all the 'five aggregates of clinging' that make up our being-in-the-world.

When we meet the 'divine messengers' at this level, they become catalysts that can induce in us a profound internal transformation. We realise that because we are frail and inescapably mortal we must make drastic changes in our existential priorities and personal values. Instead of letting our lives be consumed by transient trivia, by things that are here today and gone tomorrow, we must give weight to 'what really counts,' to aims and actions that will exert a lasting influence upon our long-range destinies—upon our final destiny in this life and upon our ultimate direction in the cycle of repeated birth and death.

Before such a revaluation takes place, we generally live in a condition that the Buddha describes by the term *pamāda*, negligence or heedlessness. Imagining ourselves immortal and the world our personal playground, we devote our energies to the accumulation of wealth, the enjoyment of sensual pleasures, the achievement of status, the quest for fame and renown. The remedy for heedlessness is the very same quality that was aroused in the Bodhisatta when he met the 'divine messengers' in the streets of Kapilavatthu. This quality, called in Pali *saṃvega*, is a sense of urgency, an inner commotion or shock which does not allow us to rest content with our habitual adjustment to the world. Instead it drives us on, out of our cosy palaces and into unfamiliar jungles, to work out with diligence an authentic solution to our existential plight.

It is at this point that the second function of the 'divine messengers' comes to prominence. For ageing, sickness and death are not only emblems of the unsatisfactory nature of mundane existence but pointers to a deeper reality that lies beyond. In the traditional legend the old man, the sick man and the corpse are gods in disguise; they have been sent down to earth from the highest heaven to awaken the Bodhisatta to his momentous mission, and once they have delivered their message they resume their celestial forms. The final word of the Dhamma is not surrender, not an injunction to resign ourselves stoically to old age, sickness and death. This is the preliminary message, the announcement that our house is ablaze. The final message is other: an ebullient cry that there is a place of safety, an open field beyond the flames, and a clear exit sign pointing the way of escape.

If in this process of awakening we must meet old age, sickness and death face to face, it is because the place of safety can be reached only by honest confrontation with the stark truths about human existence. We cannot reach safety by pretending that the flames that engulf our home are nothing but bouquets of flowers: we must see them as they are, as real flames. When, however, we do look at the 'divine messengers' squarely, without embarrassment or fear, we will find that their faces undergo an unexpected metamorphosis. Before our eyes, by subtle degrees, they change into another face—the face of the Buddha, with its serene smile of triumph over the army of Māra, over the demons of Desire and Death. The divine messengers point to what lies beyond the transient, to a dimension of reality where there is no more ageing, no more sickness, and no more death. This is the goal and final destination of the Buddhist path—Nibbāna, the Unageing, the Unailing, the Deathless. It is to direct us there that the divine messengers have appeared in our midst, and the good news of deliverance is their message.

From BPS Newsletter No. 32, 1ˢᵗ Mailing 1996.

34. DHAMMA AND GLOBALISATION

Over the past three decades the world has been dramatically transformed in ways that none but a handful of prophets and visionaries could have foreseen even a hundred years ago. From a multitude of loosely connected nation-states it has quickly evolved into a tightly knit global community linked together by rapid means of transportation and instantaneous media of communication. Old barriers of space and time have dropped away, confronting us with new vistas of self-understanding and forcing us to recognise the hard truth that we all face a common human destiny. The claims to special privilege of a particular people, nation, race or religion now sound hollow. As occupants of the same planet—a bright blue jewel suspended in the frigid blackness of infinite space—we either flourish together or perish together. In the long run, between these two alternatives no middle ground is feasible.

But while our proud technology has enabled us to split the atom and unscramble genetic codes, the daily newspapers remind us that our mastery over the external world has not ushered in the utopia that we had so confidently anticipated. To the contrary, the shrinking of global boundaries has given rise to fresh problems of enormous scope—social, political and psychological problems so grave that they throw into question the continued survival of our planet and our race. The problems that challenge the global community today come in diverse shapes and sizes. They include the depletion of the earth's natural resources and the despoliation of the environment; regional tensions of ethnic and religious character; the continuing spread of nuclear weapons; disregard for human rights; the widening gap between the rich and the poor. While such problems have been extensively discussed from social, political and economic points of view, they also cry out for critical examination from a religious viewpoint as well.

A spiritually sensitive mind would not look upon these problems as isolated phenomena to be treated by piecemeal solutions but would insist on probing into unexplored areas for hidden roots and subtle interconnections. From such a perspective, what is most striking when we reflect upon our global ailments as a whole is their essentially symptomatic character. Beneath their outward diversity they appear to be so many manifestations of a common root, of a deep and hidden spiritual malignancy infecting our social organism. This common root might be briefly characterised as a stubborn insistence on placing short-term, narrowly considered self-interests (including the interests of the limited social or ethnic groups to which we happen to belong) above the long-range, vital good of the broader human community. The multitude of social ills that assail us cannot be adequately accounted for without bringing into view the powerful human drives that lie behind them. And what is distinctive about these drives is that they derive from a pernicious distortion in the functioning of the human mind which sends us blindly in pursuit of factional, divisive, circumscribed ends even when such pursuits threaten to be ultimately self-destructive.

The most valuable contribution that the Buddha's teaching can make to helping us resolve the great dilemmas facing us today is twofold: first, its uncompromisingly realistic analysis of the psychological springs of human suffering; and second, the ethically ennobling discipline it proposes as the solution. The Buddha explains that the hidden springs of human suffering, in both the personal and social dimensions of our lives, consist of three mental factors called the unwholesome roots. These three roots—which may be regarded as the three prongs of the ego-consciousness—are greed, hatred and delusion. The aim of the Buddhist spiritual path is to gradually subdue these three unwholesome roots by cultivating the mental factors that are directly opposed to them. These are the three *wholesome* roots, namely: non-greed—which is expressed as generosity, detachment and contentment; non-hatred—which becomes manifested as loving kindness, compassion, patience and forgiveness; and non-delusion—which arises as wisdom, insight and understanding.

If we contemplate, in the light of the Buddhist analysis, the dangers that hang over us in our globalised world order, it will become clear that they have assumed such precarious proportions due to the unrestrained proliferation of greed, hatred and delusion as the basis of human conduct. It is not that these dark forces of the mind were first awakened with the Industrial Revolution; they have indeed been the deep springs of so much suffering and destructiveness since time immemorial. But the one-sided development of humankind—the development of outward control over nature, coupled with the almost complete neglect of any attempts to achieve self-understanding—has today given the unwholesome roots an awesome, unprecedented power that veers ever closer to the catastrophic.

Through the prevalence of greed the world has become transformed into a global marketplace where human beings are reduced to the status of consumers, even commodities, and where materialistic desires are provoked at volatile intensities. Through the prevalence of hatred, which is often kindled by competing interests governed by greed, national and ethnic differences become the breeding ground of suspicion and enmity, exploding in violence and destruction, in cruelty and brutality, in endless cycles of revenge. Delusion sustains the other two unwholesome roots by giving rise to false beliefs, dogmatic views and philosophical ideologies devised in order to promote and justify patterns of conduct motivated by greed and hatred.

In the new era marked by the triumph of the free-market economy the most pernicious delusion that hangs over us is the belief that the path to human fulfilment lies in the satisfaction of artificially induced desires. Such a project can only provoke more and more greed, leading to more and more reckless degrees of selfishness, and from the clash of self-seeking factions, the result will necessarily be strife and violence. If there is any validity in the Buddhist diagnosis of the human situation, the task incumbent on humankind today is clear. The entire drive of contemporary civilisation has been towards the conquest and mastery of the external world. Science probes ever more deeply into the hidden secrets of matter and life, while technology and industry join hands to harness the discoveries of science for their practical applications. No doubt science and technology have made appreciable contributions towards alleviating human misery and have vastly improved the quality of our lives. Yet because the human mind, the ultimate agent behind all the monumental achievements of science, has pitifully neglected itself, our patterns of perception, motivations and drives still move in the same dark channels in which they moved in earlier centuries—the channels of greed, hatred, and delusion—only now equipped with more powerful instruments of destruction.

As long as we continue to shirk the task of turning our attention within, towards the understanding and mastery of our own minds, our impressive accomplishments in the external sphere will fail to yield their proper fruits. While at one level they may make life safer and more comfortable, at another they will spawn baneful consequences of increasing severity and peril, even despite our best intentions. For the human race to flourish in the global age, and to live together happily and peacefully on this shrinking planet, the inescapable challenge facing us is that of coming to understand and transform ourselves.

It is here that the Buddha's Teaching becomes especially timely, even for those who are not prepared to embrace the full range of Buddhist religious faith and philosophical doctrine. In its diagnosis of greed, hatred and delusion as the underlying causes of human suffering, the Buddha-Dhamma enables us to see the hidden roots of our private and collective predicaments. By defining a practical path of training which helps us to remove what is harmful and to foster the growth of what is beneficial, the Teaching offers us an effective remedy for tackling the problems of the globe in the one place where they are directly accessible to us: in our own minds. Because it places the burden of responsibility for our redemption on ourselves, calling for personal effort and energetic application to the taming of the mind, the Buddha's Teaching will inevitably have a bitter edge. But by providing an acute diagnosis of our illness and a precise path to deliverance, it also offers us in this global era an elevating message of hope.

From BPS Newsletter No. 34, 3rd Mailing 1996.

35. Aims of Buddhist Education

I deally, education is the principal tool of human growth, essential for transforming the unlettered child into a mature and responsible adult. Yet everywhere today, both in the developed world and the developing world, formal education is in serious trouble. Classroom instruction has become so routinized and flat that children often consider school an exercise in patience rather than an adventure in learning. Even the brightest and most conscientious students easily become restless, and for many the only attractive escape routes lie along the dangerous roads of drugs, sexual experimentation, and outbursts of senseless violence. Teachers too find themselves in a dilemma, dissatisfied with the system which they serve but unable to see a meaningful alternative.

One major reason for this sad state of affairs is a loss of vision regarding the proper aims of education. The word "education" literally means "to bring forth," which indicates that the true task of this undertaking is to draw forth from the mind its innate potential for understanding. The urge to learn, to know and comprehend, is a basic human trait, as intrinsic to our minds as hunger and thirst are to our bodies. In today's turbulent world, however, this hunger to learn is often stifled, deformed by the same moral twists that afflict the wider society. Indeed, just as our appetite for wholesome food is exploited by the fast-food industry with tasty snacks that our nutritionally valueless, so in our schools the minds of the young are deprived of the nutriment they need for healthy growth. In the name of education the students are passed through courses of standardised instruction intended to make them efficient servants of the social system. While such education may be necessary for social cohesion and economic stability, it does little to fulfil the higher end of learning, the illumination of the mind with the light of truth and goodness.

A major cause of our educational problems lies in the "commercialisation" of education. The industrial growth model of society, which today extends its tentacles even into the largely agrarian societies of South and Southeast Asia, demands that the educational system prepare students to become productive citizens in an economic order governed by the drive to maximize profits. Such a conception of the aim of education is quite different from that consistent with Buddhist principles. Practical efficiency certainly has its place in Buddhist education, for Buddhism propounds a middle path which recognises that our loftiest spiritual aspirations depend on a healthy body and a materially secure society. But for Buddhism the practical side of education must be integrated;

with other requirements designed to bring the potentialities of human nature to maturity in the way envisioned by the Buddha. Above all, an educational policy guided by Buddhist principles must aim to instil values as much as to impart information. It must be directed, not merely towards developing social and commercial skills, but towards nurturing in the students the seeds of spiritual nobility.

Since today's secular society dictates that institutional education is to focus on preparing students for their careers, in a Buddhist country like Sri Lanka the prime responsibility for imparting the principles of the Dhamma to the students naturally falls upon the Dhamma schools. Buddhist education in the Dhamma schools should be concerned above all with the transformation of character. Since a person's character is moulded by values, and values are conveyed by inspiring ideals, the first task to be faced by Buddhist educators is to determine the ideals of their educational system. If we turn to the Buddha's discourses in search of the ideals proper to a Buddhist life, we find five qualities that the Buddha often held up as the hallmarks of the model disciple, whether monk or layperson. These five qualities are faith, virtue, generosity, learning, and wisdom. Of the five, two—faith and generosity—relate primarily to the heart: they are concerned with taming the emotional side of human nature. Two relate to the intellect: learning and wisdom. The fifth, virtue or morality, partakes of both sides of the personality: the first three precepts—abstinence from killing, stealing, and sexual abuse—govern the emotions; the precepts of abstinence from falsehood and intoxicants help to develop the clarity and honesty necessary for realisation of truth. Thus Buddhist education aims at a parallel transformation of human character and intelligence, holding both in balance and ensuring both are brought to fulfilment.

The entire system of Buddhist education must be rooted in faith (*saddhā*)—faith in the Triple Gem, and above all in the Buddha as the Fully Enlightened One, the peerless teacher and supreme guide to right living and right understanding. Based on this faith, the students must be inspired to become accomplished in virtue (*sīla*) by following the moral guidelines spelled out by the Five Precepts. They must come to know the precepts well, to understand the reasons for observing them, and to know how to apply them in the difficult circumstances of human life today. Most importantly, they should come to appreciate the positive virtues these precepts represent: kindness, honesty, purity, truthfulness, and mental sobriety. They must also acquire the spirit of generosity and self-sacrifice (*cāga*), so essential for overcoming selfishness, greed, and the narrow focus on self-advancement that dominates in present-day society. To strive to fulfil the ideal of generosity is to develop compassion and renunciation, qualities which sustained the Buddha throughout his entire career. It is to learn that cooperation is greater than competition, that self-sacrifice is more fulfilling than self-aggrandisement, and that our true welfare is to be achieved through harmony and good will rather than by exploiting and dominating others.

The fourth and fifth virtues work closely together. By learning (*suta*) is meant a wide knowledge of the Buddhist texts, which is to be acquired by extensive reading and persistent study. But mere learning is not sufficient. Knowledge only fulfils its proper purpose when it serves as a springboard for wisdom (*paññā*), direct personal insight into the truth of the Dhamma. Of course, the higher wisdom that consummates the Noble Eightfold Path does not lie within the domain of the Dhamma school. This wisdom must be generated by methodical mental training in calm and insight, the two wings of Buddhist meditation. But Buddhist education can go far in laying the foundation for this wisdom by clarifying the principles that are to be penetrated by insight. In this task learning and wisdom are closely interwoven, the former providing a basis for the latter. Wisdom arises by systematically working the ideas and principles learnt through study into the fabric of the mind, which requires deep reflection, intelligent discussion, and keen investigation.

It is wisdom that the Buddha held up as the direct instrument of final liberation, as the key for opening the doors to the Deathless, and also as the infallible guide to success in meeting the mundane challenges of life. Thus wisdom is the crown and pinnacle of the entire system of Buddhist education, and all the preliminary steps in a Buddhist educational system should be geared towards the flowering of this supreme virtue. It is with this step that education reaches completion, that it becomes illumination in the truest and deepest sense, as exclaimed by the Buddha on the night of his Awakening: "There arose in me vision, knowledge, wisdom, understanding, and light."

From BPS Newsletter No. 35, 1ˢᵗ Mailing 1997.

36. SUBRAHMĀ'S PROBLEM

Today, in both East and West, a general breakdown of law and order has planted in us an implacable sense of unease that assails us on the streets, in our workplace, and even in our homes. The rising number of drug addicts, the increase in petty thuggery, the decline of respect for others—all these have jointly led to an intensified atmosphere of suspicion that infects our most ordinary human encounters. Many people only feel at ease behind double-locked doors, with windows secured by metal bars and gates guarded by high-alert sensors. Yet, it is often only when we have armoured ourselves with the most impregnable defence systems that we discover a still more intrusive source of insecurity. This sense of fear and dread, which can eat away at our most precious moments of enjoyment, does not stem from outside threats but swells up inexplicably from within. Though it may wrap itself around our everyday affairs, sparking off thoughts of worry and concern, its true cause is not so much external dangers as an unlocalised anxiety floating dizzily along the edges of the mind.

A little known sutta tucked away in the Devaputta-saṃyutta gives us an insight into the nature of this hidden anguish far more poignant and realistic than our most astute existentialist philosophers. In this short sutta, only eight lines of print in the Pāli Canon, a young god named Subrahmā appears before the Awakened One and explains the problem weighing on his heart:

> "Always frightened is this mind,
> The mind is always agitated,
> About unarisen problems,
> And about arisen ones.
> If there exists release from fear,
> Being asked, please explain it to me."

It is perhaps ironic that it takes a deva to express so succinctly, with such elegant simplicity, the dilemma at the crux of the human condition. Subrahmā's confession also makes it clear that neither the deva world nor any other set of outer conditions offers a final refuge from anguish. Luxurious mansions, lucrative jobs, unchallenged authority, high-alert security systems: none of these can guarantee inner stillness and peace. For the source of all problems is the mind itself, which follows us wherever we may go.

To understand Subrahmā's distress we need only sit down quietly, draw our attention inward, and watch our thoughts as they tumble by. If we do not fix on any one thought but simply observe each thought as it passes by, we will almost surely find waves of anxiety, care and worry running through and beneath this ceaseless procession. Our fears and concerns need not assume vast proportions, booming forth bold metaphysical decrees; still beneath the melody of constantly changing thoughts, punctuating them like the thumping of the bass in a jazz quintet, is the persistent throb of worry and care, the second rhythm of the heart.

Subrahmā underscores the predicament he faced—the predicament faced by all 'unenlightened worldlings'—by repeating the words "always" (*niccaṃ*) in the first two lines. This repetition is significant. It does not mean that every thought we think is plagued by worry and dread, nor does it rule out the joy of successful achievement, the pleasure of requited love, or courage in the face of life's daunting challenges. But it does underscore the stubborn persistence of anxious dread, which trails behind us like a gruffy mongrel—growling when we cast a backward glance, ready to snap at our heels when we're off guard.

Fear and anxiety haunt the corridors of the mind because the mind is a function of time, a rolling glimmer of awareness that flows inexorably from a past that can never be undone into a future that teases us with a perpetual, indecipherable 'not yet.' It is just because the mind attempts to clamp down on the passage of time, wrapping its tentacles around a thousand projects and concerns, that the passage of time appears so formidable. For time means change, and change brings dissolution, the breaking of the bonds that we have forged with so much toil. Time also means the uncertainty of the future, plummeting us into unexpected challenges and inevitable old age and death.

When Subrahmā came to the Buddha with his urgent plea for help, he was not seeking a prescription of Prozac that would tide him through his next round of business deals and his dalliance with celestial nymphs. He wanted nothing less than total release from fear, and thus the Buddha did not have to pull any punches with his answer. In four piquant lines he told Subrahmā the only effective remedy that could heal his inner wound, heal it with no danger of relapse:

> "Not apart from awakening and austerity,
> Not apart from sense restraint,
> Not apart from relinquishing all,
> Do I see any safety for living beings."

The ultimate release from anxiety, the Buddha makes clear, is summed up in four simple measures. The most decisive are "awakening" (*bodhi*) and "relinquishment" (*nissagga*), wisdom and release. These, however, do not arise in a vacuum but only as a consequence of training in virtue and meditation, expressed here as restraint of the sense faculties and "austerity" (*tapa*), the energy of contemplative endeavour. The entire program is directed to digging up the hidden root of anguish, which the existentialists, with all their philosophical acumen, could not discern. That root is clinging. Asleep in the deep night of ignorance, we cling to our possessions, our loved ones, our position and status; and most tenaciously of all, we cling to these 'five aggregates' of form, feeling, perception, volitional activity and consciousness, taking them to be permanent, pleasurable and a truly existent self.

To cling to anything is to aim at preserving it, at sealing it off from the ravenous appetite of time. Yet to make such an attempt is to run smack up against the fixed decree written into the texture of being: that whatever comes to be must pass away. It is not only the object of clinging that must yield to the law of impermanence. The subject too, the one who clings, and the very act of clinging, are also bound to dissolve, perish, and pass away. To sit back trying to shape a world that will conform to our heart's desires is to fight against the inflexible law of change. But try as we may there is no escape: the sonorous truth swells up from the depths of being, and we can either heed its message or continue to stuff our ears.

The cutting irony in the solution the Buddha holds out to Subrahmā lies in the fact that the prescription requires a voluntary assent to the act we instinctively try to avoid. The final escape from anxiety and care is not a warm assurance that the universe will give us a cheerful hug. It is, rather, a call for us to take the step that we habitually resist. What we fear above all else, what causes the tremors of anxiety to ripple through our heart, is the giving up of what we cherish. Yet the Buddha tells us that the only way to reach true safety is by giving up all: "Not apart from relinquishing all do I see any safety for living beings." In the end we have no choice: we must give up all, for when death comes to claim us everything we identify with will be taken away. But to go beyond anxiety we must let go now—not, of course, by a premature act of renunciation, which in many cases might even be harmful or self-destructive— but by wearing away the clinging, attachment and acquisitiveness that lie within as the buried root of fear.

This relinquishment of clinging cannot come about through the forcible rejection of what we love and cherish. It arises from wisdom, from insight, from awakening, from breaking through the deep dark sleep of ignorance. The sovereign remedy is to see that right now, at this very moment, there is nothing we can truly claim as ours, for in reality "All this is empty of self and of what belongs to self." Form, feeling, perception, volition and consciousness: all are to be given up by seeing them as they really are, as "not mine, not I, not my self." To see the truth that all conditioned things are impermanent, disintegrating and bound to perish, is to turn away from clinging, to relinquish all. And to relinquish all is to find ourselves, not barren and empty-handed, but rich with the wealth of the noble ones. For one without clinging, there is no fear, no tremor of agitation, no dark winds of anxiety. The one without clinging is *akutobhaya*, one who faces no danger from any quarter. Though dwelling in the midst of ageing, sickness, and death, he has reached what lies beyond ageing, sickness and death. Though the leaves fall and world systems shimmer, he sees security everywhere.

From BPS Newsletter No. 37, 3rd Mailing 1997.

37. To Live With Dignity

I s it possible to live with dignity in today's world, and if so, how can this be done? To raise such a question may sound strange in an age like our own, when our frantic struggle to make ends meet hardly allows us the leisure to ponder such abstract matters. But if we do pause long enough to give this question a little thought, we would realise soon enough that it is not merely the idle musing of someone with too much time on his hands. The question touches on the very meaning of our lives, and goes even beyond our personal quest for meaning to the very springs of contemporary culture. For if it isn't possible to live with dignity then life has no transcendent purpose, and our only aim in the brief time allotted to us should be to snatch whatever thrills we can before the lights go off for good. But if we can find a basis for living with dignity, then we need to consider whether we are actually living as we should and whether our culture as a whole supports a dignified lifestyle.

Though the idea of dignity seems simple enough at first sight, it is actually more complex than one might suppose. My *Webster's Collegiate Dictionary* published in 1936 defines it as 'elevation of character, intrinsic worth, excellence, nobleness of manner, aspect, or style.' My *Roget's Thesaurus* published in 1977 groups it with 'prestige, esteem, repute, honour, glory, renown, fame'—evidence that over the last forty years the word's epicentre of meaning has undergone a shift. When we inquire about living with dignity, our focus should be on the word's older nuance. What I have in mind is living with the conviction that one's life has intrinsic worth, that we possess a potential for moral excellence that resonates with the hymn of the galaxies.

The conscious pursuit of dignity does not enjoy much popularity these days, having been crowded out by such stiff competitors as wealth and power, success and fame. Behind this devaluation of dignity lies a series of developments in Western thought that emerged in reaction to the dogmatic certainties of Christian theology. The Darwinian theory of evolution, Freud's thesis of the Id, economic determinism, the computer model of the mind: all these trends, arisen more or less independently, have worked together to undermine the notion that our lives have inherent worth. When so many self-assured voices speak to the contrary, no longer can we view ourselves as the crowning glory of creation. Instead we have become convinced we are nothing but packets of protoplasm governed by selfish genes, clever monkeys with college degrees and business cards plying across highways rather than trees.

Such ideas, in however distorted a form, have seeped down from the halls of academia into popular culture, eroding our sense of human dignity on many fronts. The free-market economy, the task master of the modern social order, leads the way. For this system the primary form of human interaction is the contract and the sale, with people themselves reckoned simply as producers and consumers, sometimes even as commodities. In vast impersonal democracies, the individual becomes a mere face in the crowd to be manipulated by slogans, images and promises into voting for this candidate or that. Cities have expanded into sprawling urban jungles, dirty and dangerous, whose dazed occupants seek to escape the pangs of wounded pride with the help of drugs and loveless sex. Escalation in crime, political corruption, upheavals in family life, the despoliation of the environment: these all speak to us as much of a deterioration in how we regard ourselves as in how we relate to others.

Amidst this wreckage, can the Dhamma help us recover our lost sense of dignity and thereby give new meaning to our lives? The answer to this question is yes, and in two ways: first, by justifying our claim to innate dignity, and second, by showing us what we must do to actualise our potential dignity.

For Buddhism the innate dignity of human beings does not stem from our relationship to an all-mighty God or our endowment with an immortal soul. It stems, rather, from the exalted place of human life in the broad expanse of sentient existence. Far from reducing human beings to children of chance, the Buddha teaches that the human realm is a special realm standing squarely at the spiritual centre of the cosmos. What makes human life so special is that human beings have a capacity for moral choice that is not shared by other types of beings. Though this capacity is inevitably subject to limiting conditions, we always possess, in the immediate present, a margin of inner freedom that allows us to change ourselves and thereby to change the world.

But life in the human realm is far from cosy. It is, rather, inconceivably difficult and complex, rife with conflicts and moral ambiguities offering enormous potential for both good and evil. This moral complexity can make of human life a painful struggle indeed, but it also renders the human realm the most fertile ground for sowing the seeds of enlightenment. It is at this tauntingly ambiguous crossroads that we can either rise to the heights of spiritual greatness or fall to degrading depths. The two alternatives branch out from each present moment, and which one we take depends on ourselves.

While this unique capacity for moral choice and spiritual awakening confers intrinsic dignity on human life, the Buddha does not emphasise this so much as he does our ability to acquire active dignity. This ability is summed up by a word that lends its flavour to the entire teaching, *ariya* or noble. The Buddha's teaching is the *ariyadhamma*, the noble doctrine, and its purpose is to change human beings from 'ignorant worldlings' into noble disciples resplendent with noble wisdom. The change does not come about through mere faith and devotion but by treading the Buddhist path, which transmutes our frailties into invincible strengths and our ignorance into knowledge.

The notion of acquired dignity is closely connected with the idea of autonomy. Autonomy means self-control and self-mastery, freedom from the sway of passion and prejudice, the ability to actively determine oneself. To live with dignity means to be one's own master: to conduct one's affairs on the basis of one's own free choices instead of being pushed around by forces beyond one's control. The autonomous individual draws his or her strength from within, free from the dictates of craving and bias, guided by an inward perception of righteousness and truth.

The person who represents the climax of dignity for Buddhism is the arahant, the liberated one, who has reached the pinnacle of spiritual autonomy: release from the dictates of greed, hatred and delusion. The very word arahant suggests this sense of dignity: the word means 'worthy one,' one who deserves the offerings of gods and humans. Although in our present condition we might still be far from the stature of an arahant, this does not mean we are utterly lost, for the means of reaching the highest goal are already within our reach. The means are the Noble Eightfold Path with its twin pillars of right view and right conduct. Right view is the first factor of the path and the guide for all the others. To live with right view is to see that our decisions count, that our volitional actions have consequences that extend beyond themselves and conduce to our long-term happiness or suffering. The active counterpart of right view is right conduct, action guided by the ideal of moral and spiritual excellence. Right conduct in body, speech and mind brings to fulfilment the other seven factors of the eightfold path, culminating in true knowledge and deliverance.

In today's hectic world humankind is veering recklessly in two harmful directions. One is the path of violent struggle and confrontation, the other that of frivolous self-indulgence. Beneath their apparent contrasts, what unites these two vicious extremes is a shared disregard for human dignity: the former violates the dignity of other people, the latter undermines one's own dignity. The Buddha's Noble Eightfold Path is a middle way that avoids all harmful extremes. To follow this path not only brings a quiet dignity into one's own life but also sounds an eloquent rejoinder to the cynicism and hollow pretensions of our age.

From BPS Newsletter No. 38, 1st Mailing 1998.

38. Lifestyles and Spiritual Progress

Newcomers to Buddhism often ask whether a person's lifestyle has any special bearing on their ability to progress along the Buddha's path, and in particular whether the Buddha had a compelling reason for establishing a monastic order governed by guidelines quite different from those that hold sway over the lay Buddhist community. "Doesn't it seem," they ask, "that a lay person who follows the Buddhist precepts in daily life should be able to advance just as rapidly as a monk or nun and attain the same level of enlightenment? And if this is so, doesn't that mean that the entire monastic lifestyle becomes something superfluous, or at best a mere matter of personal choice no more relevant to one's spiritual development than whether one trains to become a doctor or an engineer?"

If we suspend concern for questions of status and superiority and simply consider the two modes of life in their ideal expression, the conclusion would have to follow that the monastic life, lived *in the way envisioned by the Buddha*, is the one that conduces more effectively to the final goal. According to the Pali canon, the ultimate goal of the Dhamma is the attainment of Nibbāna: the destruction of all defilements here and now and ultimate release from saṃsāra, the round of rebirths. This attainment comes about by eliminating craving and ignorance through the practice of the Noble Eightfold Path. The Eightfold Path is open equally to both monastics and lay followers; monastic ordination does not confer any privileged access to the path or an empowerment that enables a monk or nun to make more rapid progress than a lay follower. But while this is so, the fact remains that the monastic life was expressly designed by the Buddha to facilitate complete dedication to the practice of the path in its three stages of virtue, concentration and wisdom, and thus provides the optimal conditions for spiritual progress.

The monastic lifestyle does so precisely because the final goal is a state of renunciation, 'the relinquishment of all acquisitions' (*sabbūpadhipaṭinissagga*), and from the outset the monk's life is rooted in renunciation. In 'going forth,' the monk leaves behind family, possessions, and worldly position, and even the outer marks of personal identity, symbolized by hair, beard and wardrobe. By shaving the head and donning the yellow robe, the monk has given up—in principle at least—any claim to a unique identity as his own. Outwardly indistinguishable from a hundred thousand other monks, he has become simply a 'Sakyaputtiya samaṇa,' an ascetic who follows the Sakyan son (i.e., the Buddha).

The life of the monk involves radical simplicity, contentment with the barest requisites, the need to be patient in difficulty. The monastic lifestyle places the monk in dependence on the generosity and kindness of others, and imposes on him an intricate code of discipline, the Vinaya, designed to foster the essential renunciant virtues of simplicity, restraint, purity and harmlessness. These virtues provide a sound basis for the higher attainments in concentration and insight, which are essentially stages in the progressive purification of the mind and the deepening of insight.

Of prime importance, too, is the external freedom ideally provided by the monastic life. The monastic schedule leaves the monk free from extraneous demands on his time and energy, allowing him to devote himself fully to the practice and study of the Dhamma. Of course, as the monastic life is lived today, monks take on many responsibilities not originally mentioned in the canonical texts, and in a traditional Buddhist country the village temple has become the hub of religious activity, with the monks functioning as virtual priests for the wider Buddhist community. But here we are concerned with the canonical picture of the monastic life. If the monk's life so conceived did not promote smoother progress toward the goal, it seems there would have been no sound reason for the Buddha to have established a monastic order or to have encouraged men and women so inclined to "go forth from the home life into homelessness."

While the attainment of Nibbāna is the ultimate goal of early Buddhism, it is not the only goal, and one of the shortcomings in the way Theravada Buddhism has been presented to the West is the one-sided emphasis placed on the final goal over the provisional aspect of the Teaching. In traditional Buddhist lands few Buddhists see Nibbāna as an immediately realistic prospect. The great majority, both lay and monastic, regard the path as a course of 'gradual practice, gradual progress and gradual achievement' extending over many lives. Their practice as Buddhist followers centres around the performance of meritorious deeds and methodical mental purification, rooted in the confidence that the kammic law of causality and the spiritual power of the Dhamma will sustain them in their quest for deliverance.

To make clear the choices facing the lay follower we might posit two alternative models of the Buddhist lay life. In the first model, lay life is seen as a field for gradual progress toward the goal through the development of wholesome qualities such as generosity, moral virtue, kindness and understanding. The immediate aim is not direct realization of the highest truth, but the accumulation of merits leading to a happy rebirth and gradual progress toward Nibbāna. The second model recognizes the capacity of lay followers for reaching the stages of awakening in this life itself, and advocates strict moral discipline and strenuous effort in meditation to attain deep insight into the truth of the Dhamma. While there are in Buddhist countries lay people who follow the path of direct realization, their number is much smaller than those who pursue the alternative model. The reason should be obvious enough: the stakes are higher, and include a capacity for inward renunciation rare among those who must raise a family, work at a full-time job and struggle to survive in a ruggedly competitive world. We should note further a point of prime importance: this second model of the Buddhist lay life becomes effective as a means to higher attainment precisely because it emulates the monastic model. Thus, to the extent that a lay follower embarks on the practice of the direct path to realization, he or she does so by conforming to the lifestyle of a monk or nun.

These two conceptions of the lay life need not be seen as mutually exclusive, for an earnest lay follower can adopt the first model for his or her normal routine and also stake out periods to pursue the second model, e.g., by curtailing social engagements, devoting time to deep study and meditation and occasionally going on extended retreats. Though a monastic lifestyle might be more conducive to enlightenment than a busy life within the world, when it comes to individuals rather than models, all fixed preconceptions collapse. Some lay people with heavy family and social commitments manage to make such rapid progress that they can give guidance in meditation to earnest monks, and it is not rare at all to find sincere monks deeply committed to the practice who advance slowly and with difficulty. While the monastic life, lived according to the original ideal, may provide the optimal outer conditions for spiritual progress, the actual rate of progress depends on personal effort and on the store of qualities one brings over from previous lives, and often it seems individuals deeply enmeshed in the world are better endowed in both respects than those who enter the Saṅgha.

In any case, whether for monk, nun, or layperson, the path to Nibbāna is the same: the Noble Eightfold Path. Whatever one's personal circumstances may be, if one is truly earnest about realizing the final goal of the Dhamma one will make every effort to tread this path in the way that best fits the particular circumstances of one's life. As the Buddha himself says: "Whether it be a householder or one gone forth, it is the one of right practice that I praise, not the one of wrong practice" (SN 45:24).

From BPS Newsletter No. 39, 2nd Mailing, 1998.

39. BETTER THAN A HUNDRED YEARS

O ne day not too long ago I picked up on my short-wave radio an interview with an American futurist whose name I didn't catch. A futurist, as the word implies, is one whose job it is to predict the future. By collating a vast amount of information about developments presently taking place in various fields, he discovers the most prominent trends at work beneath the surface of events, and by projecting from these trends he constructs a picture of the future over increasingly longer time frames—over the coming decade, century, and millennium. Naturally, as temporal distance from the present increases, the picture he paints becomes proportionally more liable to error; but though an element of conjecture is unavoidable in all long-range forecasts, what the futurist holds is that his projections are based squarely on the trajectory along which we are travelling today.

The questions the interviewer posed drew out from the futurist an astonishing picture of things to come. In his cheery view, the great perennial springs of human suffering are about to yield to the insistent pressure of our ingenuity and determination to create a better world. The next century will usher in an era of unprecedented progress, prosperity, and justice, with radical changes taking place even on the most primordial frontiers of biology. Couples who want children will no longer be dependent on natural processes vulnerable to chance and tragedy: they will be able to specify the precise features they would like their children to have and they'll get exactly what they want. Medical science will find cures for cancer, AIDS, and other dreaded illnesses, while virtually every vital organ will be replaceable by a synthetic counterpart. Biologists will discover how to halt the process of ageing, enabling us to preserve our youthfulness and vitality well into our twilight years. By the end of the next century our life span itself will be extended to 140 years. And before the next millennium draws to a close, science will have found the key to immortality: "That's a hundred percent certain," he assured us.

While I listened to this intelligent, articulate man ramble on with such optimistic verve, I felt a sense of uneasiness gnawing away in my gut. "What's wrong with this picture?" I kept on asking myself. "What's missing? What's so troubling?" Here he was, depicting a world in which humanity would triumph over every ancient nemesis, perhaps even over death itself; and yet I felt that I just couldn't buy it, that I would prefer this wretched, fragile, vulnerable existence nature has conferred on us by birth. Why?

For one thing, it seemed to me that his glowing picture of the future depended on some pretty big assumptions—assumptions which could only work by conveniently turning a blind eye to other present trends which are very far from comforting. He was presupposing that advances in technology will bring only benefits without entailing new problems just as formidable as those that taunt us today; that by sheer cleverness we will be able to rectify old blunders without having to curb the greed that caused those blunders in the first place; that people will spontaneously place the common good above the promptings of naked avarice; that the spread of material affluence will suffice to eliminate the suspicion, hatred, and cruelty that have bred so much misery throughout history.

But, as I continued to reflect, I realised that this was not all that was troubling me about the futurist's picture; I felt there was something still deeper scratching at the back of my mind. At its root, I came to see, my disquietude revolved around the issue of orientation. The picture he presented showed a future in which human beings are completely immersed in temporal concerns, absorbed in the battle against natural limitations, oriented entirely to the conditioned world. What was conspicuously absent from his picture was what might be called "the dimension of transcendence." There was no hint that human existence is not a self-enclosed circle, that it unfolds in a wider spiritual context from which it gains its meaning, that the quest for true fulfilment requires reference to a domain beyond everything finite and temporal.

By deleting all mention of a "dimension of transcendence" the futurist could portray a humanity pledged to the idea that the ultimate good is to be realised by gaining mastery over the external world rather than mastery over ourselves. Given that life involves suffering, and that suffering arises from the clash between our desires and the nature of the world, we can deal with suffering either by changing the world so that it conforms to our desires or by changing ourselves so that our desires harmonise with the world. The picture drawn by the futurist showed a future in which the first alternative prevailed; but the Buddha, and all humanity's other great spiritual teachers as well, unanimously recommend the second route. For them our task is not so much to manipulate the outer conditions responsible for our discontent as it is to overcome the subjective roots of discontent, to vanquish our own selfishness, craving, and ignorance.

In preferring the more ancient approach I don't mean to suggest that we must passively submit to all the frailties to which human life is prone. Stoic resignation is certainly not the answer. We must strive to eliminate debilitating diseases, to promote economic and social justice, to fashion a world in which the basic amenities of health and happiness are as widely distributed as possible. But when the driving engine of civilisation becomes sheer innovation in techniques· we risk venturing into dangerous areas. To struggle with Promethean audacity to bend nature to our will so that all the objective causes of our suffering will be obliterated seems an exercise in hubris—in arrogance and presumption—and, as we know from Greek tragedy, hubris inevitably provokes the wrath of the gods. Even if our reckless tinkering with the natural order does not unleash a cosmic cataclysm, we still risk a gradual descent into the trivialisation and mechanisation of human life. For by making technological ingenuity the criterion of progress we lose sight of the moral depth and elevation of character which have always been the classical hallmarks of human greatness. We flatten out the vertical dimensions of our being, reducing ourselves to a purely horizontal plane in which all that matters is technical expertise and organisational efficiency. Thereby we veer closer to the situation described by T.S. Eliot, "The world ends not with a bang but a whimper."

While I reflected on the futurist's predictions, there came to my mind a series of verses from the Dhammapada which offer a strikingly different picture of the challenge facing us in our lives. The verses occur in the "Chapter of the Thousands," vv.110–15. The first four stanzas tell us that it is not how long we live that really counts, but how we live, the qualities we embody in our being: "Better than to live a hundred years immoral and unconcentrated is it to live a single day virtuous and meditative. Better than to live a hundred years foolish and unconcentrated is it to live a single day wise and meditative. Better than to live a hundred years lazy and dissipated is it to live a single day with energy firmly aroused. Better than to live a hundred years without seeing the rise and fall of things is it to live a single day seeing the rise and fall of things."

In these verses the Buddha tells us that our primary task, the task to which all others should be subordinate, is to master ourselves. The challenge he throws at us is not to remove all the thorns strewn over the earth, but to put on sandals, to vanquish the desires responsible for our suffering in the very place where they arise: in our own minds. As long as our lives are ruled by desire, there will never be an end to discontent, for the elimination of one obstacle will only give rise to a new one in a self-replicating cycle. What is essential is not to prolong life by readjusting biological processes so that they fulfil our wildest dreams, but to ennoble life by sober mental training within the humble limits of our natural condition. And this is achieved, as the Buddha repeatedly stresses, by the triple discipline of moral restraint, meditation, and deep insight into the impermanence of all conditioned things.

The last two verses in this series introduce the end towards which this training points, which is also the goal towards which our lives should be steered: "Better than to live a hundred years without seeing the Deathless is it to live a single day seeing the Deathless. Better than to live a hundred years without seeing the Supreme Truth is it to live a single day seeing the Supreme Truth." If human progress is not to be reduced to a mere pageant of technological stunts pushing back our natural limits, we require some polestar towards which to steer our lives, something which enables us to transcend the limits of both life and death. For Buddhism that is Nibbāna, the Deathless, the Supreme Truth, the state beyond all limiting conditions. Without this transcendent element we might explore the distant galaxies and play cards with the genetic code, but our lives will remain vain and hollow. Fullness of meaning can come only from the source of meaning, from that which is transcendent and unconditioned. To strive for this goal is to find a depth of value and a peak of excellence that can never be equalled by brazen technological audacity. To realise this goal is to reach the end of suffering: to find deathlessness here and now, even in the midst of this imperfect world still subject, as always, to old age, illness, and death.

From BPS Newsletter No. 41, 1ˢᵗ Mailing 1999.

40. Two Paths to Knowledge

M any of the formidable social and cultural problems we face today are rooted in the sharp schism that has divided Western civilisation between science and religion, where science claims invincible knowledge based on the empirical investigation of the natural world, while religion can do little more than call for faith in supernatural creeds and obedience to codes of ethics that require restraint, self-discipline, and self-sacrifice. Since religion, as traditionally understood, often rests on little more than blithe promises and pompous threats, its appeals to our allegiance seldom win assent, while the ethical ideals it advocates stand hardly a fighting chance against the constant injunction—thrust upon us by TV, radio and signboard—to enjoy life to the hilt while we can. As a result, a vast portion of humankind today has become alienated from religion as a meaningful guide to life, left with no alternative but to plunge headlong into the secular religion of consumerism and hedonism. Too often those in the religious camp, sensing the threat secularism poses to their own security, feel driven towards an aggressive fundamentalism in a desperate bid to salvage traditional loyalties.

The quest to establish a sound basis for conduct in today's world has been made particularly difficult because one consequence of the dominance of the scientific world-view has been the banishment of values from the domain of the real. While many scientists in their personal lives are staunch advocates of such ideals as world peace, political justice and greater economic equality, the world-view promulgated by modern science grants to values no objective grounding in the grand scheme of things. From this perspective their root and basis is purely subjective, and thus they bring along all the qualities that the notion of subjectivity suggests: being personal, private, relative, even arbitrary. The overall effect of this scission, despite the best intentions of many responsible scientists, has been to give a green light to lifestyles founded on the quest for personal gratification and a power drive aimed at the exploitation of others.

In contrast to the classical Western antithesis of religion and science, Buddhism shares with science a common commitment to uncover the truth about the world. Both Buddhism and science draw a sharp distinction between the way things appear and the way they really are, and both offer to open our minds to insights into the real nature of things, normally hidden from us by false ideas based on sense perception and 'common sense.' Nevertheless, despite this affinity, it is also necessary to recognise the great differences in aim and orientation that separate Buddhism and science. While both may share certain conceptions about the nature of reality, science is essentially a project designed to provide us with objective, factual knowledge, with information pertaining to the public domain, while Buddhism is a spiritual path intended to promote inner transformation and the realisation of the highest good, called enlightenment, liberation or Nibbāna. In Buddhism, the quest for knowledge is important not as an end in itself, but because the main cause of our bondage and suffering is ignorance—not understanding things as they really are, and thus the antidote needed to heal ourselves is knowledge or insight.

Again, the knowledge to be acquired by the practice of the Dhamma differs significantly from that sought by science in several major respects. Most importantly, the knowledge sought is not simply the acquisition of objective information about the constitution and operations of the physical world, but a deep personal insight into the real nature of one's personal existence. The aim is not to understand reality from the outside but from the inside, from the perspective of one's own living experience. One seeks not factual knowledge but insight or wisdom, a personal knowledge, inescapably subjective, whose whole value lies in its transformative impact on one's life. Concern with the outer world arises only in so far as the outer world is inextricably implicated in experience as an object of knowledge. As the Buddha says: "It is in this body with its perception and thought that I declare is the world, the origin of the world, the cessation of the world, and the way to the cessation of the world."

Because Buddhism takes personal experience as its starting point, without aiming to use experience as a springboard to an impersonal, objective type of knowledge, it includes within its domain the entire spectrum of qualities disclosed by personal experience. This means that Buddhism gives prime consideration to values. But even more, values for Buddhism are not merely projections of subjective judgements which we fashion according to our personal whims, social needs or cultural conditioning; to the contrary, they are written into the texture of reality just as firmly as the laws of motion and thermodynamics. Hence values can be evaluated, rated in terms of truth and falsity, ranked as valid or invalid, and part of our task in giving meaning to our life is to unearth the true scheme of values. To determine the true gradation of values we must turn our attention inwards and use subjective criteria of investigation; but what we find, far from being private or arbitrary, is an integral part of the objective order, permeated by the same lawfulness as that which governs the movements of the planets and the stars.

Affirmation of the objective reality of value implies another major distinction between Buddhism and science. In order for the liberating knowledge of enlightenment to arise, the investigator must undergo a profound personal transformation guided by inner perception of the genuine values. While natural science can be undertaken as a purely intellectual discipline, the Buddhist quest in its entirety is an existential discipline which can only be implemented by regulating one's conduct, purifying one's mind, and refining one's capacity for attention to one's own bodily and mental processes. This training requires compliance with ethics all the way through, and thus ethical guidelines support and pervade the entire training from its starting point in right action to its culmination in the highest liberation of the mind.

What is especially noteworthy is that the ethical thrust of the Buddhist training and its cognitive thrust converge on the same point, the realisation of the truth of selflessness (*anatta*). It is just here that contemporary science approaches Buddhism in its discovery of the process nature of actuality, implying the lack of an ultimate substance concealed behind the sequence of events. But this correspondence again points to a fundamental difference. In Buddhism the impermanent and substanceless nature of reality is not simply a factual truth apprehended by objective knowledge. It is above all an existential truth, a transformative principle offering the key to right understanding and right liberation. To use this key to open the door to spiritual freedom, its sole purpose, we must govern our conduct on the premise that the idea of a substantial self is a delusion. It is insufficient merely to give intellectual assent to the idea of selflessness and turn it into a plaything of thought. The principle must be penetrated by training ourselves to discover the absence of selfhood in its subtlest hiding place, the deep recesses of our own minds.

It is to be hoped that Buddhist thinkers and open-minded scientists, by sharing their insights and reflections, can show us an effective way to heal the rift between objective knowledge and spiritual wisdom and thus bring about a reconciliation between science and spirituality. In this way spiritual practice will become an integral part of the discipline aimed at knowledge, and spiritual practice and knowledge in combination will become the tools for achieving the highest good, enlightenment and spiritual freedom. This has always been the position of Buddhism, as evidenced by the most ancient texts themselves. We must remember that the Buddha, the Enlightened One, is not only, like the scientist, a *lokavidū*, 'a knower of the world' but also, above all, a *vijjācaraṇasampanno*, 'one complete in both knowledge and conduct.'

From BPS Newsletter No. 42, 2nd Mailing 1999.

41. ANICCĀ VATA SAṄKHĀRĀ

nicca vata saṅkhārā—"Impermanent, alas, are all formations!"—is the phrase used in Sri Lanka and other Buddhist lands to announce the death of a loved one. Here, however, I have not quoted this line in order to begin an obituary, but simply to introduce the subject of this essay, the word *saṅkhārā* itself. Sometimes a single Pali word has such rich implications that merely to sit down and draw them out can bring as much insight into the Dhamma as a long expository article. This is indeed the case with the word *saṅkhārā*. The word stands squarely at the heart of the Dhamma, and to trace its various strands of meaning is to get a glimpse of the Buddha's own vision of reality.

The word *saṅkhārā* is derived from the prefix *saṃ*, meaning "together," joined to the noun *kāra*, "doing, making." *Saṅkhāras* are thus "co-doings," things that act in concert with other things, or things that are made by a combination of other things. Translators have rendered the word in many different ways: formations, confections, activities, processes, forces, compounds, compositions, fabrications, determinations, synergies, constructions. All are attempts to capture the meaning of a philosophical concept for which we have no exact parallel, and thus all English renderings are bound to be imprecise. I myself use "formations" and "volitional formations," aware this choice is as defective as any other.

However, though it is impossible to discover an exact English equivalent for *saṅkhārā*, by exploring its actual usage we can still gain insight into how the word functions in the "thought world" of the Dhamma. In the suttas the word occurs in three major doctrinal contexts. One is in the twelvefold formula of dependent origination (*paṭicca-samuppāda*), where the saṅkhāras are the second link in the series. They are said to be conditioned by ignorance and to function as a condition for consciousness. Putting together statements from various suttas, we can see that the saṅkhāras are the kammically active volitions responsible for generating rebirth and thus for sustaining the onward movement of saṃsāra, the round of birth and death. In this context *saṅkhārā* is virtually synonymous with *kamma*, a word to which it is etymologically akin.

The suttas distinguish the saṅkhāras active in dependent origination into three types: bodily, verbal, and mental. Again, the saṅkhāras are divided into the meritorious, demeritorious, and "imperturbable," i.e., the volitions present in the four formless meditations. When ignorance and craving underlie our stream of consciousness, our volitional actions of body, speech, and mind becoɩ e forces with the capacity to produce results, and of the results they prodɩ ce the most significant is the renewal of the stream of consciousness folloᴠ ing death. It is the saṅkhāras, propped up by ignorance and fuelled by craviŋg, that drive the stream of consciousness onwards to a new mode of rebirth, and exactly where consciousness becomes established is determined by the kammic character of the saṅkhāras. If one engages in meritorious deeds, the saṅkhāras or volitional formations will propel consciousness towards a happy sphere of rebirth. If one engages in demeritorious deeds, the saṅkhāras will propel consciousness towards a miserable rebirth. And if one attains the formless meditations, these "imperturbable" saṅkhāras will propel consciousness towards rebirth in the formless realms.

A second major domain where the word saṅkhāras appears is among the five aggregates. The fourth aggregate is the *saṅkhāra-khandha*, the aggregate of volitional formations. The texts define the *saṅkhāra-khandha* as the six classes of volition (*cha cetanākāyā*): volition regarding forms, sounds, smells, tastes, tactile objects, and ideas. Though these saṅkhāras correspond closely to those in the formula of dependent origination, the two are not in all respects the same, for the *saṅkhāra-khandha* has a wider range. The aggregate of volitional formations comprises all kinds of volition. It includes not merely those that are kammically potent, but also those that are kammic results and those that are kammically inoperative. In the later Pali literature the *saṅkhāra-khandha* becomes an umbrella category for all the factors of mind except feeling and perception, which are assigned to aggregates of their own. Thus the *saṅkhāra-khandha* comes to include such ethically variable factors as contact, attention, thought, and energy; such wholesome factors as generosity, kindness, and wisdom; and such unwholesome factors as greed, hatred, and delusion. Since all these factors arise in conjunction with volition and participate in volitional activity, the early Buddhist teachers decided that the most fitting place to assign them is the aggregate of volitional formations.

The third major domain in which the word *saṅkhārā* occurs is as a designation for all conditioned things. In this context the word has a passive derivation: it denotes whatever is formed by a combination of conditions; whatever is conditioned, constructed, or compounded. In this sense it might be rendered simply "formations," without the qualifying adjective. As bare formations, saṅkhāras include all five aggregates, not just the fifth. The term also includes external objects and situations such as mountains, fields, and forests; towns and cities; food and drink; jewellery, cars, and computers.

The fact that saṅkhāras can include both active forces and the things produced by them is highly significant and secures for the term its role as the cornerstone of the Buddha's philosophical vision. For what the Buddha emphasises is that the saṅkhāras in the two active senses—the volitional formations operative in dependent origination, and the kammic volitions in the fourth aggregate—construct the saṅkhāras in the passive sense: "They construct the conditioned; therefore they are called volitional formations. And what are the conditioned things that they construct? They construct the body, feeling, perception, volitional formations, and consciousness; therefore they are called volitional formations" (SN 22:79).

Though external inanimate things may be due to purely physical causes, the saṅkhāras that make up our personal being—the five aggregates—are all products of the kammically active saṅkhāras that we engendered in our previous lives. In the present life as well the five aggregates are constantly being maintained, refurbished, and extended by the volitional activity we engage in now, which again becomes a condition for future existence. Thus, the Buddha teaches, it was our own kammically formative saṅkhāras that built up our present edifice of personal being, and it is our present formative saṅkhāras that are now building up the edifices of personal being we will inhabit in our future lives. These edifices consist of nothing other than saṅkhāras as conditioned things, the conditioned formations comprised in the five aggregates.

The most important fact to understand about saṅkhāras, as conditioned formations, is that they are all impermanent: "Impermanent, alas, are formations." They are impermanent not only in the sense that in their gross manifestations they will eventually come to an end, but even more pointedly because at the subtle, subliminal level they are constantly undergoing rise and fall, forever coming into being and then, in a split second, breaking up and perishing: "Their very nature is to arise and vanish." For this reason the Buddha declares that all saṅkhāras are suffering (*sabbe saṅkhārā dukkhā*)—suffering, however, not because they are all actually painful and stressful, but because they are stamped with the mark of transience and thus cannot provide stable happiness and security.

To win complete release from suffering—not only from experiential suffering, but from the unsatisfactoriness intrinsic to all conditioned existence—we must gain release from saṅkhāras. And what lies beyond the saṅkhāras is that which is not constructed, not put together, not compounded. This is Nibbāna, accordingly called the Unconditioned—*asaṅkhata*—the opposite of what is *saṅkhata*, a word which is the passive participle corresponding to *saṅkhāra*. Nibbāna is called the Unconditioned precisely because it's a state that is neither itself a *saṅkhāra* nor constructed by saṅkhāras; a state described as *visaṅkhāra*, "devoid of formations," and as *sabbasaṅkhāra-samatha*, "the stilling of all formations."

Thus, when we put the word *saṅkhāra* under our microscope, we see compressed within it the entire worldview of the Dhamma. The active saṅkhāras consisting in kammically active volitions perpetually create the saṅkhāras of the five aggregates that constitute our being. As long as we continue to identify with the five aggregates (the work of ignorance) and to seek enjoyment in them (the work of craving), we go on spewing out the volitional formations that build up future combinations of the aggregates. These aggregates—impermanent, unreliable, and deceptive—are the suffering from which we need deliverance.

When, however, we take up the practice of the Dhamma, we apply a brake to this relentless generation of saṅkhāras. We learn to see the true nature of the saṅkhāras, of our own five aggregates: as impermanent, prone to suffering, and devoid of a substantial self. Thereby the engine driven by ignorance and craving is arrested at its root and the process of kammic construction, the production of active saṅkhāras, is effectively deconstructed. By putting an end to the constructing of conditioned reality, we open the door to what is ever-present but not constructed, not conditioned: the *asaṅkhata-dhātu*, the unconditioned element. This is Nibbāna, the Deathless, the stilling of volitional activities, the final liberation from all conditioned formations and thus from impermanence and death. Therefore our verse concludes: "The subsiding of formations is blissful!"

From BPS Newsletter No. 43, 3d Mailing 1999.

42. NAVIGATING THE NEW MILLENNIUM

Although our calculations of times passage carries no more weight against the vastness of the cosmic process than a feather before a storm, still, being human, it is natural for us to nurture hope on reaching the threshold of a new millennium. Almost all people entertain hopes for themselves and those close to them: for good health, for an unexpected change in fortune, for the fulfilment of their deepest wishes. We must also cherish hope for our world, for humanity as a whole hope that despite the dark predictions of dangers lying ahead, the change of digits will usher in a new era of peace, general prosperity, and good will.

Adherents of different religions also turn their thoughts towards the new millennium, and as Buddhists we might briefly ponder the question what the Dhamma can offer the world in the years that lie before us. From one angle it could be said that what Buddhism can offer humankind today is exactly what it has been holding out for the past twenty-five centuries: an acute diagnosis of the human condition and a clear path to full liberation from suffering. But while this statement is correct as far as it goes, it is not yet sufficient; for it does not take account of the fact that in any age the aspects of the Dhamma to be emphasised, and the way they are to be expressed, must address the particular problems faced by the people living in that age. The Buddha'a teaching acquires its incisive relevance, not merely by the cogency of its broad generalities, but by attuning its formulations to the precise problems that loom so large in the consciousness of the particular period in which it has taken root. Thus for the Dhamma to recover its vitality and strength, it is not enough merely to repeat hallowed formulas inherited from the past, however true they might be in their own right. Rather, we must focus the lens of the Buddha'a teaching on the deep problems faced by human beings today and determine how the teachings can help to resolve those problems as efficiently as possible. If what the Buddha taught is _only suffering and the cessation of suffering, then the starting point for any convincing presentation of the way to sufferings cessation must be the specific forms of suffering characteristic of our time.

In the last decades of the twentieth century, two manifestations of suffering have become so prevalent that they seem almost the defining characteristics of the modern era. One is an invidious sense of meaninglessness, a feeling of alienation from life, now becoming almost as common in the more modernised quarters of Asia as in the West. The other, most marked in the Third World, is collective violence. The first problem has its locus in the individual consciousness, the second in the relationships among communities at different levels of social order. If the Dhamma is to bring benefits to humanity in the coming years and decade, it must show us a way out of the abyss of meaningless and offer guidelines for reducing the severity of collective violence.

The sense of meaninglessness as a widespread social phenomenon set in with the rise of modern industrial civilisation. As each new breakthrough in natural science dealt a fresh blow to the organic Christian world view that had prevailed during the mediaeval period, human beings could no longer regard themselves as the pinnacle of creation, the beloved children of an all-loving Father who had created the universe expressly as the stage for our unfolding march towards salvation. Instead, under the influence of the mechanistic sciences, we came to see ourselves as chance products of purely natural causes, born and dying in a universe cold and indifferent to our hopes. Our existence was inexplicable in terms of any objective source of meaning, and did not embody any higher purpose than the brute struggle to survive and propagate our genes before death draws the curtain closed on all our restless strivings.

The loss of meaning was further aggravated by the break-up of traditional forms of social order under the impact of industrial capitalism. The rise of the city and the compulsive work routine of office and factory cut the bonds of social solidarity, so that each individual came to see himself or herself as an isolated entity pitted against others in stark competition for dominance. The individual ego thus became the ultimate centre of experience and the sole determinant of value, but it was an isolated ego on whom the other-regarding virtues inculcated by religious ethics, such as generosity and self-sacrifice, no longer had any claims. Altruism and restraint were eclipsed by the new creed of self-indulgence, which gave precedence to wealth, power, and conspicuous consumption as the supreme goals of life.

As Western technology and its offshoot, the consumerist culture, spread to the far corners of the world, the breakdown of meaning and the sense of self-alienation became endemic to many lands, and today this sense of meaninglessness has reached a truly global scale. The culture of narcissism, which exalts the reckless quest for self-aggrandisement, has spread its tentacles everywhere, leaving behind the same debris: agitated minds and hollow lives. Bent on quick and easy gratification, we pass our lives perpetually shadowed by a fear that all our achievements are worthless, unable to deliver any deep and stable satisfaction. And when this fear reveals itself, the abyss opens up, the realisation that we have wasted our lives in the pursuit of empty dreams. Thus the high incidence of mental illness, drug dependence, alcoholism, and suicide, particularly in the more affluent parts of the world.

It is a telling sign that despite the impressive achievements of science and technology, a culture built on mere mastery over external nature is far from successful in meeting the deep demands of the human spirit. For those adrift in the sea of meaninglessness, the Buddha'a teaching offers a sense of meaning stemming from a profound spiritual tradition that combines metaphysical depth with psychological astuteness and the highest ethical standards. Without calling for blind faith in dogmatic creeds or speculative postulates, the Buddha points directly to the invariable universal laws that underlie happiness and suffering. He insists that we can discover these for ourselves, simply by clear reflection on our own immediate experience, and he offers us methods of practice by which we can gradually dig up the buried roots of suffering and cultivate the causes culminating in the highest happiness.

His appeal is to immediate experience. We can see for ourselves that suffering prevails in a mind driven by greed, hatred, and delusion, and that happiness grows when the mind is suffused by the virtues of generosity, kindness, and understanding. On the basis of this experimental test, which lies within the scope of any thinking person, we can then extrapolate and see that for a mind fully liberated from all self-centred defilements and adorned with perfect detachment, love, and wisdom, happiness and peace will have become boundless and irreversible. Thus by showing us the way to inner peace and happiness, the Dhamma offers us an outlet from the abyss of meaninglessness, a way to confer on our lives an exalted meaning and purpose.

The second type of suffering that has become so pervasive in our epoch is social violence, which still wreaks so much misery across the globe. To be sure, communal violence is by no means peculiar to our era nor a product of modern civilisation, but has infected human relations from the days of our prehistoric past. But what has become so disturbing in the present-day world is the eruption of violence between different ethnic communities that in the past had managed to coexist in a relatively stable degree of mutual acceptance. We have witnessed these outbreaks of enmity recently in the Balkans, Russia, Indonesia, Central Africa, northern India, and sadly in our own Sri Lanka. Violence manifests itself, moreover, not only in the conflicts that rage between groups of different ethnic stocks and communal loyalties, but also in economic oppression, in the widening gap between the rich and the poor, in the gargantuan arms industries that thrive on violent conflict, in the sexual exploitation of women and children, in the drug trade, and also in the reckless devastation of the environment, by which we risk ripping away the life support systems that sustain our life on earth.

While Buddhism cannot pretend to offer a detailed solution to all the countless forms that violence takes in the present-day world, the values emphasised by the Dhamma show what is required to arrive at any lasting solution. What is necessary for true peace and harmony to prevail among human beings is not the hammering out of a comprehensive treaty by which the various parties to a conflict compromise their hard and volatile demands. What is truly required is a new mode of perception, the acquiescence to a universal consciousness that transcends the narrow standpoint of egocentric or ethnocentric self-interest. This is a consciousness that regards the other as not essentially different from oneself, which detaches itself from the insistent voice of self-interest and rises up to a universal perspective from which the welfare of all appears as important as ones own good.

We can see the germ of this universal perspective in a principle that stands at the base of Buddhist ethics, even more fundamental to its ethical ideals than the Five Precepts or any other formal code of conduct. This is the principle of taking oneself as the criterion for determining how to treat others. When we apply this principle we can understand that just as we each wish to live happily and to be free from suffering, so all other beings wish to live happily and to be free from suffering; just as we are each averse to pain and hardship and want to live in peace, so all others are averse to pain and hardship and want to live in peace. When we have understood this common core of feeling that we share with all other beings, not as a mere idea but as the fruit of clear reflection, we will treat others with the same kindness and care that we would wish them to treat us. And this must apply at a communal level just as much as in our personal relations. We must learn to see other communities as essentially similar to our own, and entitled to the same benefits as we wish for the group to which we belong. Even if we cannot reach any expansive feelings of love and compassion for the others, we will at least realise that the moral imperative requires that we treat them with justice and kindness.

Thus the message of the Dhamma to human beings in the next millennium might be briefly summed up in these twin gifts. In the personal domain it gives us a precisely defined path that confers on life a deep sense of purpose, a purpose grounded in the cosmic order but which can be actualised in ones own immediate experience. In the communal dimension of human existence it holds out an ethical guideline to right action which, if diligently applied, can arouse a conscientious commitment to a life of non-violence. Though it is far too much to expect that these two blessings will become the common heritage of all humanity, we can at least hope that enough people will accept them to make the twenty-first century a brighter and happier century than the one we are about to leave behind.

From BPS Newsletter No. 44, 1ˢᵗ Mailing 2000.

43. TWO STYLES OF INSIGHT MEDITATION

Today the practice of insight meditation has gained global popularity, yet in achieving this success it has undergone a subtle metamorphosis. Rather than being taught as an integral part of the Buddhist path, it is now often presented as a secular discipline whose fruits pertain more to life within the world than to supramundane release. Many meditators testify to the tangible benefits they have gained from the practice of insight meditation, benefits that range from enhanced job performance and better relationships to deeper calm, more compassion and greater awareness. However, while such benefits may certainly be worthwhile in their own right, taken by themselves they are not the final goal that the Buddha himself holds up as the end point of his training. That goal, in the terminology of the texts, is the attainment of Nibbāna, the destruction of all defilements here and now, and deliverance from the beginningless round of rebirths.

Perhaps the most powerful pressure that has shaped the contemporary expression of insight meditation has been the need to transplant the practice into a largely secular environment remote from its traditional matrix of Buddhist faith and doctrine. Given the skeptical climate of our age, it is quite appropriate that newcomers to Dhamma be invited to explore for themselves the potential inherent in the practice. Perhaps the last thing they need is to have the full agenda of Buddhist doctrine thrust upon them from the start.

However, though we may initially take up meditation with an open and explorative mind, at a certain point in our practice we inevitably arrive at a crossroads where we are faced with a choice. Either we can continue the meditation as a purely naturalistic, non-religious discipline, or we can transpose the practice back into its original setting of Buddhist faith and understanding. If we choose the first route, we might still deepen our meditation and reap more abundantly the same benefits we have obtained so far—deeper calm, more equanimity, greater openness, even a kind of penetration of the here and now. Nevertheless, as desirable as these fruits might be in themselves, viewed against the Buddha's word they remain incomplete. For the practice of insight meditation to achieve the full potential ascribed to it by the Buddha, it must be embraced by several other qualities that rivet it to the framework of the teaching.

Foremost among such qualities is the complementary pair of faith and right view. As a factor of the Buddhist path, faith (saddhā) does not mean blind belief but a willingness to accept on trust certain propositions that we cannot, at our present stage of development, personally verify for ourselves. These propositions concern both the nature of reality and the higher reaches of the path. In the traditional map of the Buddhist training, faith is placed at the beginning, as the prerequisite for the later stages comprised in the triad of virtue, concentration and wisdom. The canonical texts do not seem to envisage the possibility that a person lacking faith in the tenets specific to the Dhamma could take up the practice of insight meditation and reap positive results. Yet today such a phenomenon has become extremely widespread. It is quite common now for meditators to make their first contact with the Dhamma through intensive insight meditation, and then to use this experience as a touchstone for assessing their relationship to the teaching.

At this juncture, the choice they make divides meditators into two broad camps. One consists of those who focus exclusively on the tangible benefits the practice yields here and now, suspending all concern with what lies beyond the horizons of their own experience. The other consists of those who recognize the practice to flow from a fount of understanding far deeper and broader than their own. To follow this wisdom to its source, such meditators are prepared to subordinate their own familiar assumptions to the disclosures of the teaching and thus embrace the Dhamma as an integral whole.

The fact that insight meditation can be seriously practised even outside the domain of Buddhist faith raises an interesting question never explicitly posed by the canon and commentaries. If insight meditation can be pursued solely for its immediately visible benefits, then what role does faith play in the development of the path? Certainly, faith as a full acceptance of Buddhist doctrine is not a necessary condition for Buddhist practice. As we have seen, those who do not follow the Dhamma as a path to spiritual deliverance might still accept the Buddhist ethical precepts and practise meditation as a way to inner peace.

Faith must therefore play a different role than that of a simple spur to action, but the exact nature of this role remains problematic. Perhaps the solution will emerge if we ask what faith actually means in the context of Buddhist practice. It should be clear at once that faith cannot be adequately explained simply as reverence for the Buddha, or as some alloy of devotion, admiration and gratitude. For while these qualities often exist alongside faith, they may all be present even when faith is absent.

If we examine faith more closely, we would see that besides its emotive ingredients, it also involves a cognitive component. This consists in a readiness to accept the Buddha as the unique discoverer and proclaimer of liberating truth. Seen from this angle, faith necessarily involves a decision. As the word 'decision' implies (namely, to decide = to cut off), to place faith in something is to exercise an act of discrimination. Thus Buddhist faith entails, at least implicitly, a rejection of the claims of other spiritual teachers to be bearers of the liberating message on a par with the Buddha himself. As a decision, faith also entails acceptance. It involves a willingness to open oneself to the principles made known by the Enlightened One and adhere to them as trustworthy guides to knowledge and conduct.

It is this decision that separates those who take up the practice of insight meditation as a purely naturalistic discipline from those who practise it within the framework of the Buddhist faith. The former, by suspending any judgment about the picture of the human condition imparted by the Buddha, limit the fruits of the practice to those that are compatible with a secular, naturalistic worldview. The latter, by accepting the Buddha's own disclosure of the human condition, gain access to the goal that the Buddha himself holds up as the final aim of the practice.

The second pillar that supports the practice of insight meditation is the cognitive counterpart of faith, namely, right view *(sammādiṭṭhi)*. Though the word 'view' might suggest that the practitioner actually sees the principles considered to be right, at the outset of the training this is seldom the case. For all but a few exceptionally gifted disciples, right view initially means right belief, the acceptance of principles and doctrines out of confidence in the Buddha's enlightenment. Though Buddhist modernists sometimes claim that the Buddha said that one should believe only what one can verify for oneself, no such statement is found in the Pali canon. What the Buddha does say is that one should not accept his teachings blindly but should inquire into their meaning and attempt to realize their truth for oneself.

Contrary to Buddhist modernism, there are many principles taught by the Buddha as essential to right understanding that we cannot, in our present state, see for ourselves. These are by no means negligible, for they define the framework of the Buddha's entire program of deliverance. Not only do they depict the deeper dimensions of the suffering from which we need release, but also they point in the direction where true liberation lies and prescribe the steps that lead to realization of the goal.

These principles include the tenets of both 'mundane' and 'transcendent' right view. Mundane right view is the type of correct understanding that leads to a fortunate destination within the round of rebirths. It involves an acceptance of the principles of kamma and its fruit; of the distinction between meritorious and evil actions; and of the vast expanse and multiple domains of saṃsāra within which rebirth may occur. Transcendent right view is the view leading to liberation from saṃsāra in its entirety. It entails understanding the Four Noble Truths in their deeper ramifications, as offering not merely a diagnosis of psychological distress but a description of saṃsāric bondage and a program for final release. It is the transcendent right view that comes at the head of the Noble Eightfold Path and steers the other seven factors toward the cessation of suffering.

While the actual techniques for practicing insight meditation may be identical for those who pursue it as a purely naturalistic discipline and those who adopt it within the framework of Dhamma, the two styles of practice will nevertheless differ profoundly with respect to the results the techniques can yield. When practised against the background of a naturalistic understanding, insight meditation can bring greater calm, understanding and equanimity, even experiences of insight. It can purify the mind of the coarser defilements and issue in a tranquil acceptance of life's vicissitudes. For these reasons, this mode of practice should not be disparaged. However, from a deeper point of view, this appropriation of Buddhist meditation remains incomplete. It is still confined to the sphere of conditioned existence, still tied to the cycle of kamma and its fruit.

When, however, insight meditation is sustained from below by deep faith in the Buddha as the perfectly enlightened teacher, and illuminated from above by the wisdom of the teaching, it acquires a new capacity that the other approach lacks. It now functions with the support of dispassion, moving toward ultimate deliverance. It becomes the key to open the doors to the Deathless, the means to gain a freedom that can never be lost. With this, insight meditation transcends the limits of the conditioned, transcends even itself, to arrive at its proper goal: the eradication of all the fetters of existence and release from the beginningless round of birth, ageing and death.

From BPS Newsletter No. 45, 2nd Mailing 2000.

44. Does Rebirth Make Sense?

Newcomers to Buddhism are usually impressed by the clarity, directness and earthy practicality of the Dhamma as embodied in such basic teachings as the Four Noble Truths, the Noble Eightfold Path and the threefold training. These teachings, as clear as daylight, are accessible to any serious seeker looking for a way beyond suffering. When, however, these seekers encounter the doctrine of rebirth, they often baulk, convinced it *just doesn't make sense.* At this point, they suspect that the teaching has swerved off course, tumbling from the grand highway of reason into wistfulness and speculation. Even modernist interpreters of Buddhism seem to have trouble taking the rebirth teaching seriously. Some dismiss it as just a piece of cultural baggage, 'ancient Indian metaphysics', that the Buddha retained in deference to the world-view of his age. Others interpret it as a metaphor for the change of mental states, with the realms of rebirth seen as symbols for psychological archetypes. A few critics even question the authenticity of the texts on rebirth, arguing that they must be interpolations.

A quick glance at the Pāli suttas would show that none of these claims has much substance. The teaching of rebirth crops up almost everywhere in the Canon, and is so closely bound to a host of other doctrines that to remove it would virtually reduce the Dhamma to tatters. Moreover, when the suttas speak about rebirth into the five realms—the hells, the animal world, the spirit realm, the human world and the heavens—they never hint that these terms are meant symbolically. To the contrary, they even say that rebirth occurs "with the breakup of the body, after death," which clearly implies they intend the idea of rebirth to be taken quite literally.

In this essay I won't be arguing the case for the scientific validity of rebirth. Instead, I wish to show that the idea of rebirth *makes sense.* I will be contending that it 'makes sense' in two ways: first, in that it is *intelligible,* having meaning both intrinsically and in relation to the Dhamma as a whole; and second, in that it helps us to *make sense,* to understand our own place in the world. I will try to establish this in relation to three domains of discourse: the ethical, the ontological, and the soteriological. Don't be frightened by the big words, the meaning will become clear as we go along.

First, the teaching of rebirth makes sense in relation to *ethics.* For early Buddhism, the conception of rebirth is an essential plank of its ethical theory, providing an incentive for avoiding evil and doing good. In this context, the doctrine of rebirth is correlated with the principle of kamma, which asserts that all our morally determinate actions, our wholesome and unwholesome deeds, have an inherent power to bring forth fruits that correspond to the moral quality of those deeds. Read together, the twin teachings of rebirth and kamma show that a principle of moral equilibrium obtains between our actions and the felt quality of our lives, such that morally good deeds bring agreeable results, bad deeds disagreeable results.

It is only too obvious that such moral equilibrium cannot be found within the limits of a single life. We can observe, often poignantly, that morally unscrupulous people might enjoy happiness, esteem and success, while people who lead lives of the highest integrity are bowed down beneath pain and misery. For the principle of moral equilibrium to work, some type of survival beyond the present life is required, for kamma can bring its due retribution only if our individual stream of consciousness does not terminate with death. Two different forms of survival are possible: on the one hand, an eternal afterlife in heaven or hell; on the other hand, a sequence of rebirths. Of these alternatives, the hypothesis of rebirth seems far more compatible with moral justice than an eternal afterlife, for any finite good action it seems must eventually exhaust its potency, and no finite bad action, no matter how bad, should warrant eternal damnation.

It may be the case that this insistence on some kind of moral equity is an illusion, an unrealistic demand we superimpose on a universe that is cold and indifferent to our hopes. There is no logical way to prove the validity of rebirth and kamma. The naturalist might just be right in holding that personal existence comes to an end at death, and with it all prospects for moral justice. Nevertheless, I believe such a thesis flies in the face of one of our deepest moral intuitions, a sense that some kind of moral justice must ultimately prevail. To show that this is so, let us consider two limiting cases of ethically decisive action. As the limiting case of immoral action, let us take Hitler, who was directly responsible for the dehumanizing deaths of perhaps ten million people. As the limiting case of moral action, let us consider a man who sacrifices his own life to save the lives of total strangers. Now if there is not survival beyond death, both men reap the same ultimate destiny. Before dying, perhaps, Hitler experiences some pangs of despair; the self-sacrificing hero enjoys a few seconds knowing he is performing a noble deed. Then beyond that, there is nothing, except in others' memories. Both are obliterated, reduced to lifeless flesh and bones.

Now the naturalist might be correct in drawing this conclusion, and in holding that those who believe in survival and retribution are just projecting their own wishes out upon the world. But I think something within us resists consigning both Hitler and our compassionate hero to the same fate. The reason we resist is because we have a deep intuitive sense that a principle of moral justice is at work in the world, regulating the course of events in such a way that our good and bad actions rebound upon ourselves to bring the appropriate fruit. Where the naturalist holds that this intuition amounts to nothing more than a projection of our own ideals out upon the world, I would contend that the very fact that we can conceive a demand for moral justice has a significance that is more than merely psychological. However vaguely, our subjective sense of moral justice reflects an objective reality, a principle of moral equilibrium that is not mere projection but is built into the very bedrock of actuality.

The above considerations are not intended to make belief in rebirth a necessary basis for ethics. The Buddha himself does not try to found ethics on the ideas of kamma and rebirth, but uses a purely naturalistic type of moral reasoning that does not presuppose personal survival or the working of kamma. The gist of his reasoning is simply that we should not mistreat others—by injuring them, stealing their belongings, exploiting them sexually or deceiving them—because we ourselves are averse to being treated in such ways. Nevertheless, though the Buddha does not *found* ethics on the theory of rebirth, he does make belief in kamma and rebirth a strong inducement to moral behaviour. When we recognize that our good and bad actions can rebound upon ourselves, determining our future lives and bringing us happiness or suffering, this gives us a decisive reason to avoid unwholesome conduct and to diligently pursue the good.

The Buddha includes belief in rebirth and kamma in his definition of right view, and their explicit denial in wrong view. It is not that the desire for the fruits of good kamma should be one's main motive for leading a moral life, but rather that acceptance of these teachings inspires and reinforces our commitment to ethical ideals. These twin principles open a window to a wider background against which our pursuit of the moral life unfolds. They show us that our present living conditions, our dispositions and aptitudes, our virtues and faults, result from our actions in previous lives. When we realize that our present conditions reflect our kammic past, we will also realize that our present actions are the legacy that we will transmit to our kammic descendants, that is, to ourselves in future lives. The teaching of rebirth thus enables us to face the future with fortitude, dignity and courage. If we recognize that we can still redeem ourselves no matter how debilitating or limiting our present conditions might be, we will be spurred to exercise our will for the achievement of our future good. By our present actions of body, speech, and mind, we can transform ourselves, and by transforming ourselves, we can surmount all inner and outer obstacles and advance toward the final goal.

The teachings of kamma and rebirth have a still deeper ethical significance than as simple pointers to moral responsibility. They show us not only that our personal lives are shaped by our own kammic past, but also that we live in an ethically meaningful universe. Taken in conjunction, they make the universe a *cosmos,* an orderly, integrated whole, with dimensions of significance that transcend the merely physical. The levels of order that we have access to by direct inspection or scientific investigation do not exhaust all the levels of cosmic order. There is system and pattern, not only in the physical and biological domains but also in the ethical, and the teachings of kamma and rebirth reveal just what that pattern is. Although this ethical order is invisible to our fleshly eyes and cannot be detected by scientific apparatus, this does not mean it is not real. Beyond the range of normal perception, a moral law holds sway over our deeds and via our deeds over our destiny. It is just the principle of kamma, operating across the sequence of rebirths, that locks our volitional actions into the dynamics of the cosmos, thus making ethics an expression of the cosmos's own intrinsic orderliness.

The teaching of rebirth, taken in conjunction with the doctrine of kamma, implies that we live in a morally ordered universe, one in which our morally determinate actions bring forth fruits that in some way correspond to their own ethical quality. Though the moral law that links our actions with their fruits cannot be demonstrated experimentally in the same way that physical and chemical laws can be, this does not mean it does not exist. It means only that, like quarks and quasars, it operates beyond the threshold of sensory perception. Far from being a mere projection of our subjective ideals, the moral law locks our volitional deeds into an all-embracing cosmic order that is perfectly objective in that it functions independently of our personal desires, views and beliefs. Thus when we submit our behaviour to the rule of ethics, we are not simply acting in ways that merit moral approval. By conforming to the principles of ethics we are doing nothing less than aligning ourselves with the Dhamma, the universal law of righteousness and truth which stands at the bedrock of the cosmos.

This brings us to the *ontological* aspect of the Buddhist teaching on rebirth, its implications for understanding the nature of being. Buddhism sees the process of rebirth as integral to the principle of conditionality that runs through all existence. The sentient universe is regulated by different orders of causation layered in such a way that higher orders of causation can exercise dominion over lower ones. Thus the order of kamma, which governs the process of rebirth, dominates the lower orders of physical and biological causation, bending their energies toward the fulfilment of its own potential. The Buddha does not posit a divine judge who rules over the workings of kamma, rewarding and punishing us for our deeds. The kammic process functions autonomously, without a supervisor or director, entirely through the intrinsic power of volitional action. Interwoven with other orders in the vast, complex web of conditionality, our deeds produce their consequences just as naturally as seeds in a field bring forth their appropriate herbs and flowers.

To understand how kamma can produce its effects across the succession of rebirths we must invert our normal, everyday conception of the relationship between consciousness and matter. Under the influence of materialistic biases we assume that material existence is determinative of consciousness. Because we witness bodies being born into this world and observe how the mind matures in tandem with the body, we tacitly take the body to be the foundation of our existence and mind or consciousness an evolutionary offshoot of blind material processes. Matter wins the honoured status of 'objective reality', and mind becomes an accidental intruder upon an inherently senseless universe.

From the Buddhist perspective, however, consciousness and the world coexist in a relationship of mutual creation which equally require both terms. Just as there can be no consciousness without a body to serve as its physical support and a world as its sphere of cognition, so there can be no physical organism and no world without some type of consciousness to constitute them as an organism and world. Though temporally neither mind nor matter can be regarded as prior to the other, in terms of practical importance the Buddha says that mind is the forerunner. Mind is the forerunner, not in the sense that it arises before the body or can exist independently of a physical substratum, but in the sense that the body and the world in which we find ourselves reflect our mental activity.

It is mental activity, in the form of volition, that constitutes kamma, and it is our stock of kamma that steers the stream of consciousness from the past life into a new body. Thus the Buddha says: "This body, O monks, is old kamma, to be seen as generated and fashioned by volition, as something to be felt" (SN 11:37). It is not only the body, as a composite whole, that is the product of past kamma, but the sense faculties too (see SN 25:146). The eye, ear, nose, tongue, body-sense and mind-base are also fashioned by our past kamma, and thus kamma to some degree shapes and influences all our sensory experience. Since kamma is ultimately explained as volition (*cetanā*), this means that the particular body with which we are endowed, with all its distinguishing features and faculties of sense, is rooted in our volitional activities in earlier lives. Precisely how past volition can influence the development of the zygote lies beyond the range of scientific explanation, but if the Buddha's words are to be trusted such an influence must be real.

The channel for the transmission of kammic influence from life to life across the sequence of rebirths is the individual stream of consciousness. Consciousness embraces both phases of our being—that in which we generate fresh kamma and that in which we reap the fruits of old kamma—and thus in the process of rebirth, consciousness bridges the old and new existences.

Consciousness is not a single transmigrating entity, a self or soul, but a stream of evanescent acts of consciousness, each of which arises, briefly subsists, and then passes away. This entire stream, however, though made up of evanescent units, is fused into a unified whole by the causal relations obtaining between all the occasions of consciousness in any individual continuum. At a deep level, each occasion of consciousness inherits from its predecessor the entire kammic legacy of that particular stream; in perishing, it in turn passes that content on to its successor, augmented by its own novel contribution. Thus our volitional deeds do not exhaust their full potential in their immediately visible effects. Every volitional deed that we perform, when it passes, leaves behind a subtle imprint stamped upon the onward-flowing stream of consciousness. The deed deposits in the stream of consciousness a seed capable of bearing fruit, of producing a result that matches the ethical quality of the deed.

When we encounter suitable external conditions, the kammic seeds deposited in our mental continuum rise up from their dormant condition and produce their fruits. The most important function performed by kamma is to generate rebirth into an appropriate realm, a realm that provides a field for it to unfold its stored potentials. The bridge between the old existence and the new is, as we said above, the evolving stream of consciousness. It is within this stream of consciousness that the kamma has been created through the exercise of volition; it is this same stream of consciousness, flowing on, that carries the kammic energies into the new existence; and it is again this same stream of consciousness that experiences the fruit. Conceivably, at the deepest level all the individual streams of consciousness are integrated into a single all-embracing matrix, so that, beneath the surface of events, the separate kammic accumulations of all living beings crisscross, overlap, and merge. This hypothesis—though speculative—would help account for the strange coincidences we sometimes meet that prick holes in our assumptions of rational order. ·

The generative function of kamma in the production of new existence is described by the Buddha in a short but pithy sutta preserved in the Aṅguttara Nikāya (AN 3:76). Venerable Ānanda approaches the Master and says, "'Existence, existence' is spoken of, venerable sir. In what way is there existence?" The Buddha replies: "If there were no kamma ripening in the sensory realm, no sense-sphere existence would be discerned. If there were no kamma ripening in the form realm, no form-sphere existence would be discerned. If there were no kamma ripening in the formless realm, no formless-sphere existence would be discerned. Therefore, Ānanda, kamma is the field, consciousness the seed, and craving the moisture for beings obstructed by ignorance and fettered by craving to be established in a new realm of existence, either low (sense-sphere), middling (form-sphere), or high (formless-sphere)."

As long as ignorance and craving, the twin roots of the round of rebirths, remain intact in our mental continuum, at the time of death one especially powerful kamma will become ascendant and propel the stream of consciousness to the realm of existence that corresponds to its own 'vibrational frequency'. When consciousness, as the seed, becomes planted or 'established' in that realm, it sprouts forth into the rest of the psycho-physical organism, summed up in the expression 'name and form' *(nāma-rūpa)*. As the organism matures, it provides the site for other past kammas to gain the opportunity to produce their results. Then, within this new existence, in response to our various kammically induced experiences, we engage in actions that engender fresh kamma with the capacity to generate still another rebirth. Thereby the round of existence keeps turning from one life to the next, as the stream of consciousness, swept along by craving and steered by kamma, assumes successive modes of embodiment.

The ultimate implication of the Buddha's teaching on kamma and rebirth is that human beings are the final masters of their own destiny. Through our unwholesome deeds, rooted in greed hatred, and delusion, we create unwholesome kamma, the generative cause of bad rebirths, of future misery and bondage. Through our wholesome deeds rooted in generosity, kindness and wisdom, we beautify our minds and thereby create kamma productive of a happy rebirth. By using wisdom to dig more deeply below the superficial face of things, we can uncover the subtle truths hidden by our preoccupation with appearances. Thereby we can uproot the binding defilements and win the peace of deliverance, the freedom beyond the cycle of kamma and its fruit.

From BPS Newsletters Nos 46 and 47, 3rd Mailing 2000 and 1st Mailing 2001.

45. WHAT DOES IT MEAN TO BE ENLIGHTENED?

The word 'buddha' was already known and in circulation before the Buddha appeared on the Indian scene. The word means 'enlightened' and spiritual seekers would commonly discuss the question "Who is a Buddha? Who is enlightened?"

Once an aged brahmin named Brahmāyu heard that the ascetic Gotama, a man rumoured to be a Buddha, had arrived in his town and he decided to pay him a visit. When the old brahmin arrived, the Buddha was in the midst of a discussion with many people. Since the old brahmin was highly distinguished, when he came into the midst of the crowd, everyone gave way to him. The Buddha too realized that this was a highly respected brahmin, the teacher of several generations of pupils, so he asked Brahmāyu to come right up to the front of the assembly and to take a seat beside him.

Brahmāyu then said to him, "Honorable Gotama, I would like to ask you some questions." The Buddha invited him to ask what was on his mind, and the brahmin phrased his questions in a four-line verse, the basic point of which was, "How can one be called a Buddha, an Enlightened One?" The Buddha responded in verse:

> "What has to be known, that I have known;
> What has to be abandoned, that I have abandoned;
> What has to be developed, that I have developed;
> Therefore, O brahmin, I am a Buddha."

This answer tells us, very concisely, three characteristics of an Enlightened One. These are not only three characteristics of a Buddha; they are also three objectives at which we aim in following the Buddha's teaching. If someone were to ask, "What is your fundamental purpose in taking refuge in the Triple Gem? What is your purpose in following the precepts? What is your purpose in practising meditation?" your answer should come down to the same three points: to fully know what should be known; to abandon what should be abandoned; and to develop what should be developed. These are the goals of the Buddhist path and the three accomplishments that mark the attainment of enlightenment.

If you are familiar with the Buddha's First Sermon, you would immediately recognize that these three tasks are aligned with three of the Four Noble Truths. The first noble truth is the noble truth of *dukkha*, usually translated as suffering, unsatisfactoriness or stress. What is the task to be performed in relation to this noble truth of suffering? The noble truth of suffering is to be correctly **known**, fully known, fully understood. The noble truth of the origin, or cause, of suffering is craving, and the task to be performed in relation to this truth is abandonment: craving is to be **abandoned**. The fourth noble truth, the Noble Eightfold Path, is the truth that has to be **developed**. The one noble truth that isn't mentioned in the Buddha's verse is the third truth, the noble truth of the cessation of suffering. This has its own task as well: the cessation of suffering is to be 'realized.' But when the other three tasks are accomplished, realization of the noble truth of the cessation of suffering will naturally follow.

What does it mean to say that our task is "to know that which should be known"? What we have to know, what we have to understand, is that which is closest to ourselves, what we usually refer to as our self. What we usually refer to as our self is this complex of body and mind. For most of us, from the time we are born right up to the time of our death, our minds face outwardly, engaged in a tireless quest for pleasure and sensual gratification, for the enhancement of our self, for the confirmation of our sense of ego-identity. Very few people stop and turn around to consider the question, "What is it that I call 'my self'? What is the 'I' behind the reference I make to myself?" And yet, if you reflect for just a moment, you will see that this is the most important question we can ask. If, from the day of your birth until the day you draw your final breath, the best you can do when you are asked, "Who are you? What is your identity?" is to pull out your driver's license or show your birth certificate, without really knowing who you are or what you are, then you've made a pretty bad job of your journey from birth to death.

Our task in following the Buddha's teaching is to investigate what it is we refer to as 'I,' as 'my self,' as 'what I am.' We usually take these terms to refer to some kind of persisting entity, an ego, a substantial self possessing a real identity. But the Buddha teaches that all such ideas are deceptions. When we look, when we investigate the referents of the terms, 'I', 'me' and 'myself,' what we find are just components of bodily and mental experience.

To aid investigation, the Buddha has neatly classified these components of bodily and mental experience into five groups. These are called the 'five aggregates of clinging' because they are the things that we ordinarily cling to with the ideas "This is mine, this is what I am, this is my true self."

So we find, underlying these notions of 'I' and 'self,' just these five aggregates: the aggregate of *bodily form*, the material substance that constitutes our bodies; the aggregate of *feeling*: pleasant, painful, and neutral feelings; the aggregate of *perception*: the mental function of identifying the characteristics of things, acts of identifying, recognizing, and remembering; the aggregate of *volitional formations,* the various functions connected with volition; and the aggregate of *consciousness:* the light of awareness arising on the basis of the six sense bases.

For each of us, this is the totality of what we call our self. Our task in following the Buddha's teaching is to come to know, to come to understand, the true nature of these five aggregates. We thereby come to know what constitutes our real identity. From birth through adulthood to old age and death, this whole process of life is just a succession of the five aggregates bound together as conditions and conditionally-arisen phenomena. The bodily aggregate or form is the basis, and on this basis, the mental aggregates arise and pass away. Through meditation practice, we examine very deeply, with a fine focus, the nature of these five aggregates as they occur from moment to moment. We see them arising, standing, and dissolving, which gives us the insight into impermanence. From the understanding of impermanence comes the insight into suffering, the unsatisfactory nature of the five aggregates. We then realize that these changeable five aggregates are undependable, insecure, unreliable, and therefore cannot be taken as our self: they are empty or selfless.

The second project the Buddha's teaching sets for us is "to abandon that which should be abandoned." What should be abandoned are the defilements, all the mental states that cause suffering and unhappiness in our lives. The Buddha's teaching sets out a detailed method for investigation of the mind which enables us to understand how the mind works. But this investigation is not undertaken in the value-free way in which contemporary psychology might describe the workings of the mind. Buddhist psychology defines its values clearly and sharply. It draws definite ethical distinctions, draws them without hesitation or ambiguity, because these ethical distinctions have vital implications for our desire to achieve happiness and avoid suffering.

According to the Buddha's teaching, unethical actions and impure mental states can never give rise to true and lasting happiness. Rather, unethical actions and defiled mental states inevitably germinate in unhappiness, in suffering. It is true that defiled states of mind, especially greed and craving, are accompanied by pleasure and enjoyment. If that weren't the case, the world would be filled with enlightened people. And yet the pleasure that accompanies present craving and greed is just a superficial coat that covers a bad seed. When that seed germinates and bears its fruits, it will bring pain and suffering either in this life, or if not in this life, then in future lives. In contrast, wholesome states of mind may sometimes be accompanied by present pain, because to develop them we have to go against the current, against the natural grain of the mind. But when those wholesome states bear their fruits, inevitably they will lead to happiness, to peace, and to inner well-being. Again, this is part of the same law, the law of moral causation.

The unwholesome mental states are called *kilesas*. The word can be translated *afflictions* because they bring suffering. It can also be translated *defilements* because they defile and corrupt the mind. The Buddha has analyzed the nature of the defilements and has beautifully explained how they can all be traced to the three 'root defilements' of greed, hatred and delusion. Our task in following the Buddha's teaching, in practising the Dhamma, is to overcome, to eliminate, to abandon the defilements of greed and hatred that give rise to many other branch defilements. But greed and hatred spring ultimately from delusion or ignorance. And thus to eliminate all the defilements, we have to eliminate ignorance.

Ignorance is what covers up the five aggregates, what we refer to as 'I', 'mine' and 'myself'. Thus the way to overcome ignorance or delusion is through the first task "knowing that which should be known." When we know that which should be known, ignorance falls away—greed, hatred, and all the other defilements fall away. It isn't possible, however, to accomplish this merely by having the desire to do so. We can't expect simply to think, "I want to know that which should be known;" and immediately it is known. That's why the whole practice of Buddhism is a process of *walking a path*. The great gift that the Buddha offers the world is not simply a profound philosophy, not simply a penetrating psychology, but a practical, systematic, step-by-step path that we can cultivate in every aspect of our lives.

To cultivate the path means "to develop that which should be developed." This is the third project the Buddha speaks of in his four-line verse: "That which should be developed, that I have developed." So what the Buddha has developed is what we have to develop. One cultivates the path in order "to abandon that which should be abandoned," namely, the defilements. And again, one cultivates the path in order "to know that which should be known," the five aggregates.

How does developing the path do this? Again, the path is structured in such a way that it proceeds not suddenly, not abruptly, but in a gradual step-by-step manner to help us climb the ladder to the ultimate freedom of enlightenment. One has to begin by keeping the coarser expression of the defilements under control. One does this by observing the precepts. One observes the Five Precepts or the Eight Precepts. These control the coarser expressions of the defilements, the defilements that erupt in the form of unwholesome actions.

Observing the precepts is not merely a matter of abstaining from negative actions. One also has to cultivate their counterparts: virtuous, wholesome actions. These suffuse the mind with pure and purifying qualities. One has to be compassionate and kindly towards others, to be honest in one's dealings with others, to be constantly truthful in one's communications, to be responsible to one's family and society, to observe right livelihood, to be diligent, to be respectful of others, to be patient under difficult conditions, to be humble and upright. All these virtues gradually help to purify the mind and make the mind bright, clean and radiant.

To develop what must be developed, it isn't sufficient merely to cultivate morality. One must go further and cultivate concentration. When we try to collect and concentrate the mind, we begin to understand how our minds work. We gain insight into the workings of our own minds. By understanding the workings of our own minds, we're gradually changing the shape of the mind. First, we are beginning to weaken and undermine those unwholesome qualities that defile the mind. We are scraping away the soil in which the unwholesome roots have been lodged. We have to remember that the unwholesome roots have been lodged in our minds throughout beginningless time. The process isn't a quick or easy one, but requires gradual, persistent, and dedicated effort.

As one practises consistently, the mind will eventually settle into firm concentration. It acquires the skills needed to remain settled upon an object consistently, without wavering, and this provides the opportunity for wisdom to arise. Wisdom is the third quality that needs to be developed. Wisdom comes through examination, through investigation.

To be sure, wisdom does not arise only from meditative concentration. Even in your day-to-day life, when you study the Buddha's teachings, especially the important discourses on the development of wisdom such as the teachings on the five aggregates, dependent origination and the Four Noble Truths, you are investigating the Dhamma and thereby creating the conditions for wisdom. You are generating a conceptual wisdom that is already starting to dig away at the root of ignorance. So just by studying the teaching and reflecting on the teaching, you are already shaking the deep root of ignorance.

But the ultimate wisdom is experiential. When one has developed a strongly concentrated mind, one uses that mind to investigate the five aggregates. As one observes one's own experience, one directly sees into their real nature, into 'the true characteristics of phenomena.' Generally, one first sees the arising and falling away of the five aggregates. That is, one sees their impermanence. One sees that because they're impermanent, they're unsatisfactory. There's nothing worth clinging to in them. And because they're impermanent and unsatisfactory, one cannot identify with any of them as a truly existing self. This is the empty or self-less nature of the five aggregates. This marks the arising of true insight wisdom.

With insight-wisdom, one cuts deeper and deeper into the root of ignorance until one comes to fully understand the nature of the five aggregates. When one does so, one can then say that one has "known that which should be known."

And by fully knowing that which should be known, the defilements "that should be abandoned have been abandoned;" and the path "that should be developed has been developed." One then realizes that which should be realized, the extinction of suffering right here and now. And, in the Buddha's own words, that is what makes an Enlightened One.

From BPS Newsletter No. 55, 1ˢᵗ Mailing 2006.

46. Spiritual Friendship

People new to Buddhism often take the Dharma to be a purely individual path of spiritual development. They imagine that the only correct way to follow the Dharma is to lock oneself up in one's room, turn off the lights, and devote all one's efforts to practising meditation. However, if we look at the Buddhist texts, we would see that the Buddha again and again stressed the value of spiritual friendship as a support for the Buddhist path throughout the entire course of its practice. On one occasion the Venerable Ānanda, the Buddha's attendant, came to the Buddha and said that in his view half the spiritual life revolves around spiritual friendship. The Buddha immediately corrected him and said, "Do not say this, Ānanda! Do not say this, Ānanda! Spiritual friendship is not half the spiritual life. It's the entire spiritual life!" Then, with reference to himself, the Buddha added, "In this whole world, I am the supreme spiritual friend of living beings, because it is in dependence upon me, by relying upon me, that those who are subject to birth, old age, and death become liberated from birth, old age, and death."

I want to make a distinction between two types of spiritual friendship, which might be called the "horizontal type" and the "vertical type." What I call horizontal spiritual friendship is friendship between people who are at roughly the same level in following the path; this is the friendship between "partners" in following the path, and what unites them as spiritual friends is a common dedication to following the Buddhist path.

People come together and unite as friends for various reasons. We usually take the gregarious side of human nature for granted, but to understand the nature and importance of friendship it's instructive to reflect on the factors that bring people together and unite them as friends. To do so, will give us a standard for evaluating our own friendships and seeing which are helpful and which harmful.

The Buddha says that it is because of an "element" that people come together and unite. What is meant by "element" here is the basic disposition or trait of character. Thus the Buddha says that those of inferior disposition come together and unite with those of inferior disposition, whereas those of superior disposition come together and unite.

So, if we cast our mental eye out upon the world, we can see that on a given Saturday night many people will go out to night clubs to enjoy themselves dancing; others will go to bars to enjoy drinking and chatting together; others might go to sports matches; others will get together and watch crude films. That is what unites them in friendship. So this is how people of inferior disposition come together and unite.

But others come together to listen to Dharma talks, participate in meditation retreats, and study the Dharma. In this case, what unites them is a shared dedication to the Dharma. So, the defining characteristic of spiritual friendship is dedication to a common teaching, in this case, the Buddha's teaching. This is dedication to a common teaching, dedication to the practice of the same path, dedication based on similar ideals and aspirations, unity based on engagement in similar practices. To unite with others in a common dedication to the spiritual path has a strengthening and uplifting effect upon our own practice. When we try to practise the path alone, we may feel as though we are walking through a desert. It can be very lonesome, the landscape around us is rough and barren, and we have no refreshment, no inspiration from others to replenish our energies. But when we unite with others in spiritual friendship based upon common aspirations, this reinforces our own energies. When we walk a common path and engage in common practices, we gain encouragement, strength, and inspiration to continue in our practice. This is like crossing the desert in a caravan: others help us carry the supplies, we can pause for conversation, we have a sense of sharing the trials along the way, and we rejoice together as we approach our destination.

When we unite with others in spiritual friendship, this not only transforms our approach to the practice, but also has an impact upon the very nature of our friendships.

In our worldly life, our friendships are very closely connected with personal attachments, which in turn are rooted in our own egocentric needs. Even when we think we love the other person, often we really love that person because this relationship in some way satisfies a deep need within ourselves. When the other person fails to satisfy this deep need within us, our feelings quickly become embittered and our love turns into resentment or even enmity.

But when we enter into a spiritual friendship based upon dedication to a common goal, this friendship helps us to transform our attachments and ego-centred drives. Even more, it helps us to transcend the very idea of the ego-self as a substantive reality. Spiritual friendship, we discover, is not about satisfying my personal needs, or even about my satisfying the other person's personal needs. It's about each of us contributing as best we can to uplift each other, and to bring each other closer to the ideals of the Dharma.

In spiritual friendship we are concerned with the other person not because of the ways that person satisfies us, but because we want to see the other person grow and develop in the direction of greater wisdom, greater virtue, greater understanding. We want the other person's wholesome qualities to attain maturity and bring forth fruits for the benefit of others. This is the essence of "horizontal" spiritual friendship: a keen interest in helping our friends grow and develop in the practice of the Dharma, in maturing their potential for goodness, for understanding, for wholesomeness.

The other aspect of spiritual friendship is what I call "vertical" friendship. This is the spiritual friendship between people who are at widely different levels on the path. We might also call this "asymmetrical" friendship, in that the relationship between the two members is not one of equality. This type of spiritual friendship is the bond between senior and junior followers on the path, especially the bond between a teacher and a student.

Because the relationship between the two is not equal or symmetrical, if this relationship is to be mutually beneficial, different qualities are required of the teacher and the student. In a relationship that revolves around the Dharma, the ideal teacher should have wide knowledge of the Buddhist scriptures and also abundant practical experience in following the teaching. Few teachers measure up to the ideal in all respects, and thus most students must be ready to settle for teachers who, like themselves, are still far from perfect. But two essential qualities in a teacher are a clear understanding of the fundamental principles of the Dharma and a sincere dedication to the proper practice. Besides knowledge and practical experience, the teacher must be willing or eager to teach. This willingness or eagerness to teach, however, shouldn't stem from personal ambition or egotism, from the desire to be an outstanding teacher surrounded by a flock of admiring disciples. Rather, the teacher should regard himself as a humble transmitter of the tradition, and his desire to teach should be motivated by compassion for his students and by a sincere wish to uplift the students by improving their knowledge and practical experience.

The teacher should treat the students with kindness and gentleness when they are well disciplined and obedient; but though he should be kind and gentle, he should not treat his students too leniently but should know how to maintain the proper distance needed to preserve his own dignity as a teacher. And if he's a true spiritual teacher and not just one who is imparting knowledge, he should be ready to discipline his students when necessary by admonishing them, pointing out their faults, and attempting to correct their faults.

The student should adopt the proper attitude in relation to the teacher. In Buddhist spiritual training, the attitude required is quite different from that of a student at a university. The attitude required of a student is one directed toward spiritual understanding and realisation. Whereas academic study can lead to success independently of the personal character of the student, in the study of the Dharma, success is directly proportional to the purification of one's character. Thus at the outset students need the qualities conducive to spiritual growth.

Students should have faith in the teacher, confidence that the teacher is a superior person able to help them, to guide them in their spiritual development. This, of course, is not a blind faith, but a trusting confidence in the spiritual capacities of the teacher. It is the trust that the teacher has invested a long period of time in his own spiritual training and thus is sufficiently qualified to guide the student at least a few steps further in the practice of the Dharma. Both teacher and student are united in a common faith, faith in the Triple Gem, faith in the efficacy of the Dharma as a path to liberation and to the realisation of the ultimate good. But students should assume that the teacher, by reason of his role, has a faith that is deeper and more solidly grounded than their own and thus that the teacher's advice and guidance should be accepted as worthy of trust. This does not mean that the student must regard the teacher as infallible and accept every bit of advice that the teacher offers, nor does it mean that the student must docilely follow every order that the teacher issues. The Buddha respected the capacity of mature human beings to make independent judgements; he did not subscribe to the view held by many Indian religious teachers that disciples must regard their teacher's word as absolute law. In the Vinaya, the Buddhist code of monastic discipline, pupils are authorised to correct their teachers if they see them engaging in improper modes of conduct or hear them advancing wrong interpretations of the teaching. This principle, laid down over two thousand years ago, is still valid today and should regulate the relationship between teachers and their students.

But to allow students to evaluate their teachers' ideas and conduct does not mean that the students are entitled to act without respect. To the contrary, one can only advance in the Dharma if one is respectful and reverential towards one's teachers. One should never be obstinate, proud, or arrogant towards anyone, least of all towards the person one regards as one's guide to the understanding and practice of the Dharma. The practice of the Dharma aims at subduing the ego, the false sense of self, and to act in ways that inflate the sense of self is to defeat one's very purpose in following the Dharma.

The relationship between student and teacher provides an ideal field for both to work at tackling the importunate demands of the ego. The student gains this opportunity by developing a respectful attitude towards the teacher and by showing respect in bodily and verbal conduct: for example, by standing up when the teacher enters the room, by making *añjali* towards him, by speaking to him politely and with a humble demeanour. The teacher also can use the relationship to subdue his own ego: by refusing to adopt an arrogant attitude towards the pupil, by treating the pupil with kindness and consideration, by sharing his knowledge with the pupil.

One quality that the Buddha considered essential in a qualified student is called (in Pali) *suvaco*, which means being "easy to speak to." A student who is "easy to speak to" is ready to listen to his or her teacher and to accept the teacher's advice without resentment, without vindictiveness, without arguing back, without complaints. Spiritual growth in the Dharma is a process of abandoning one's faults and replacing them with the opposing virtues. Yet too often we are blind to our own faults, unable or unwilling to see them.

A skilful teacher is like a mirror: he shows us our faults clearly, insistently, without deception, reminding us of the faults we continually strive to hide from ourselves. For it is only when we are willing to see our faults that we can correct them. If we go on denying these faults, insisting that we are perfect, then we will continue to wallow in them, like a buffalo in the mud. But when we open up to the teacher and show a willingness to see our own faults, to subdue our self-will, we then take the first major step in the direction of correcting them. It is through this consistent, continuous process of removing our faults, of subduing our egocentric tendencies, that we move in the direction that the Buddha is pointing us, the direction taken by all the noble ones of the past. It is in this way that we can collect the precious jewels of the noble virtues and embed them in our own hearts and minds, so that we shine resplendent in the world. For this reason, the Dhammapada says that when the teacher points out a student's faults and tries to correct them, the student should feel as though the teacher were pointing out hidden treasure.

From BPS Newsletter No. 57, 1ˢᵗ Mailing 2007.

47. Finding a Place from Which to Start

When one sets out to choose a religion, how does one make the right choice? Different religions offer us such different perspectives on the nature of human life, and such different paths of practice, that it is impossible to find a unifying scheme capable of reconciling their opposing claims. Yet so much depends on the choice we make. Most religions tell us that the world is the creation of an all-powerful God, and they say that if we want to find salvation we must accept this God in faith and love him with all our being. The problem we face, however, is that different religions describe their God quite differently, in ways that are not mutually compatible, and we have no means at our disposal for determining which description is true and which is false; it is also possible that they are all unacceptable. Some religions teach that we live but a single life on earth and then spend eternity in another realm depending on how we behaved in this life; other religions teach that we pass through many lives, in this world and in other worlds, until we attain liberation from the chain of rebirths.

Buddhism is a non-theistic religion that teaches rebirth. It does not accept any concept of a creator God, yet it teaches that we migrate from life to life, in the human realm and in other realms, depending on our karma, our intentional actions. When I teach the Dhamma, I do not hesitate to teach these basic tenets of Buddhist doctrine. It is not unusual for newcomers to Buddhism to approach me and raise the question about how much of Buddhist doctrine they must accept before they can integrate Buddhist practices into their daily lives. Do they have to believe in rebirth? Do they have to believe in heavens and hells? Do they have to believe in gods and hungry ghosts?

I never urge others to uncritically take on board the whole package of classical Buddhist doctrines and beliefs. For me, these teachings of Buddhism are not dogmas that one has to accept blindly. In fact, I usually appreciate it more when the person who comes to me expresses honest doubts and reservations. Then I know that this person is ready to examine the teachings with full earnestness, and once they do gain confidence in the Dhamma, it is likely that this confidence will be firm and steady.

The Buddha, too, didn't expect those who came to him for guidance to surrender to him and place unquestioning faith in everything he said. Faith is critical to progress on the Buddhist path, for it is the seed out of which all wholesome qualities grow, the light that guides us through the darkness of doubt and confusion. But for faith to germinate and send down healthy roots, it has to be planted in nourishing soil, and the proper soil for faith is not a mind that has been cowered into belief by dogmatic demands, by fear of punishment and hopes of rewards in a blissful afterlife. The Buddha treated those who inquired from him as rational adults capable of arriving at informed decisions. Instead of using threats and bribes, he appealed to two capacities readily available to all of us, capacities that we can draw upon to find a suitable starting point for resolving our spiritual doubts. One is the ability to reflect on our own experience, to evaluate our own experience honestly and lucidly. The other is the ability to extrapolate from our experience, that is, to draw inferences from what lies within the range of our immediate experience to wider areas of life that are relevant to us but not directly accessible to observation.

The starting point for all reflection in Buddhism is a universal urge that lies at the bottom of our being: the desire to avoid pain and suffering and to find happiness and well-being. To acknowledge this truth does not require that we assent to any doctrines that appeal to matters beyond range of our own experience. We need only look into our own minds, and it will then become clear that the desire to avoid pain and suffering, and to achieve happiness and true well-being, underlies all our thought and action. It is this desire that shapes our lives, that comes to expression in our plans and projects, our visions and undertakings; it is this aspiration for freedom from sorrow and the realisation of happiness that becomes diffused in a thousand hopes and fears.

Beginning with this observation, we can then translate our basic aim into a pair of questions: (1) What can we do to avoid suffering? and (2) What can we do to achieve happiness? When we posit these questions, we can see that most of the time we are, in fact, acting to avoid suffering and to achieve happiness. Yet, if ordinary unguided actions, based on spontaneous instinct and calculated self-interest, automatically guaranteed us the happiness we so deeply desire, we wouldn't be discontented with our mundane lives or feel a need for spiritual guidance. Our problem is that our natural, everyday actions don't fulfil our desire for deep and superior happiness. To the contrary, they either keep us tethered to dull, wearisome routines or, if we behave unwisely, plunge us into conflict and misery. Therefore the questions that we frame have to be expressed more precisely. What we have to ask is: (1) What should we do to avoid long-term harm and suffering? and (2) What should we do to achieve long- term happiness and well-being?

This reformulation differs from the previous one in three respects. First, it qualifies the suffering that we want to avoid and the happiness we want to attain as 'long-term,' thereby indicating that what we seek is not merely transitory gratification, which may quickly be followed by bitterness and regrets, but stable, solid, and lasting benefits. Second, it links 'suffering' with 'harm,' indicating that what we seek to avoid is not only felt pain but also personal damage, which may include damage to the moral fabric of our character. And third, it links 'happiness' with 'well-being,' indicating that what we want to achieve is not only a state of felt pleasure, a peak of euphoria, but a state of inner well-being secure against future loss.

Once we put the questions in these terms, the Buddha asks us to use our own experience as a guide for determining the right answers. He first tells us where we shouldn't turn for answers. In the well-known Kālāma Sutta (Aṅguttara Nikāya III 65), he advises us not to look to authoritative traditions, to lineages of teachers, to collections of sacred texts. This does not mean that traditions, lineages, and sacred texts can't give us helpful answers. It doesn't mean that they are wrong. It just means that they aren't unsusceptible to doubt. The traditions may have been handed down impeccably, but they could be wrong. The texts might be regarded as sacred, as divine revelation, but they might be the work of human authors and their teachings might be far from holy. The Buddha also tells us not to rely on abstract logic and reasoning. Again, this doesn't mean that logic and reasoning are useless. It just means that the answers they give will always be open to doubt. A chain of reasoning can be flawless as it proceeds from premises to conclusions; but the premises are axiomatic, taken for granted, and they might be questionable. Or the movement from one step of reasoning to the next might be faulty. Hence, even when employed with utmost skill, logic can lead to contradictory conclusions. Further, the Buddha tells us not to be swept away by impressive speakers and charismatic teachers. This doesn't mean that we can't learn from others, or that the guidance given by spiritual teachers is inherently untrustworthy. It is just that different teachers, equally impressive and charismatic, might teach different things, which each claims to be the highest truth; they might give different answers to the most critical spiritual questions. We are looking, however, for an unshakeable platform on which to stand, for some truths that are beyond doubt and questioning.

What we want to find is a secure and solid base upon which we can establish faith; we don't want to begin with a demand for faith. The Buddha therefore says that we should begin with things that we can know for ourselves, and take that as our starting point. When we know for ourselves what leads to our harm and suffering, then we will know what we have to avoid; when we know for ourselves what leads to our well- being and happiness, then we will know what we have to pursue and develop. To be sure, the Buddha doesn't leave us to our own devices. Nor does he simply give us a meditation technique to practise and tell us that we don't have to think of any wider issues but just direct our minds to our meditation subject. The Buddha does not ground the spiritual life upon mere technique, but sets technique within a context, and to find an appropriate context for the technique we have to begin by clarifying the aim of our practice.

To help us get clear about our aim, the Buddha poses certain questions that steer our thinking into the proper channels. These questions do not take us into the mists of metaphysical speculation, into theories about the origin and ending of the world. They do not make any appeals for belief in things that lie beyond the range of observation. They take us, rather, towards an examination of our own minds and reflection on our own actions. The questions he asks—or wants us to ask ourselves—relate to intentionality, the fundamental motives of thought, emotion, and action. The Buddha wants us to ask ourselves whether, when greed, hatred, and ignorance arise in our minds, they arise for our good or for our harm. The answer, naturally, will be that greed, hatred, and ignorance arise for our harm. They might give us pleasure, but what they bring is a transient pleasure, which may well be followed by long-term harm. We can see that they arise for our own harm, and they also drive us to act in ways that bring harm and suffering to others. The degree of harm and suffering they cause may not be particularly obvious in every individual instance, but when we consider the consequences of greed, hatred, and ignorance functioning as motives for action on a global scale, the danger becomes staggering. On reflection, we can see that actions springing from greed, hatred, and ignorance can be terribly destructive. Indeed, such reflection would reveal to us very much the world that leaps out at us from our daily news reports: a world afflicted by senseless violence and brutality, by agonising wars, by reckless over-exploitation of our natural resources; a world, moreover, in which those most responsible for harm shamelessly resort to mendacious stratagems to avoid taking responsibility for their actions. But if we can see this when the picture is blown up globally, we can then return to any given instance of greed, hatred, and delusion, and recognise that it is from these small seeds, these unwholesome driving forces of thought and action, that terrible calamities arise and bring so much misery. We can then further realise that if we are to secure our own well-being and happiness, and to promote the well-being and happiness of others, it is necessary for us to restrain and overcome our own greed, hatred, and delusion. This then becomes the first requirement of a spiritual path.

The next series of questions the Buddha poses brings to light the opposite side of the mind. He asks us to consider whether, when non-greed, non-hatred, and non-delusion arise in our minds, they arise for our good or for our harm. These three terms, formulated in the negative, are synonymous with generosity, loving- kindness, and wisdom. When we reflect, we can see that generosity, loving kindness, and wisdom arise for our welfare and happiness. When we are able to give freely to others, out of concern for their well-being, we experience lightness and peace, freedom from the grip of attachment. When our hearts rise above anger and hatred and radiate loving kindness, a genuine wish for the welfare and happiness of others, we experience joy and harmony.

When our minds are illuminated with the light of understanding, when we see and understand true principles, we experience brightness and clarity. We can then realise that if we are to secure our own well-being and happiness, and to promote the well-being and happiness of others, it is necessary for us to cultivate generosity, loving kindness, and wisdom. This then becomes the second requirement of a spiritual path.

Thus, we can understand, right here and now, that greed, hatred, and delusion are the roots of harm and suffering, while non-greed, non-hatred, and non- delusion—or generosity, loving kindness, and wisdom—are the roots of happiness and well-being. On this basis, we can be certain that whatever else we require from a spiritual teaching, whatever other principles it might teach, it must take as its principal aim the elimination of greed, hatred, and delusion, and it must esteem such values as generosity, love, and wisdom.

For the Buddha, this understanding does not yet mark the achievement of right view, the view that leads onward towards the ultimate goal of his teaching, liberation from suffering. Right view begins with an acceptance of the principle of karma, which holds that our actions inevitably bring their fruits or results, and this principle depends upon acceptance of its corollary, the idea of rebirth. But an understanding of the immediately visible consequences of the unwholesome and wholesome roots offers a starting point for placing confidence in the Buddha as one who teaches a doctrine that is good and beneficial in all respects, a teaching that cannot lead astray. Once one gains confidence in the Buddha by examining those aspects of his teaching that come into range of one's immediate experience, one can then place trust in him as one who speaks truthfully about things that lie beyond range of one's immediate experience. And on the basis of this trust one can devote oneself wholeheartedly to the practice of his teaching.

But even the final goal of the Buddha's teaching is continuous with the certitude that we achieve as our starting point. At the beginning, through reflection, we gain confidence that a worthy spiritual discipline must be one that leads to the overcoming of greed, hatred, and delusion. The final goal of the Buddha's path is Nibbāna, and in the suttas we find Nibbāna defined precisely as "the extinguishing of greed, the extinguishing of hatred, the extinguishing of delusion." The practice of the Dhamma is a gradual process of removing greed, hatred, and delusion, of replacing them with greater generosity, with greater loving kindness and compassion, with greater wisdom and understanding. The confidence that comes by gaining faith in the Buddha is the confidence that it is possible to eradicate greed, hatred, and delusion entirely. With faith, one takes up the practice of the Buddha's path in the confidence that this path leads to the end of greed, hatred, and delusion.

From BPS Newsletter No 58 , 2ⁿᵈ Mailing 2007.

48. A Buddhist Social Ethic for the New Century

The arrival of a new century is always a time of great ferment and great expectations, and when the new century also marks the dawn of a new millennium our expectations are likely to be especially intense. An inherent optimism makes us think that the new is always bound to be better than the old, that the arrival of the next year or century will inevitably bring our wildest dreams to fulfilment. Unfortunately, however, life is not so simple that the mere ticking of the clock and the change of calendars are enough to undo the knots with which we have tied ourselves up by our rash decisions and ill-considered actions through all the preceding months, years, and decades.

One fact that past experience should deeply impress on us is the need to look carefully beneath the surface of events for hidden tendencies that portend future harm. The importance of this guideline is brought home for us by reflection on the transition from the nineteenth to the twentieth century. In the Western world the end of the nineteenth century was a period of fervent optimism, of Utopian dreams quickened by an unflinching faith in a glorified ideal called progress. The twin leaders of the cult of progress were science and technology. Science was the new Prometheus, an unstoppable Prometheus that had snatched nature's hidden secrets and passed them on to a humanity brimming over with ardent hopes. In each decade, one major breakthrough in knowledge followed another, each fresh theoretical advance being matched by corresponding success in harnessing nature's powers to our needs. The result was a tremendous surge in the growth of technology that promised to liberate humankind from its most stubborn historical limitations.

The next century showed just how short-sighted this optimism really was. Indeed, for those who looked deeply enough, the seeds of destruction were already visible right beneath the feet of the proud conquistadors. They could be seen on the home front, in the miserable lives of millions of workers condemned to degrading toil in the factories, mines, and sweatshops; in the ruthless colonization of the non-Western world, the rape of its resources and subjugation of its peoples; in the mounting friction and tensions between ambitious empires competing for global domination. During the first half of the twentieth century the tensions exploded twice, in two world wars with a death count of many millions. These wars, and the ensuing cold war, brought into the open the dark primordial forces that had long been simmering just a little beneath the polished veneer of Western civilization. It is surely significant that our discovery of nature's most arcane secret—the convertibility of matter and energy—conferred on us the capacity for total self-annihilation: unlimited power and total destruction arriving in the same package.

Today, as we stand at the beginning of the twenty-first century, our world has become a living paradox. It is a world of immense wealth, but also of grinding poverty where 1.3 billion people—a quarter of the world's population—live in constant want. It is a world of tremendous advances in medicine and health care, where eleven million people die annually from diseases that are easily treatable. It is a world where the daily trade in lethal weapons numbers in the millions of dollars, yet where seven million children die of hunger each year and 800 million people are severely undernourished. And perhaps most alarming of all, it is a world bent on unlimited economic growth on a planet whose finite resources are rapidly dwindling. Thus, with all our bold strides towards the future, our world still suffers from painful wounds, and the need for a solution, for a cure, has become ever more insistent if humanity is to survive intact through to the end of the new century.

In the course of this essay I wish to formulate a Theravada Buddhist response to the need to heal the wounds of the world. In popular textbooks on world religions, Theravada Buddhism is generally depicted as a religion of individual salvation which holds up as its ideal a purely private enlightenment to be reached through renunciation and meditation. Though Theravada Buddhism does stress the inescapably personal nature of the ultimate goal, if we carefully examine the discourses of the Buddha, we would see that the Buddha was keenly aware of the problems human beings face in the social dimensions of their lives, and he formulated his teaching to address these problems just as much as to show the way to final liberation. Although these texts are nowhere as numerous as those dealing with personal ethics, meditation, and philosophical insight, they remain remarkable testimonials to the clear sociological acumen of the Awakened One. Even today they still offer clear-cut practical guidelines in devising a social ethic capable of addressing the problems peculiar to the present age.

The first principle that the Buddha's teaching gives us in responding to these problems is a methodological one: not to rush to foregone conclusions but to investigate the underlying causes at all levels, and not to stop until we have reached the deepest roots. However, the common tendency today in tackling social problems is quite different. Particularly in political and economic circles, obstinate human dilemmas with subterranean roots are treated simply as technical snags that can be resolved merely by the application of the right technical solution. Thus, it is held, to counter the danger of global warming we must hammer out a treaty on reducing emissions of greenhouse gases; if crime and violence are on the increase, we need a larger and tougher police force; if drug addiction has reached alarming proportions among our youth, we need more effective controls against drug trafficking. Such measures may indeed be expedient safeguards against the grosser manifestations of the problems they are intended to rectify, but however effective and efficient they may be in the short run, on their own they do not provide long-term solutions. What they offer is cosmetic treatment, stop-gap measures that should not be taken as substitutes for alternatives that operate at the level of the deeper root-causes.

When we adopt a Buddhist perspective on the wounds that afflict our world today, we soon realize that these wounds are symptomatic: a warning signal that something is fundamentally awry with the way we lead our lives. We would see these outer wounds as outgrowths of a more malignant wound hidden deep within, eating away at our vital strength and discharging its venom into our air, rivers, and oceans; into our forests and farmlands; into our family lives and homes; into our social relationships and political agendas. Thus, from the Buddhist point of view, what we really need to heal our common wounds is radical surgery, a far-reaching change in our collective views, attitudes, and lifestyles. The word that enjoys currency these days as an expression for our need is 'Values.' We are told that the reason social conditions have degenerated so widely is because people have abandoned traditional values, and all we need to solve our problems is a revival of those values. While such a recommendation can stir up waves of nostalgia in those disturbed by the spread of moral disorder, we must bear in mind that the mere call for a revival of traditional values will be utterly ineffective unless we are prepared to make some bold changes in the foundation on which values rest, namely, the aims, purposes and sense of meaning that determine the social dimension of our existence. To attempt to revive private values in a corrupt and degrading society is like trying to beautify a chemical dump by planting roses along the banks: as long as the dump remains, the roses will only grow up stunted and deformed.

The transformation we need has to go further than the merely personal. It must embrace both aspects of our existence, the internal and the external, the personal and the social. These two dimensions of our lives are inseparably intertwined and mutually conditioning, so that our values reflect social and economic realities, while social and economic realities are shaped by our values. Thus, while it is in our personal lives that we have the most power to instigate direct change, any alterations in our personal lifestyles must also reach outwards and exercise an impact on our interpersonal relations, our social order, our political agenda, and our relationship to the natural environment. To avoid turning personal values into a lovely facade covering up social disorder and decay, critical and even painful self-examination is essential. We must be ready to examine with complete honesty our own priorities and to see the dangers for ourselves and others in letting ourselves drift along with the current of egotism and selfishness that sweeps across the world. Without such honest self-criticism, any cry for a recovery of values, even Buddhist values, is bound to end in little more than pious platitudes— personally consoling, perhaps, but powerless to bring effective change.

When we set out to diagnose our global problems from a Buddhist perspective, we should recognize that an adequate diagnosis must take account of multiple levels of causality. One of the Buddha's most striking insights is that phenomena do not arise from a single cause but from a complex concurrence of many conditions operating at different levels. Whereas specialist studies deal with problems from within a closed and narrow frame of reference, a Buddhist approach would adopt a comprehensive point of view that takes account of many levels of causation, which criss-cross and overlap, reinforcing each other at various turns. This allows for a more comprehensive solution, for when problems are approached from a limited frame of reference, the angle taken in viewing the problems already implies the solution. It is only when this 'wide angle' perspective is adopted that we can grasp the various dimensions in which the problem projects itself, and thereby we can see the multitude of factors that must be addressed in drawing up a solution.

We also have to give heed to the 'specific gravity' of the different types of causation, that is, to the relative contribution they make to the problem as a whole. According to the Buddha the most powerful and weighty causal factor operative in human life is the mind. Though the mind is invisible, intangible, weightless, and dimensionless, it is the hidden vector behind all the other modes of causality—social, political, and economic. The mind does not operate in a vacuum, however: inevitably, it is always embedded in a specific historical and personal context, subject to the impact of a wide variety of influences which shape its perspectives and determine its dispositions. But while this is so, we must also note that all these other factors influencing the mind are at some level themselves manifestations of mental activity. Thus the other orders of causality affecting the mind—social, economic, cultural, and political—can in turn be considered objectifications of mind, embodying and 'externalizing' specific attitudes, views and psychological agendas. For this reason the Buddha says that "all conditions are preceded by the mind, dominated by the mind, fashioned by the mind" (*Dhammapada*, vv. 1-2).

When we recognize the enormous contribution the mind makes to every other level of causality, we can see at once that in order to heal the wounds that afflict our world today our most urgent task is to heal the wounds in our minds. Down the centuries, especially since the start of the Scientific

Revolution in the West, we have been obsessed with the challenge of extending our control and mastery over the external world, but in our enthusiasm to master the outer world and exploit it for our material ends, we have neglected an even more vital dimension of our being, namely, our own minds.

For this reason our triumphs in scientific knowledge and technology have been painfully lopsided. While we have made astounding strides in understanding the world, we have made very little progress in understanding ourselves; while we have tapped the hidden powers of nature and made them our servants, we have done very little to tame the controller of nature. For just this reason, our proud triumphs in science and technology have had a very mixed impact on humanity as a whole. Along with their unquestionable material blessings, they have brought devastation and deprivation, waste and carnage, impoverishment and misery for many millions.

The basic needs of human beings are really very simple, and in principle they should be easily met in ample measure for everyone. They include an acceptable standard of material security, fresh air and clean water, nourishing food, comfortable housing, medical care, education and information, and sufficient leisure to develop one's talents and faculties. Under the present system, however, a tiny percentage of people, hardly more than a handful, live in greater luxury than the emperors of ancient Rome, while over a billion people, a quarter of the world's population, are condemned to live below the poverty line. Isn't it ironic that while we can send out spacecraft to distant planets and manipulate them with hairpin accuracy, we still cannot feed all the world's children? Isn't it alarming that while all indicators point to the massive threat to health and life from escalating pollution, unprecedented climate change, and the depletion of our natural resources, the nations most responsible for this crisis insist on pursuing unchecked their wasteful, exorbitant lifestyles? What prevents us from meeting the basic needs of all people on earth is not a scarcity of means but a failure of will, a failure rooted in selfishness and greed.

In the Buddha's teaching, the dark forces of the mind responsible for human suffering are called the defilements (*kilesa*), of which the most powerful are the three 'unwholesome roots'—greed, hatred, and delusion. In its classical expression, the Buddha's teaching focuses upon the role of the defilements in our personal lives, showing how they are the determinants of psychological and existential suffering. Today, however, as our world has become tightly integrated into a single global order, a shift in emphasis is necessary if we are to analyse and address our common plight. Since institutions and organizations have become ever more influential in moulding our circumstances and determining our destiny, we must closely investigate how the defilements assume a collective expression. We must lay bare the detrimental impact of our economic and political structures and discover how our forms of social organization, both national and international, sustain the grip of greed, hatred, and delusion upon our minds. For these structures do not merely objectify the mind's defilements; they also reinforce those defilements and make their grip ever more difficult to cast off. By powerful strategies often hidden by camouflage and deceit, they nurture and support the mass of distorted views, unhealthy attitudes, and risky policies that wreak so much havoc in our societies and our lives.

Perhaps the most glaring example of this destructive potential in the last decade of the twentieth century is the unregulated free-market economic system, which today has acquired a global reach. The massive transnational corporations that dominate this economic order, driven by the quest for commercial profit, have turned into institutional embodiments of greed. Despite their impressive public-relations propaganda, their fundamental purpose is not to meet genuine human needs but to generate maximum profit at minimum cost. Profit is the fuel of corporate growth, and every profit target met generates only a still higher target; the ideal is never a state of stable equilibrium, but the achievement of limitless profit at zero cost.

For the commanders of the corporate culture nothing else ultimately matters but economic success. Carefully documented studies have shown that in the pursuit of greater financial gain the corporations are quite prepared to jeopardize the welfare of the work force, the health of the customers, the stability of the society, traditional norms and values, the harmony of the community, and the sustainability of the natural environment. In their view, if the net result is a larger profit margin, all these can be sacrificed with barely a shrug of the shoulders.

The corporate economy is not only driven by its own inherent greed; its very success depends on arousing greed in others. For a company to sell its products, to grow and expand, it has to induce in others a desire to buy these products, and to the extent that these products do not meet genuine human needs (which is often the case), the desires must be provoked by deliberate strategies. Hence the twin disciplines of market research and advertising, which exploit every means available to push their clients' products. Television and radio, signboard and newspaper, pictures and jingles, slogans and songs, all are to be used to hammer home the message: "Buy this, buy that." The psychological sophistication that underlies the advertising industry is astounding. There is hardly a human weakness it hesitates to play upon to promote sales: sexual attraction and status, pride and cupidity, fear and worry, arrogance and vanity—all are fair game in the drive to boost profits.

Behind the specific advertising appeals there lies a more general assumption, an assumption never explicitly proposed but made absolutely compelling through countless images and slogans. This is the idea that consumption is the key to happiness. We are made to believe that the way to become happy is to indulge our desires. Happiness is identified with the acquisition of wealth and the enjoyment of commodities, and the more costly and luxurious the goods, the more lavish is the promise of happiness. In the consumerist vision, the enjoyment of goods is nothing less than 'The Good', the final, all-sufficient goal of human life.

If we use the Buddha's teachings as a lens to examine the corporate economic system and its offshoot, the consumerist culture, we will see that it is ultimately detrimental to the well-being of both its masters and servants alike. Drawing upon the tools of Buddhist analysis, let us briefly sketch the inner dynamics of this system. We see in the first instance that such a social order is founded upon ignorance or delusion (*avijjā*, *moha*), namely, the supposition that material wealth and consumption are the criteria of the good life. According to the Buddhist texts, when ignorance infiltrates our cognitive systems it issues in a series of 'distortions' (*vipallāsa*) which infect our perception (*saññā*), thinking (*citta*), and views (*diṭṭhi*). The Buddha mentions four such distortions: the notions that the impermanent is permanent, that the painful (or suffering) is pleasant, that the insubstantial is a self, and that the unbeautiful is beautiful. At the most basic level we perceive things by way of these distortions; when these distorted perceptions are taken up for reflection, we start thinking in terms of them; and finally, under the combined influence of distorted perception and thought, we adopt views—that is, beliefs, doctrines, and ideologies—that affirm the mistaken notions of permanence, pleasure, selfhood, and beauty.

In modern commercial culture these distortions—conceptual manifestations of ignorance—dominate the thinking, attitudes, principles, and policy lines of both producers and consumers alike. The illusions of permanence, pleasure, self, and beauty are sustained by the images that have become such an intimate part of our lives: the happy family using a particular brand of soap, the beautiful woman standing beside the latest model car, the rugged cattle man smoking this particular brand of cigarettes, the self-assured executive drinking that particular brand of whisky. The inevitable outcome of this commercially aggressive campaign is the exaltation of craving and greed as the fuel of social and economic activity. In free-market economics, production is not geared towards the satisfaction of real need but towards the enhancement of commercial profit, which means that human desires must be subtly manipulated and expanded in a bid to enhance profits.

In subservience to the internal demands of this system, the elementary need for material sustenance, for the basic requisites of life, becomes blown up into an insatiable urge for status, power, and luxury. The masters of commerce strive to create in us a perpetual discontent, to induce feelings of inadequacy, to stir up the need to purchase more. As a result, envy and resentment replace contentment; titillation replaces satisfaction; prestige value eclipses life value. The one word to be banished from the dictionaries is 'enough.' For the corporate-based economy to flourish there must never be enough, but always a thirst for more: for the bigger, faster, and better; for novelty and variety.

In a newly affluent society perhaps the segment of the population most vulnerable to the tactics of commercial advertising is the youth. The promoters of consumerism know this well. They know how to capitalize on the tender psychological needs of the young—their rebelliousness and audacity, their compulsions and anxieties—and on the basis of this understanding they attempt to create a specific culture of youth that attaches prestige and prominence to the appropriate commodities. They also know how to control fashions and styles, to make the acquisition of replacements a recurring demand that triggers off regular sprees of buying. For religious cultures that thrive on such traditional values as simplicity, contentment, and self-control, the impact of the global corporate culture can be traumatic, rupturing the lifeline that sustains the transmission of traditional values from one generation to the next.

In sum, the glorification of the profit motive gives rise to a social order in which the underlying springs of social activity are the twin defilements of ignorance and craving. The experts who defend this system, the advocates of free trade and globalization, tell us that the unrestrained functioning of the economy is the precondition for general human happiness, "the greatest happiness of the greatest number." But what the Buddha teaches is just the opposite. In a social order governed by ignorance and craving, in which greed, reckless growth, and competition are the spurs to mass-scale human activity, the inevitable outcome has to be suffering and conflict. In the formula of the Four Noble Truths we find this expressed in psychological terms: "Craving is the origin of suffering." Elsewhere the Buddha has made the same point with specific reference to the breakdown of social cohesion: "From craving comes the search for profit, from searching comes the gain of profit, from gain comes discrimination, thence comes desire and lust, thence attachment, thence possessiveness, thence selfishness, thence hoarding; and from hoarding come many evil unwholesome things, such as the taking up of clubs and knives, quarrels, conflicts, and disputes, recrimination, slander, and falsehood" (*Mahānidāna Sutta*).

Ironically, the linking together of the world's population in the globalized economy is accompanied by a progressive atomization of individuals which undermines their ability to function as cooperative, responsible members of their societies. This happens because the ultimate effect of corporate culture is to reduce the person to a mere consumer whose whole being centres on the intensity and variety of private experience. In subtle ways that operate below the threshold of perception, the consumerist conception of the good life cuts away at the bonds of community that unite the members of a social order into a unified whole. By appealing to those values that inflame egotism and selfish interest, it replaces social cohesion with a social atomism that locks each individual into a self-enclosed world of his or her own private concerns. The union of autonomous, responsible, disciplined individuals essential to a true community gives way to a 'culture of narcissism' in which each person is obsessed with maximizing his or her own status, wealth, position, and power—the outward signs of material success. If we are puzzled why social discipline and responsibility have become so rare today, reflection on the above may provide an answer.

In such a culture as we find in the 'developed' countries of the West, it is hardly surprising that the most basic unit of social formation, the family, has been virtually rent asunder. In the United States, the pioneer in establishing the 'new world order,' roughly half the marriages end prematurely in divorce and almost fifty per cent of American children grow up in one-parent homes. Even when family bonds endure, the atmosphere of family life has drastically changed from what it used to be in the past. No longer is the family a close harmonious unit held together by ties of love, respect, self-sacrifice, and cooperation. Instead it has become a symbiotic pact, a union of convenience, in which each member seeks his or her personal advantage, often by exploiting and hurting the other members.

Earlier we saw that the internal dynamics of consumerist culture begin with ignorance or delusion, the assumption that happiness can be achieved through acquisitiveness and the enjoyment of goods. This belief conditions craving, the desire to acquire and enjoy, and the ultimate outcome is frustration, competitiveness, and conflict; in short, personal and collective suffering. In a social order governed by the Dhamma—and I use this word here not with narrow reference to Buddhism, but more broadly to signify the universal law of righteousness and truth—the inner dynamics would be the diametric opposite of the one governing the consumerist model. In a righteous society the role played by ignorance will be exercised by knowledge or wisdom, a basic shared understanding of the fundamental laws of wholesome living. In a predominantly Buddhist society this would include the law of *kamma* and its fruit, the benefits of generosity and ethical conduct, and some insight into the Four Noble Truths and the three characteristics of existence. Those whose lives are guided by this knowledge need not be perfect saints, and indeed in mass society very few will even approximate to any degree of sanctity. But when people are guided by the principles of the Dhamma they will understand where their true welfare is to be found, and this understanding will enable them to distinguish clearly between what is truly in their interest and what appears attractive on the outside but eventually leads to harm.

From the standpoint of practical life, this is the critical distinction. A person enveloped in ignorance easily falls prey to craving, blindly pursues wealth, power and status, and brings suffering upon himself as well as others. A person guided by the Dhamma understands the true good, the highest goal of life. This understanding stimulates desire, but a kind of desire that is the exact opposite of craving. Craving is blind desire, a self-centred drive for sensual pleasure, power, and status. In contrast, the desire awakened by true knowledge is a wholesome desire, called in the texts 'desire for the good' (*atthakāma*) or 'desire for truth' (*dhamma-chanda*). Motivated by this wholesome desire, a person will engage in virtuous activities that lead to the realization of the good, and these activities will promote the well-being of both the individual and the community.

For Buddhism the highest goal is Nibbāna, liberation from ignorance and craving, release from the repetitive cycle of rebirths. In this paper I do not want to give a philosophical explanation of Nibbāna, but a practical one which will highlight the bearings the Dhamma has on our search for a viable social ethic. To go about this task, I intend to examine the experiential dimension of Nibbāna in a way that is not rigidly tied to the specific principles of Buddhist doctrine. One of my reasons for adopting such a general approach is to sketch a model for a righteous social order that can be readily appropriated by followers of other religious traditions, and also by those of no religious conviction who recognize the need for a sane alternative to the consumerist ideal. The task of 'healing the wounds of the world' is not one that any single spiritual tradition can handle alone. We live in a pluralistic society in a pluralistic world, and what is needed is a cooperative effort by all men and women of spiritual sensitivity regardless of their faith. While each religion and spiritual path has its own unique perspectives, underlying their obvious differences is a shared perception of the inherent dignity of the human person. It is this perception that must be recovered and safeguarded against the dehumanizing impact of the free-market economy and its offshoot, the consumerist society.

In terms of living experience, the ultimate goal of Buddhism combines four primary attributes: happiness, peace, freedom, and security. In Pali, the language of the early Buddhist canon, Nibbāna is called *parama sukha*, the highest happiness; *anuttara santivarapada*, the supreme state of sublime peace; *vimutti*, liberation or deliverance; and *anuttara yogakkhema*, the supreme security from bondage. While these aspects of Nibbāna may seem far removed from our present condition, a little thought will show that they link up with our most basic aspirations, indeed with the most basic desires of all human beings regardless of religious affiliation. When we consider the true motivation behind all our actions, it should be immediately clear that what we really desire most is a state that combines these four qualities: happiness, peace, freedom, and security The reason we fail to attain them is not that we desire their opposites—for no one deliberately seeks to be miserable, distressed, enslaved, and imperilled—but because we misconceive them and thus do not know how to attain them.

Under the influence of ignorance and delusion (*avijjā*), we seek our true good in the wrong direction, like a man who wants to go from Kandy to Colombo by heading north on the Matale road:

(1) We cannot distinguish *true happiness* from sensual gratification, and thus we seek happiness by frantically pursuing sensual pleasures, which are transient, degrading, and bound up with anxiety. To try to extract real happiness from sensual pleasures, however, is like trying to satisfy one's thirst by drinking sea water: the more one drinks, the thirstier one becomes.

(2) Again, we think that *peace* means the absence of conflict; thus we try to gain peace by subduing our opponents and by bullying our environment to serve our desires, unaware that this process is ultimately self-destructive.

(3) We identify *freedom* with license, the freedom to act on impulse, to do whatever we wish; thus we demand the right to act impetuously, without having to pay the price, without having to bear responsibility for our irresponsible actions.

(4) We think of *security* as protection from external harm; thus we shield ourselves in high-walled homes equipped with high-alert security systems, yet we never feel completely safe but live in the shadow of fear, of an anxiety that swells up from within.

What the Buddha teaches so clearly is that we must look within to achieve the vital goal towards which we aspire. He points out that real happiness, peace, freedom and security have to be attained by overcoming the mental fetters that bind us so tightly to suffering. These fetters are the mind's defilements: greed, hatred, and delusion, along with their many offshoots such as anger, malice, jealousy, stinginess, hypocrisy, obstinacy, conceit, arrogance, vanity and heedlessness. Thus to win our goal, we must turn the beam of our searchlight upon the mind itself and invest our energy in the task of self-purification.

While Nibbāna itself, in its fullness, may be remote from the common person mired in mundane responsibilities, this does not mean it is completely inaccessible to us. For Nibbāna is defined as the destruction of greed, hatred, and delusion, and this means that the goal must be reached by a gradual process which centres on the task of diminishing greed, hatred, and delusion in our everyday lives. We might even speak of the goal as 'bending back' or 'reaching down' and intersecting with our everyday concerns, spelling out the prerequisites for its own attainment. To advance towards Nibbāna from where we presently stand means that we must work to attenuate the influence of the defilements in our daily conduct: in our deeds, words, and thoughts. What we must do is replace greed with non-greed: with generosity, detachment, contentment and simplicity. Instead of hoarding and accumulating things, Buddhism emphasizes the value of giving: the practice of generosity is the most effective way to erase the greed from one's own mind as well as to confer benefits on others. Instead of nurturing hatred and resentment, we are to develop loving-kindness and compassion towards others, to cooperate with them in meeting our common goals, and to bear adversity with patience and equanimity. And instead of remaining in the clouds of delusion, we are to develop wisdom: to acquire understanding and insight into the invariable laws that underlie human existence.

The work of self-purification is to be undertaken by treading the Noble Eightfold Path, with its three divisions of virtue, concentration, and wisdom. Each of these three divisions of the path is intended to check and remove the defilements at successively subtler levels. The training in virtue, which comprises right speech; right action, and right livelihood, checks the outward expression of the defilements in transgressive action, in conduct that violates the norms of the moral life. The training in concentration, which comprises right effort, right mindfulness, and right concentration, aims at eliminating the active eruption of the defilements into our thought processes. And the training in wisdom, which comprises right view and right intention, aims at eradicating the defilements at the most fundamental level, as subtle seeds in the deep recesses of the mind. It is only when these defilements have been completely uprooted by wisdom, by direct insight into the true nature of phenomena, that ignorance is completely removed and knowledge fulfilled. And it is this that brings the realization of Nibbāna, the highest happiness, peace, freedom, and security right in this very life.

I want to emphasize here that while the practice of the Noble Eightfold Path is inescapably personal, requiring individual effort and diligence, this practice has consequences that are profoundly and inextricably social. As I pointed out earlier, society is not an abstract entity but the aggregate-mass of its individual members. If we compare society to an organism, then its members are like the cells; and just as the health of a body's cells affects the well-being of the physical organism, so the conduct, attitudes and values of a society's members inevitably influence the health of the social organism.

We need cherish no illusions that it will be feasible to marshal an entire society to walk along the Noble Eightfold Path. It is difficult enough even to get people to live a decent upright life governed by sound moral guidelines. The forces of darkness, of materialism and consumerism, have become so powerful, so seductive, so overwhelming, that it is only too easy to accept their propaganda as invincible truth. With the trend towards the globalized economy, those who dominate the corporate culture have brought virtually all the media under their control, and thus to dispel the consumerist mirage is a most formidable challenge indeed. Yet the seeds of this system's own destruction have already sprung up from within itself: in its growing polarization of the world into the rich and the poor; in its aggressive assault on every obstacle to corporate profit; in its disregard for basic human values; and of most importance today, in its reckless exploitation of the earth's own life-support systems.

Today we stand at a forked road, a road whose branches extend in two different directions. The choice of which road to take will decide our fate—our own personal fate and that of our planet. The road that has brought us to our present impasse is that of untrammelled development guided by a profit-oriented economic system. By extending our understanding of the physical world, science has conferred on us commanding powers over nature, a degree of control that is truly staggering. But the mastery we have won over the external world has been gained at the neglect of mastery over ourselves. To continue in this way, focused exclusively on more external development, is to place our very survival in jeopardy. That this risk is very real can be seen from the Conference on Climate Change in Kyoto (1997): virtually every country that participated, West and East, insisted on the right to pursue the path of unrestricted economic growth, even though this means that in the future, the pollution of our air and water will become unbearable and unpredictable climate change may cause large-scale calamities. Indeed, one gets the impression that in their rush to win a share of the good life, people are ready to flirt with the prospect that by their unbridled greed they may rip away the very support systems that make life on earth possible.

The other road does not involve a rejection of science and technology, but a recognition of their proper place in the scale of human values. Their function is to serve the human community, to alleviate want, and to help provide the material prosperity needed as a basis for the pursuit of other goals—cultural, intellectual, and spiritual development. What we need most urgently today is a shift in emphasis from external development to internal development. To focus upon internal development is not to escape into a private realm of subjective fantasy or to spurn the demands of social responsibility, but to organize our priorities in the way that brings the fullest realization of the human potential at the deepest level. The great spiritual teachers tell us that the goals of human life are governed by a scale of values, and that within this scale the highest value belongs to the highest goal. For Buddhism this is the attainment of enlightenment and liberation, the attainment of Nibbāna, to be won by treading the Noble Eightfold Path.

While the laws of the spiritual life have always held true, what we are being compelled to see today, with a clarity never before so striking, is the inextricable dependence of the external, material dimension of our existence on the internal, psychological dimension. In countless ways the point is being driven home to us that the world we share is a collective reflection of our minds, its social, economic and political structures the outward projections of our thought patterns and value schemes. For this reason our common welfare, perhaps even our survival as a species, depends on a large-scale transformation of consciousness. This transformation must cut clear across all boundaries—East and West, North and South—dissolving obstinate attitudes and assumptions that are ultimately self-destructive. If I were to sum up in concise terms the implications that the Buddha's message has for us today, as we slide into the twenty-first century, it would be this: that we must recognize that the wounds that afflict our world are symptoms of the wounds that afflict our minds. Our collective problems, from child prostitution to ecological devastation, from political corruption to corporate imperialism, are warning signs writ large of the destructive distortions in views and values that have sunk so deeply into our hearts. The bright side of the Buddha's message is that human beings can change. They are not held helpless captives of the mind's dark defilements, but by acknowledging their predicament, their suffering and anguish, they can begin the slow hard task of tackling the causes and thereby set about freeing themselves.

Surely such goals as social justice, relief from poverty, an end to communal conflict, and the protection of our natural environment deserve a top place on our agendas. But what the Buddha's teaching leads us to see is that we cannot reasonably expect to resolve these formidable social problems as long as we continue, in our personal lives, to move in the same familiar ruts of greed, carelessness, and selfishness. To heal the wounds of our world we must work to heal the wounds of our heart, the deep hidden wounds of greed, hatred, and delusion. The message, admittedly, is a difficult one, for inner changes always require greater effort than outer achievements, especially when the first step is self-understanding. In the final analysis, however, it is the only approach that will work, and this certainly makes it worthy of our attention.

I wish to close this paper with some words referring specifically to the condition of Buddhism within Asia. When we look at the way of life gaining ascendency in Buddhist Asia today, it seems that the true Dhamma is rapidly losing its influence. There may be plenty of temples, gigantic Buddha images looking out on us from the hills and roadways, and monks visible in all the major cities and towns. But a life inspired and guided by the Dhamma, based on moral rectitude, on loving-kindness and compassion, on respect and care for others: all this is in alarming decline. To prevent the true Dhamma from disappearing, radical and far-sighted steps will have to be taken.

To keep the Dhamma alive through the coming generations it is most essential to find ways to make the teaching meaningful to the younger generation. Given the way Buddhism is practised in Asia today, it seems that an educated young person will see in it little more than a system of rites and rituals, useful perhaps as a reminder of one's cultural and ethnic identity, but with very little relevance to our present concerns. The youth are the ones who will have to see that Buddhism survives into the next generation and that it will be able to offer its rich insights and spiritual practices to the global community. If we lose the youth to materialism and the cult of self-indulgence, we have lost the future of Buddhism, and at best all that will survive will be the outer crust of the religion, not its vital essence.

Success in keeping Buddhism alive requires that the true spiritual core of the Dhamma be extracted from its often constricting and deadening institutional embodiments. Above all, this task demands that the Dhamma be treated not as a basis for ethnic identity or cultural pride but as a living path of spiritual development and personal transformation that touches our most fundamental attitudes, goals, and values. It is only when the Dhamma is appropriated in such a way that it will serve to heal the wounds in our own minds and hearts, and it is only by healing the wounds within that we can face the momentous task of helping to heal the wounds of the world.

From Facing the Future: Four Essays on the Social Relevance of Buddhism, *The Wheel Publication No. 438/400, 2000. Originally given as the Centenary Lecture of the Young Men's Buddhist Association, Colombo, 8th January 1998.*

49. A Buddhist Approach to Economic and Social Development

In this paper I will be using the Buddha's teachings as a lens through which to examine the conception of economic and social development prevalent in today's world. If, as I contend, a Buddhist model of development is fundamentally incompatible with the dominant one, it is important to understand the reasons why. Thus I will first examine, from a Buddhist point of view, the model of development currently endorsed by most mainline economists and social analysts. Having shown the flaws in this model, I will then sketch some guideposts towards an alternative programme of economic and social development based on Buddhist principles. Since I am not by training an economist and really have little knowledge of this area, my comments will have to be very general, but as long as they are in accordance with the spiritual and ethical principles of the Dhamma even generalities can be helpful.

The notion of economic and social development has today become the rallying call of politicians, business leaders, and policy planners clear across the globe. This notion thus exercises a tremendous influence on the lives of all human beings, both at the personal level and as a determinant of social policy. Although the Buddhist texts prescribe certain principles to guide human beings in their economic and social activities, the notions of economic and social development that dominate current policy formulation have no precise parallels in earlier epochs. Thus to give adequate treatment to our topic it is not enough merely to listen to the canonical texts. Rather, we must draw out the implications of such ideas as economic and social development in their bearings on present-day social policy. Then we must use the profound perspectives offered us by the Dhamma as a tool for evaluating them and judging their worth.

The goal of economic and social development currently being pursued by most developing nations is governed by a model represented by the West, particularly by the United States. Political leaders and business magnates, both East and West, take it for granted that the Western economic system provides the standard for the rest of the world to follow, offering the panacea for humanity's most persistent social problems—poverty, violence, and injustice. The word 'development' implies a scale along which countries can be ranked according to their relative success in fulfilling this ideal. Those countries which successfully implement the ideal are called developed; those which haven't yet made the grade are said to be developing. It is assumed as a matter of course that all countries are moving along a single track in the same direction, with the West out ahead and the rest of the world struggling to catch up.

The chief characteristic of a developed country in this sense is determined almost exclusively by its economy. A developed country is understood to be one in which the economy is driven by the application of high technology to industrial production and commercial services. The trajectory of development is defined by both vertical and horizontal axes: the vertical axis is innovation in techniques and products, the horizontal axis, expansion in production and distribution. In such a society the rest of the social order is subordinated to the economy in such a way as to enable the economy to function with maximum efficiency. The rationalization offered to explain this form of social organization is that an efficient economy, marked by mass-scale production and wide distribution of goods, is the indispensable means for promoting the general welfare. By constantly raising levels of production and distribution, its proponents hold, a super-abundance of wealth will be created which will eventually trickle down to everyone, thus ensuring that everyone gets a share of the cake.

It is on this theoretical foundation that the West has pursued unchecked economic growth since the days of the Industrial Revolution, and it is in awe of the West's enormous technological prowess and material affluence that the rest of the world has chosen to follow its lead. This model has deeply impressed the leaders of Asian countries throughout the Buddhist world, who seem, almost without exception, committed to developing an economy geared to industrial production and the use of high technology. Thus it is of paramount importance to those responsible for guiding the future of Buddhism in those countries to contemplate this model in its many ramifications.

A detailed examination of this conception of economic and social development would require at least a full-length paper, but in this short presentation I intend to raise two simple questions. First: Is it really feasible for the rest of the world to emulate the Western model? And second: If it is feasible, is it really desirable for us to take this route? The first question is quite independent of a Buddhist point of view, since it involves considerations that do not hinge on any particular religious commitment. The second question, however, brings in a Buddhist perspective and asks whether the Western approach to development is truly compatible with the spirit that animates the Buddha's teaching.

Is It Feasible for All?

The first question can be answered very simply. Not only is it unfeasible for the rest of the world to pursue the road to development taken by the West, but it is virtually impossible for the Western economies (and those of the 'newly industrialized countries') to continue along this track much longer without jeopardizing everyone. The pursuit of economic development through high technology and industrialization has brought in its trail consequences that verge on disaster, threatening to undermine the very support systems on which sentient life depends.

The human economy does not operate in an infinite expanse capable of providing an inexhaustible supply of resources. It operates, rather, in an ecosystem which is closed, finite, and extremely fragile. When the economy expands, it does so by absorbing into itself more and more of the resource base of the ecosystem and by burdening the ecosystem in turn with its waste. The ecosystem imposes a limit of 100%, beyond which nothing more remains for consumption. But long before the human economy reaches that limit, it will cross a threshold point beyond which the delicate fabric of the ecosystem will be damaged so badly it can no longer sustain higher forms of life.

We may already be very close to that threshold; we have no sure way to know in advance, and as natural systems can disintegrate from below very slowly the final catastrophe may not become evident at once. With the human population due to increase by 50% over the next half century, the stress on the environment is bound to rise to even more perilous levels, levels which will be stretched still further by the global pursuit of economic growth. Not only is it reckless and irresponsible for the countries of the Third World to head down the road of expansive industrial production, but our very survival as a species will require that we place unrelenting pressure on the North to drastically cut down on current high levels of production and consumption and adopt new models of economic organization more conducive to the ecological health of the world.

Is It Desirable at All?

The second question I posed assumes (contrary to actual fact) that the Western model of economic development is ecologically feasible, and asks whether it would still be desirable from a Buddhist point of view. Once we have seen that the model portends ecological disaster, it might seem unnecessary even to raise this question. Such would indeed be the case if human beings were really as rational as they claim to be, but like moths heading towards a flame, our leaders and policy planners still seem drawn towards economic growth as the master solution to the weighty social problems pressing so heavily on their lands. Therefore a brief discussion of this question is warranted.

In reply, I would say succinctly that the Western model is not desirable, on the grounds that it has inescapable economic, social, and cultural consequences which, from a Buddhist perspective, are unmistakably pernicious. Let us briefly examine each category in turn.

(a) *Economic.* The proponents of global capitalism advocate continuous growth as the means to eliminate poverty and ensure general prosperity. The slogan that expresses this bit of conventional wisdom is 'the rising tide will lift all boats.' However, after over fifty years of incessant global development, we find the gap between rich and poor wider than ever before and increasing almost in tandem with the degree of economic growth. The gap has widened both between the rich and poor nations of the world, and also between the rich and poor within most of the world's nations. Over the past half century economic growth has expanded fivefold, international trade twelve fold, and direct foreign investment by 24-36 times. Yet today a higher proportion of the world's population is living below the poverty line than ever before. The population of the North, which makes up 20% of the world total, receives 80% of world income, while the bottom 20% takes in only 1.4%. The combined incomes of the top 20% are 60 times larger than those at the bottom 20%; this is twice as high as in 1950, when they were only 30 times larger. In short, the economic growth of fifty years has not brought the universal benefits promised in such glowing terms. To the contrary, the wealth generated has accrued to a minuscule minority, the corporate and financial elite, while increasing numbers, now in the West as well, sink deeper into insecurity and poverty.

(b) *Social.* The social consequences of the industrial growth economy are equally grim. A traditional Buddhist society is characterized by a high degree of social cohesion and a strong sense of community, its members linked in a rich web of relationships, from the family on up, that confer a deep sense of personal anchorage. Most people earn their living by subsistence agriculture, craftsmanship, and small-scale trade, occupations which bring them into direct contact with those who purchase and consume their products. Spiritual guidance comes from the Saṅgha, the order of monks and nuns, who not only pass on to the lay community the teachings of the Buddha but also stand at the acme of civil society as living examples of the spiritual virtues needed to win the ultimate goal, Nibbāna.

Enter the market economy, beginning from the colonial era, and the complex web of sustaining relationships is twisted into a tangle. Small farms are dismantled in favour of large estates used to grow cash crops for sale on the global market. Small industries are driven into extinction by the arrival of the transnational corporation, artisans rendered superfluous by cheap mass-produced goods, the small retailer driven into bankruptcy by the spread of the supermarket and chain store.

As people are dispossessed of their land and businesses, unemployment soars, and large numbers drift towards the cities, seeking employment in factories and accommodation in the spreading slums. There they toil at tedious tasks for long hours and low wages, sometimes under dangerous conditions.

Hit by the blows of the market economy, the close bonds of community are suddenly sundered. The blow can be traumatic. People find themselves adrift in a sea of distrust, as the close personal ties so characteristic of traditional society give way to cold impersonal confrontations between nameless faces in the crowd. Instead of cooperating to promote the common good, people are subtly forced to compete with each other in a brute struggle for subsistence that can be won only by bending others to one's advantage.

Family relations also disintegrate: first the closely-knit extended family dissolves into the self-enclosed nuclear family; then the nuclear family in turn splits up, leaving behind broken marriages, lonely adults, and emotionally deprived children. The degrading nature of this social system is clearly evident in the symptoms of decline so prevalent today, both in the North and the South: homelessness, escalating crime, prostitution and child abuse, juvenile delinquency, suicide, pervasive alcoholism and drug addiction.

(c) *Cultural.* In traditional Buddhist societies, concern with the accumulation of wealth and goods is subordinate to the pursuit of ethical and spiritual virtues. The Dhamma as the peerless guide to thought and action encourages such qualities as simplicity, contentment, generosity, and self-sacrifice. Wisdom is cherished above mere cleverness, moral purity above wealth and status. But with the rise of the industrial growth society, everything changes, as the drive to acquire, own and consume turns into a tyrannical master whose demands are implacable.

The need to dissolve the attitudes enjoined by traditional Buddhist culture is inherent in the logic of global capitalism, and it is therefore naive to expect reform to come about simply by giving the giant corporations an injection of Buddhist precepts. The driving engine of the corporate economy is the need to increase profits, and to achieve this objective it must methodically undercut all those traditional values that discourage the acquisitive urge. The corporate leaders do not have to accomplish this by direct assault, and generally they will espouse moral values. But by subtly manipulating people's perceptions and ways of thinking at deep subliminal levels, the corporate system gradually transforms them into consumers whose lives centre around the unconstrained acquisition and enjoyment of technologically produced commodities. The most vulnerable targets are the young, who are encouraged to develop a culture of their own in which popularity and status are determined by what they own, wear, sing, and eat.

The avenues of invasion are manifold. They include television, the cinema, videos and music. They foster the rise of a global monoculture in which all traditional diversity is dissolved. Chain stores and shopping malls make their contribution too, providing the commodities essential to high status. But the most direct agent of attack is the advertising industry, which plants in people's minds the firm conviction that the ruling purpose of their lives is nothing more than to acquire and enjoy, without need for scruples or restraint.

Buddhist Guideposts towards Development

At the present point in history it is difficult to offer a well-designed practical plan for economic and social development that has already proved its worth. Standing at the threshold of the third millennium we are entering a new frontier, where we must work out new solutions to formidable problems by sheer trial and error. It is clear enough, however, that with the global industrial economy pushing the world towards the brink of catastrophe, we have no choice but to envision viable alternatives, and already, in various quarters, the search for new models is diligently underway. In what follows I will enumerate a few simple guideposts for a Buddhist approach to development.

The first task that Buddhism would have to undertake is to reverse a strange inversion of logic that lies at the heart of the industrial growth model of development. When we view this model in the light of the Buddha's teaching, it is at once obvious that it rests upon an extraordinary degree of abstraction from the concrete reality of lived experience. This abstraction takes place in at least two stages. First, the economy, which in traditional cultures occupies a subordinate place in the social order, is drawn out from its proper bounds and taken as the chief criterion for judging societal well-being.

Then, as if this were not enough, the health of the economy is conceived exclusively in quantitative terms, by means of such indicators as the GNP or the GDP. These indicators measure only a country's total exchange of monetary goods and services. They reveal nothing at all about the qualitative nature of the goods and services exchanged; they do not register the social and ecological costs of economic development; they say nothing about how the wealth generated is distributed among a country's population. Yet a myopic fixation on bolstering GDP captivates the attention of policy planners everywhere, guiding the formulation of economic and social policy in virtually every country on Earth. This narrowness of vision encourages a double parasitism, whereby the economy becomes a parasite on the social order and both combined gnaw away at the planet's delicate ecosystem.

The Four Noble Truths of the Buddha provide us with a powerful instrument for diagnosing the causes and results of this distortion of vision. The cause is ignorance, not seeing things as they really are, which provides a field for craving to emerge and bring entire societies under its dominion. When there is craving, as we know from the Four Truths, suffering is bound to follow, and this is amply confirmed when we survey the debris left behind by the global race towards development.

The fundamental concept that must underlie any Buddhist approach to economic and social development is 'Dhamma,' the natural, self-subsistent law of righteousness and truth realized by the Buddha through his enlightenment and communicated by his teaching. The primacy of Dhamma means that economic and social policy must be guided from start to finish by ethical norms. These norms are not mere matters of subjective judgement, personal and relative, but real and immutable laws written into the very fabric of being. This does not imply that there is one invariable form of social and economic organization valid for all people under all conditions. A wide range of alternatives are possible, as diverse as natural landscapes, but for any such system to conduce to real human welfare it must be grounded on sound ethical principles which encourage people to strive for moral integrity in their lives. A social system which runs counter to the Dhamma, which encourages or condones unethical behaviour, is bound to bring widespread misery and destitution, not only for human beings but for the entire natural order. We can see concrete proof of this in present-day corporate capitalism. Founded on the idea that selfishness, greed, and unrestrained consumption are the keys to progress, the whole juggernaut drives us steadily towards global catastrophe.

From the centrality of Dhamma to social order, two subsidiary principles follow, one especially relevant to the economic sphere, the other to the social sphere. The principle that should govern the economic sphere is 'the rule of sufficiency' which means 'simply knowing that enough is enough.' The rule of sufficiency is both a policy of mental hygiene contributing to psychological balance and a policy of ecological wisdom contributing to the preservation of the natural environment. In both respects the rule promotes a sound economy of 'home management,' encompassing the judicious ordering of both our internal home of mind and our external home, the natural world.

As a discipline of mental hygiene, the rule of sufficiency rests on the insight that human needs are hierarchical—as I will shortly explain—and that there is a point of satiation in meeting material needs beyond which continued gratification becomes deleterious. This does not imply that we must all adopt ascetic lifestyles and deny ourselves even the innocent pleasures of life. But it does mean that when people seek to acquire possessions and enjoy sensual pleasures beyond their natural capacities, they do so at the expense of other needs, social and spiritual, which are equally crucial to their fulfilment. Thereby they violate a law of human nature and bring harm to themselves and to those victimized by their avarice.

As a policy of ecological wisdom, the rule of sufficiency teaches us that there are inherent limits to economic growth dictated by the unsurmountable finitude of the ecosystem. Pursued beyond these limits, economic expansion becomes parasitic both on human health, physical and mental, and on the regenerative capacities of nature. When applied to our present-day situation, this principle teaches us that economic development, in the sense of continuously expanding production and obsessive technological innovation, is precisely what we don't need. Our economy is big enough already, far too big, and our technologies too smart, too powerful, and too much fraught with moral risk for beings as fallible as ourselves. What we need most of all is streamlining and downsizing: cutting down on weapons production, on industries dedicated to wasteful luxuries, on conspicuous consumption as the engine that drives the economy. Instead we need qualitative improvements to make our technologies more humble and humane, more benign towards the total biosphere. And above all we need greater stress on economic justice and social equity, so that no one need be deprived of a fair standard of living.

The principle that should guide social activity is the rule of cooperation and harmony. But cooperation must be infused and animated by ethical motivation. The cooperation between super-powers to dominate the global political order in their own selfish interests is not the kind of cooperation we require; the mergers, corporate takeovers, and business cartels formed to control the world economy is not the kind of cooperation that accords with the Dhamma. Our current social order promotes competition rather than cooperation; the key word bandied about today is competitiveness. Such an emphasis is bound to generate conflict and resentment, splintering the social system into a multitude of hostile factions. A society founded upon the Dhamma recognizes that each person should aim to promote the good of the greater unit to which he or she belongs, and as a minimum should never seek private fulfilment in ways that inflict harm on others. The ideal is beautifully summed up in the 'six principles of harmony and respect' taught by the Buddha to the Saṅgha: loving kindness in thought, word, and deed; sharing righteous gains; observing a common code of morality; and holding in common liberating views.

In a Buddhist approach to social and economic development, the primary criterion that would govern policy formulation should be the well-being of a society's members, and this well-being should be viewed holistically taking account of a wide range of factors. The economy would be assigned to the place where it belongs, as a subordinate domain nested within the wider social system; in turn the social system would be viewed as an integral part of the total ecosystem, the indispensable foundation for all life. Thus economic development would be guided along lines that promote the health and well-being of the social order without harming the natural systems within which human society is lodged. To the contrary, a Buddhist social policy would recognize the importance of preserving the natural environment, not simply to provide a continued supply of resources for the human economy, but as a positive good both intrinsically and in relation to the aesthetic enrichment and psychological wholeness of its members.

Society in turn must be recognized as an abstraction from the individual human beings who make up the social order. Thus, when we speak of improving the well-being of society, this ultimately means that social policy must seek to promote the welfare of individual people. How we set about promoting the welfare of people is contingent on our view of human nature. If we hold a materialistic view of human nature, then our efforts will be directed primarily to ensuring that their material needs are met, and we will see no reason to give attention to other factors. If, however, we hold a more spiritual conception of human nature, then we will recognize that other needs beyond material prosperity also call out for fulfilment.

The Buddha's teachings offer a wide-ranging conception of the human person as a complex entity having a diversity of needs which all must be met to ensure happiness and well-being. These needs fall into a well-defined hierarchy of importance, which we might here consider as threefold. At the base of the hierarchy is the physical need for the basic requisites of existence: clothing, food, a comfortable dwelling, medical care, transportation, energy, tools, and so forth. At the next level are social needs: for education, family, friendship and personal intimacy, participation in a community, and meaningful work. At the highest level are spiritual needs: for moral rectitude, mental development, and wise understanding of the true nature of life.

A social order guided by Buddhist principles would create opportunities for all these needs to be satisfied and would see that no one is frustrated in their aspirations to lead a contented life. A Buddhist social order would begin by ensuring that all members of society are able to satisfy their material needs. But because the Buddhist teaching views needs hierarchically, it does not encourage the narrow fixation on material acquisition and sensual gratification so characteristic of contemporary culture. By pointing out that the crass pursuit of luxury and abundance is a root-cause of suffering. Buddhism encourages restraint, simplicity and contentment. By extolling generosity as a basic virtue and the mark of a superior person, it promotes a wide distribution of basic necessities so that no one has to suffer deprivation.

For Buddhism, however, material satisfaction merely provides a starting point for the pursuit of higher goals. Since human beings are social creatures who naturally come together for common ends, this means that a social order guided by Buddhist principles would consist primarily of small-scale communities in which each member can make an effective contribution. Only small-scale social arrangements can rescue people from the ominous abyss of meaningless so pervasive in modern urban life. From a Buddhist perspective, the vast polluted mega-cities and impersonal bureaucracies characteristic of our era would have to be considered deviations from the natural order conducive to true human well-being. They are a travesty of our inherent need for communal participation. The local communities consonant with Buddhist principles would focus on the extended family as the primary unit of social integration. The family would be guided by Buddhist views and values, which they will serve to transmit from one generation to the next.

The model for the entire web of social relationships would be that provided in the magnificent Sigālovāda Sutta (Dīgha Nikāya No. 31), where the Buddha minutely defines the reciprocal duties of parents and children, husband and wife, employer and employee, friend and friend, teacher and students, monks and laity. The economy most compatible with such a mode of social organization would be small-scale and localized, using simple technology which does not drain natural resources. In such an economy production would be aimed principally at local consumption, so that there would be direct face-to-face contact between producers and consumers. Modalities would have to be worked out to bring about integration of the small local economies into a broader national and global economy, but the driving engine of the entire system would be the promotion of well-being both material and social, not commercial profit and unrestrained expansion.

But even a prosperous economy and a harmonious social order cannot satisfy the deepest need of the human heart: the need for meaning, for an ultimate purpose around which our lives should revolve and a path of conduct to guide us through the thickets of difficult decisions. This need can only be met by religion: religion not as a bond reinforcing a sense of communal identity, not as a legacy of traditional rituals and beliefs, but as a genuine path of self-transformation opening upon a transcendent reality. Since in the ontological order it is this reality which claims the highest place, it follows that in the hierarchy of values it is spiritual values that should claim our deepest respect.

Genuine spiritual values do not exist in a self-enclosed domain of their own, cut off from the rest of life. Rather, they spill forth and pervade all other aspects of our existence, sustaining them in a unifying vision and steering them in the direction of the highest good. Thus in a sound and healthy social order, spiritual vision will guide the formulation of economic and social policy, ensuring that the latter do not stop short at mundane ends but aim beyond themselves towards the dimension of transcendence. In a predominantly Buddhist society, the highest good is Nibbāna, and economic and social life would be seen as offering the opportunity for making progress towards Nibbāna. Though the final goal may be accessible only to those who embark on the austere road of renunciation, the Buddhist path reaches down into the mire of everyday life and spells out, with clarity and precision, the steps needed to advance in the direction of the final goal. Thus in a Buddhist social order the ceaseless struggle for mundane subsistence would be considered, not as a mere series of technical problems in need of a technological fix, but as an opportunity for cultivating the virtues of mind and heart that lead to the highest. This gives us the ultimate meaning of development for a Buddhist society: the development of morality, concentration, and wisdom culminating in full enlightenment and liberation from suffering.

A true Buddhist social order would try to make this prospect available to its members by nurturing a Saṅgha, a community of renunciant monks and nuns, and providing for their material needs. These renunciants in turn would guide the broader community in the Buddha's teaching and provide them with the inspiring example of those who have withdrawn from the cycle of production and consumption to devote themselves to a holy life.

One last word is called for. It may seem that I have just sketched a plan that is beautiful and compelling on paper, but utterly idealistic and impracticable in fact. In part I agree. To implement such a model will be extremely difficult, awakening staunch resistance from mighty sectors with immense wealth and power. But we have to recognize that in a world moving steadily to universal democracy the final say in determining the forms of social organization under which we live must rest with people, with you and me. When a system assumes forms which bring extravagant benefits to a few and great misery and deprivation to many, there is no cogent reason for it to continue. All that sustains it is the naked ambitions of the elite at its helm, and the web of deceit they weave to hide the truth from ordinary people.

Today this web of deception is dissolving on many fronts: in ecological disasters, in increasing unemployment and economic injustice, in the waves of crime, exploitation, and social degeneration so visible everywhere, especially in the Third World, where most of the world's population lives. Large numbers of people, who have seen through the mirage of technological progress and global capitalism, realize that this system is unsustainable, indeed that it is ultimately harmful for its beneficiaries as much as for its manifest victims. In many quarters—grass-roots organizations, counter-culture movements, and alternative think-tanks—the search is on for a way to preserve this planet in the new century. To such people Buddhism offers a message which is at once lofty and sublime yet capable of addressing in lucid terms the hard realities of social and economic life. It is the responsibility of the Buddhist community to sound that message, in its spiritual heights and earthly applications, for the benefit of all living beings.

From Facing the Future: Four Essays on the Social Relevance of Buddhism, *The Wheel Publication No. 438/400, 2000. Originally presented at the International Buddhist Conference on The Timeless Message of the Sammā Sambuddha, Colombo, 10th November 1998.*

50. THE CHANGING FACE OF BUDDHISM

On those rare occasions when I visit an urban Buddhist temple here in Sri Lanka, I am repeatedly struck by the stark observation that almost all the devotees present are middle aged or elderly people, perhaps accompanied by their grandchildren. In the viharas of our towns and cities young people, and even adults in the prime of life, are most conspicuous by their absence. For a country where seventy percent of the population is counted as Buddhist, such an uneven turnout at religious functions is ominous. For Buddhism to continue from one generation to the next, the flame of religious faith must be transmitted across the gap of generations. If, however, it is indeed these invisible young people who hold the future of the Sāsana in their hands, then that future does not seem very bright. Their absence is perhaps a warning that the message of the Dhamma is not hitting home, that its representatives are failing to translate its principles into a language that speaks to those most in need of its guidance. Should this trend continue, in a few more generations Buddhism may become just a relic of Sri Lanka's ancient heritage: beautiful to look upon but as lifeless as the ruins at Anuradhapura.

Outwardly, symbols of Sri Lanka's Buddhist legacy can be seen everywhere in this land. Monks still play prominent roles at public functions; gigantic Buddha images stare down at us from the hilltops; in most towns a steady stream of *pirit* chanting blares out twice daily from the loudspeakers. Paradoxically, however, these outward emblems of Buddhist piety coexist in an uneasy tension with a malignant spiritual disease whose symptoms have spread across all strata of Sri Lankan society. A bitter internecine war drags on interminably, with a brutalizing impact on the whole country. Strikes are commonplace in our essential services, holding the poor and helpless hostage. Murder, theft, rape, drug-trafficking, the sexual exploitation of children have become so widespread that even the most gruesome criminal act barely pricks our sense of moral outrage. Alcohol, drug use, and suicide are the most common escape routes, especially for the poor, but their popularity is hardly a sign that Buddhism is thriving.

If Buddhism is failing to penetrate deep into the hearts of those who profess it as their faith, we have to ask ourselves why, and also to ask what can be done to reverse these trends. I would like to approach these questions by first asking what role Buddhism is intended to play in our lives. I will deal with this question by distinguishing two aspects of Buddhism both stemming from the Buddha's original teaching. I shall call these the liberative and the accommodative strands of the Dhamma.

The liberative strand, the essential and unique discovery of the Buddha, is the message of a direct way to liberation from suffering. This strand begins with the realization that suffering originates within ourselves, from our own greed, hatred, and ignorance, above all from our drive to establish a sense of separate selfhood that pits us against all other living forms. The Buddha's radical solution to the problem of suffering is the demolition of the self-delusion in its entirety. This issues in an utterly new mode of being that the Buddha called 'Nibbāna,' the extinguishing of the fire of lust, the going out of the ego-consciousness with its flames of selfish craving.

The attainment of this goal, however, requires a price far higher than most people can pay: a strict discipline of contemplation grounded upon a radical ethic of restraint. Thus, being a skilful teacher, the Buddha modulated his teaching by including another dimension suitable for those unable to walk the steep road of renunciation. This is the accommodative strand of the Dhamma: a path of gradual transformation, extending over many lives, fulfilled by training in meritorious deeds and developing the virtues needed as a foundation for the ultimate attainment of Nibbāna. This strand of Dhamma, it must be emphasized, is not merely an expedient device, a beautiful fable invented by the Buddha as a means of offering consolation or of inculcating moral virtues. It is, rather, an integral aspect of the original teaching stemming from the Buddha's own vision into the multiple dimensions of sentient existence and the prospects for transmigration within the round of rebirths. But the function of this teaching within his system of training is provisional rather than ultimate, mundane rather than transcendent.

I call this dimension of Buddhism 'accommodative' for two reasons: first, because it accommodates the doctrine of deliverance to the capacities and needs of those unable to follow the austere path of meditation prescribed as the direct route to Nibbāna; and second because it helps to accommodate Buddhist followers within saṃsāra while offering salutary guidance to protect them from the more intense forms of worldly suffering, especially from a fall into lower spheres of rebirth. In its accommodative dimension, Buddhism provides a comprehensive world-view which gives ordinary men and women a meaningful picture of their place in the cosmos. At the same time it propounds an elevated system of values that includes ethical rules to help us live happily amidst the fluctuations of daily life and in harmony with our fellow human beings.

Although the original keynote of the Dhamma was the message of deliverance, as Buddhism spread first across India and later over wider Asia, the balance between its two strands swung away from the liberative towards the accommodative. Such a development was only natural when a spiritual teaching whose liberative core was suited for renunciants became the religion of an entire nation, as happened in Sri Lanka and elsewhere in Asia. But this aspect of Buddhism should not be disparaged or placed in competitive contrast to the liberative dimension, for both are equally essential to the aims of the Buddha's teachings. The path of renunciation leading to final liberation was always suited for the few, even within the ranks of the monastic order; for the many, the accommodative strand of Buddhism was necessary, both as a world-view and as a means of preparing the ground for practice of the liberative Dhamma.

Through the centuries, accommodative Buddhism portrayed for us an orderly universe with the Buddha as the supreme teacher, with multiple heavens inhabited by benevolent gods, governed by an ethical law connecting our present actions with our future destinies. By means of its doctrine of merit, this side of Buddhism gave people an incentive for doing good deeds, and the fruits of this were evident in the general spirit of benevolence that prevailed in traditional Buddhist societies.

From ancient times until the modern era, the picture of the universe offered by accommodative Buddhism functioned as the unchallenged bedrock for the preaching and practice of the Dhamma. However, beginning in the late fifteenth century, a challenge came from beyond the horizon that was to shatter the self-assured certainty of this world-view. The challenge took the shape of the European colonial powers who in successive waves grabbed control of the social and political institutions on which popular Buddhism depended. Foreign conquest, the proselytizing missions of the Christian churches, the secularization of education and its subordination to colonial rule—all these measures together dealt a hard blow to Buddhist self-esteem and to the sovereign role of the Dhamma in the lives of the wider Buddhist population.

This trend was reinforced by the rise of the scientific worldview. Although the basic principles of the scientific method could easily resonate with the Buddhist spirit of free inquiry, science introduced an understanding of the world that, in its materialistic bias, clashed with the spiritual vistas envisaged by Buddhist tradition. While classical Buddhism posits a multi-tiered universe inhabited by many classes of sentient beings who transmigrate from realm to realm in accordance with their karma, scientific naturalism holds that life is a purely physical process which utterly terminates at death, with no survival of personal identity in any form beyond bodily death. While Buddhist thought sees mind as primary and matter as subordinate to mind, naturalism sees matter as fundamental and mind as derivative, a by-product or aspect of material processes. While Buddhism posits a transcendent goal, a supramundane reality to be won by moral and spiritual training, naturalism sees nothing beyond the empirical world and regards all ethical and religious codes as of purely human origin. In the West also the rise of science in conjunction with an insistent demand for intellectual and moral freedom worked to dislodge Christianity from its dominant place in the Western mindset.

It was not, however, merely the theoretical power of modern science that threatened the traditional Buddhist worldview and its attendant scheme of values. In fact, in the early twentieth century Buddhist thinkers could enrol science as an ally in their struggle against Christian triumphalism. But what has turned the tables on traditional Buddhist values has not been theory but praxis—the harnessing of technology by a free-market economic system in quest of expanding profits.

This marriage between technology and the free market has given birth to a ravenous consumerist culture grounded on the premise that material affluence and sensual enjoyment are the only worthwhile goals in life. At the present time it is perhaps this culture of consumerism, stimulated by advertising and the popular media, that poses the single biggest challenge to spirituality as an effective force in people's lives. In the cities this culture enfolds the affluent elite in clouds of hedonistic self-indulgence. For the urban and rural poor— awed by its splendours as presented by television, radio and cinema—it breeds envy, resentment, and despair. Under such circumstances, is there any cause for wonder that alcoholism, drug addiction, suicide, and violent crime have escalated so sharply?

This clash of worldviews and value systems also explains why the Buddhism of the temples has become so peripheral to our younger generation. In temple Buddhism today, the language in which the teaching is couched— the ambience, the flavour, the whole tenor of the teaching—is one rooted in the worldview of medieval accommodative Buddhism. This may be lovely, ennobling, and even true in its own way, but it is hardly able to deliver the message of the Dhamma to those nurtured on the ways of modernity. The teachings of temple Buddhism stem from a culture irretrievably gone, from an era where roles were clearly defined and everything had its place in an intelligible, friendly whole. But we live, breathe, and wend our way along the streets of the modern world, where changes take place at blinding speed, where a host of aggressive voices compete for our attention, where every cosy assumption is exposed to merciless questioning. For those struggling to find a niche for themselves in such a world, the self-assured Buddhism of the temples has ceased to be 'the Dhamma,' the message of awakening that blows open our minds and floods them with light. Instead it has become just a quaint reminder of the past, still capable of evoking occasional moods of piety but barely relevant to the difficult choices we face amidst the grind of daily life.

One approach to this clash of worldviews is to retreat defensively into the past, to try to seal off our ancient cultural and religious heritage from the depredations of modernity, and to extol the superiority of Buddhism to everything modern. This is the fundamentalist stance, not necessarily an aggressive stance, but one which chooses nostalgic retreat to the past over innovative adjustment to the present. From this perspective the arrival of modern culture poses an intrinsic threat to the Dhamma, and the only way to protect the precious teaching is by rejecting modernity and attempting to preserve the heritage of tradition with minimal change.

However, for any organism to survive, it must adapt to changes in the environment. To reject the new environment and struggle to preserve the past is to risk petrifaction, to turn Buddhism into an outdated antique whose relevance has vanished and which remains only as a stimulus for feelings of devotional piety. This has been the attitude in more traditionalist Buddhist circles. Its stubborn conservatism, which weds the spiritual vistas of the Dhamma to a particular culture and social order, partly accounts for the withering relevance of Buddhism in the eyes of many in the younger generations.

Yet retreat into the past is not the only way to preserve the Dhamma from destruction. Indeed, such regressive pietism preserves only the shell, the outer forms of Buddhism, while nullifying its inner vitality. Another approach, a more optimistic one, is available to us, one which does not jump to the conclusion that the arrival of modernity will necessarily sound the death knoll of the Dhamma. Looked at from this angle, the current crisis of Buddhist culture might be seen as a means of purgation, helping us to separate the chaff from the kernel and rediscover what is truly timeless in the Buddha's message. This means that a new emphasis is required, one which might be described as a turn from the overemphasis on the accommodative dimension of Buddhism to the liberative.

When I speak about this shift in emphasis, I do not intend to say that the traditional Buddhist worldview is wrong and must be jettisoned in favour of the purely naturalistic outlook proposed by modern science. In fact, allowing for inevitable mythological elements in Buddhist tradition, I would maintain that the Buddhist world-view, with its recognition of the crucial role of the mind and the inconceivably vast dimensions of reality, is much richer and more adequate to philosophical reflection than the flattened worldview bequeathed to us through a presumptuous misapplication of the scientific method beyond its legitimate domain. In any case, one impressive feature of the Buddha's teaching is the independence of its liberative core from any particular cosmology, its ability to speak directly to our most fundamental concerns in a way that is immediately and personally verifiable no matter what cosmology one adopts. In terms of our present situation, material progress, the fulfilment of the consumerist dream, forces us to recognize that affluence does not bring real happiness but only leaves us empty, thirsting for some deeper fulfilment. Thereby we are brought to see the hard truth, enshrined in the liberative Dhamma, that craving is the cause of suffering. We can also see that release from suffering can never be won by yielding to the incessant implorations of craving, but only by mastering our minds through methodical training aimed at self-knowledge and self-transformation.

While it is difficult to predict the directions that institutional Buddhism will take in the coming decades, we can discern at work today several important trends which may actually herald a true revival of the Dhamma. One is disenchantment with the supposed blessings of consumerism. The realization that happiness cannot be bought in the shopping mall should awaken in us an urgent desire to find a more genuine sense of meaning for our lives, a peace and happiness that does not depend on outer conditions. We see signs of this already in the increasing number of lay Buddhists willing to take up the hard work of meditation, traditionally considered the preserve of the monks. For such people, the practice of Buddhism is not so much a matter of conventional rituals as an inward training to be pursued privately or in small groups with like-minded friends.

The impact of materialism thus sends us back to the original liberative strand of the Dhamma, for centuries submerged beneath the accommodationist dimension. But while the older message spoke of the goal mainly as release from the round of rebirths, the stress required today should be on the benefits of Dhamma practice visible here and now: on the happiness and fulfilment won through greater self-knowledge and mastery of the mind. This, of course, is not intended to question the veracity of the doctrine of rebirth and the conception of the goal as ultimate release from saṃsāra, but only to insist that for this ultimate goal to become meaningful and relevant to us we must first put our everyday lives in order through self-understanding and self-mastery. Otherwise it is likely to remain the Utopian fantasy that it is within much of present-day accommodative Buddhism.

However, the quest for personal peace of mind does not exhaust the promise of the Dhamma in the epoch that lies ahead. For we live at a decisive moment in history when the future of humankind, and even of our planet as a biological entity, hangs in a delicate balance. Our instantaneous media of communication and rapid means of transportation have welded people everywhere into a single family in which each member is to some degree responsible for the welfare of the whole, not only of all human beings but of the entire community of life. But while our technologies have given us the capacity to provide a decent living to everyone, grave problems of enormous scope remain. Poverty, war, hunger, exploitation, and injustice still cast their shadows over our future, claiming too many victims who cannot even voice their grievances, let alone set them right.

These problems—political, economic, social, and ecological—cry out for solutions, and one of the major tasks faced by every major religion today is to serve as the voice of humanity's conscience. To regard these problems as merely temporary snags that can easily be resolved by political and social reform is to miss the point that what underlies them all, in different ways, is a blind and stubborn selfishness pernicious in its consequences. It is precisely the role of religion, in its innermost essence, to address and rectify this malignancy. Too often in the past religion has been an inflammatory force creating divisions rather than unity, and this trend can still be seen today in the various kinds of religious fundamentalism rippling across the globe. But all the great spiritual traditions contain at their core a perception of humanity's unity, to be translated into a life guided by love and compassion. It is this side of religion, and not the divisive, that must be fostered in the immediate future.

One of the primary tasks facing Buddhism in the global world of the future is to develop a comprehensive vision of solutions to the social, economic, and political problems that loom so large today. This is not a matter of blending religion and politics, but of making an acute diagnosis of the destructive fixations of consciousness from which these problems spring. The diagnosis must lay bare how human defilements—the same greed, hatred, and ignorance responsible for private suffering—take on a collective dimension embedded in social structures. What is necessary is not only to expose the oppressive, detrimental nature of such structures, but to envisage and strive for new alternatives: fresh perspectives on social organization and human relatedness that can ensure political, economic and social justice, the preservation of the natural environment, and the actualization of our spiritual potential.

Although such a project, on so vast a scale, will be a new challenge to Buddhism, it is a challenge that can be partly met with the Buddha's insights into the origination of suffering and the means to its resolution. But only partly, for creative thought is needed to apply these insights to today's unique problems. This means in effect expanding the liberative dimension of the Dhamma by giving it a collective or even global application. In this enterprise, Buddhists must join hands with leaders of other religions committed to the same goal. Beneath their inevitable differences, the great religions concur in seeing our grave social and communal problems as stemming from a primordial blindness rooted in the delusion of self, either personal or blown up into ethnic and nationalistic identities.

From the perspective of the great spiritual traditions, what we must do to redeem ourselves and preserve humanity's place on earth is to abandon our obsession with narrow selfish goals and re-align ourselves with the fundamental law of the universe, with the timeless Dhamma. The Buddha teaches that we can only achieve our own true good when we transcend the standpoint of self and set our hearts on the welfare of all. This principle is not the preserve of any particular religion but can be understood by anyone of good will. What Buddhism gives us is a clear-cut path to master ourselves and to bring forth the wisdom and compassion so sorely needed as we enter the new millennium.

From Facing the Future: Four Essays on the Social Relevance of Buddhism, *The Wheel Publication No. 438/400, 2000. An earlier version of this paper was published in the Millennium Supplement of The Island newspaper, 1st January 2000.*

51. Sangha at the Crossroads

There can be little doubt that in Sri Lanka today Buddhism finds itself at a crossroads, its future increasingly in question. The challenge it faces is not one of numbers and power, but of relevance. Not that the Dhamma itself, the Buddha's teaching, has lost its relevance; for neither the shifting drama of history nor the undulating waves of culture can muffle the timeless message embedded in the Four Noble Truths and the Noble Eightfold Path. The problem lies not with the teaching itself, but with those responsible for bringing the teaching to life. What is lacking above all is a combination of skills that can be summed up in three simple words: *comprehension*, *commitment*, and *translation*. *Comprehension*: a clear understanding of how the teaching applies to the hard realities of human life today, to a society and world in which the old certainties of the past are being scattered like leaves before a storm. *Commitment*: the willingness to apply the teachings in the way they were intended, even when this means defying the encrustations of established tradition. *Translation*: not stereotyped 'sermons,' not sweet consolation, not religious lullabies, but solid, sober explanations of how the timeless principles of the Dhamma can resolve the distinctive problems and quandaries of our age.

As we stand at this crossroads looking towards the future, three choices offer themselves to us. One is simply to resign ourselves to the decay of the Sāsana, accepting it as a backward swing of the pendulum of history—sad but inevitable. A second is to wring our hands and complain, shifting the responsibility to others—the government, the monks, or the minorities. A third is to ask ourselves what we can do to stem the rising tide. If we adopt the third route we might begin by noting that the Sāsana does not exist in an ideal realm of its own, but only as embodied in the millions of people who call themselves Buddhists and look for refuge to the Triple Gem.

This statement might sound obvious, even trite. However, if we reflect for a few moments we will see that, though obvious, it has enormous implications, for it means that we ourselves are ultimately responsible for the prosperity and decline of the Sāsana: our own views, attitudes, and conduct decide whether the Sāsana is to thrive or wither. To recognize this is to see that the welfare of the Sāsana ultimately rests on our own shoulders, not on some state ministry or ecclesiastical council. Just as the health of the body depends on the vitality of its cells, so the strength of the Sāsana ultimately devolves on ourselves, the cells in the living organism of Buddhism.

In this article I want to focus on one particular constituency of Buddhists in present day Sri Lanka, the Bhikkhu Saṅgha, the Order of Monks. I intend to examine, albeit briefly, the problems it faces and its prospects for the future. This task is especially critical because of the central role the Saṅgha plays in guiding the destiny of the Sāsana, and it is clear that if the Saṅgha does not learn to deal with the momentous forces inundating present-day society, the future will see it increasingly relegated to the sidelines.

Buddhist tradition meticulously defines the mutual duties of Saṅgha and laity and these roles form the warp and woof of the Sāsana. The monks are to uphold the teaching by study, practice, preaching, and moral example; the lay people, to support the monks by offering them the four requisites of robes, food, lodging and medicines. This intimate relationship between the two communities has provided a stable basis for the persistence of the Sāsana through the centuries. Despite the fluctuations of Buddhist history in Sri Lanka, which at times had sunk so low that even a proper Saṅgha could not be found, whenever Buddhism thrived the relationship between the monastic order and the laity has been its lifeblood. This relationship of mutual assistance, however, found its supporting matrix in a stable agrarian society with clearly defined social roles and a lifestyle governed by common religious and ethical norms. That is precisely what has altered so radically today. A global culture, driven by exponential technological innovation and a relentless free-market economy, has made its presence felt in every corner of this land, challenging every obstacle to its dominance. In consequence, the entire social order has been shaken by upheavals that reach from the halls of economic and political power right through to the most remote villages and temples.

This modernistic onslaught does not limit itself to mere external triumphs but reaches through to the most private places in our lives: our values, world-views, and even our sense of personal identity. The result, for the ordinary Buddhist, has been a profound disorientation, a feeling of being stranded in a strange landscape where the old familiar reference points no longer hold. Looking back, we see a past of comfortable certainties that we can never recapture; looking ahead, a future that looks increasingly unpredictable. But amidst the confusion of the present, the Dhamma still appears as a stable reference point that can provide clear answers to our pressing questions and relief from existential stress.

This brings us right to the crux of our problem: the problem of relevance, of conveying the timeless message of the teaching in a language that can address the difficult, unique, complex problems we face navigating our way through the post-modern world. The most critical challenge facing the Sāsana today is that of surviving in this 'new world order' and not merely of surviving institutionally, in name and form, but of contributing to the recovery of universal human values, of helping countless men and women find a way beyond the intellectual and moral abyss. It is precisely here that the role of the Saṅgha becomes so vitally important, for it is the monks (and, I dare say, the nuns as well) who should be capable of offering a convincing refuge to 'a world gone mad'—a vision of basic sanity, selfless goodness, and serenity amidst the storms of greed, conflict, and violence. Yet it is just on this point that we face a gaping chasm: namely, that the Saṅgha today seems hardly equipped to respond to such a challenge.

What is needed most urgently, in my view, is not a reinforcement of Buddhist religious identity or a governmental policy that gives 'pride of place to Buddhism.' Nor will the construction of more Buddha images and the daily broadcasting of *pirit* chanting over the loudspeakers give the Sāsana the infusion of fresh blood it so badly needs. What is required are monks and nuns of intelligence, insight and sensitivity who can demonstrate, by their lives and characters, the spiritually ennobling and elevating power of the Dhamma. To produce monastics of such calibre is not easy, yet such a task cannot be left to chance. It will require, above all, deep-rooted changes in the entire system of monastic recruitment and education, and thus will call for serious thought and careful planning on the part of the Saṅgha elders. The task is not one to be taken at all lightly; for one can say in all truth that nothing less is at stake than the future of Buddhism in this country.

Just as the Sri Lankan government has recently reviewed the whole system of secular education in this country with the aim of reforming educational policy, a similar reformation will have to be introduced right at the heart of the Saṅgha. If one compares the system of instruction in the Buddhist monasteries with the curriculum of the Christian seminaries, the disparity is striking. In the seminaries the future priests and nuns are trained, not only in Latin, theology, and scripture, but in all the fields of modern knowledge they will need to play a leading role in today's world, including the critical and comparative study of religion. In the *piriven* or Buddhist monastic schools, so far as I can see, the young monks (never nuns!) are trained to become village priests capable of preserving a religious culture not very different from that of the sixteenth century. One can see the bizarre result when a monk educated in the *pirivena* system has to give a sermon to an audience that might include an astrophysicist, a psychiatrist, several computer analysts, and even some lay Buddhist scholars trained in the methods of critical scholarship. Is it any wonder that the listeners pass the time glancing idly at the ceiling or casting weary smiles at each other?

In what follows I will merely throw out a few random suggestions. A systematic programme would have to be worked out by those more directly involved in Saṅgha administration and the training of monks and nuns. I will speak about monks rather than nuns, since I am more familiar with their lifestyles and training. But corresponding changes should also be considered for the nuns; their status, education, and functions require drastic upgrading if Buddhism is to present a respectable face to a world moving rapidly towards complete gender equality.

For the monks, radical change might be needed at the very beginning—in the system of recruitment. The method of recruitment that currently prevails in the Saṅgha is the induction of young boys who are far from mature enough to make their own decisions. Often they are 'offered' to the Saṅgha by their parents as a way for the parents to earn merit. If the parents would sacrifice a youth who seems temperamentally inclined to the religious life, the ultimate effect such a system has on the Sāsana might be a positive one. Indeed, in the past it was usually 'the best and the brightest' who would be given to the monastery. Today, however, the child selected is too often the one who appears unlikely to succeed in worldly life: the mischief-maker, the maverick, the dullard.

I am aware that this system of childhood ordination is deeply entrenched in Sri Lankan Buddhist culture, and I would not propose abolishing it. Despite its faults, the system does have its positive points. For one thing, it enables the youngster to enter the path of renunciation before he has been exposed to the temptations of worldly life; thus from an early age it helps promote the inner purity and detachment needed to withstand the rigours of the monastic training. Another advantage is that it gives the young monk the opportunity to study the Dhamma and the textual languages (Pali and Sanskrit) while the mind is as yet fresh, open, receptive, and retentive. Thereby it conduces to the wide erudition which is one of the traditional hallmarks of the cultured monk.

However, while I would not go so far as to suggest abolishing adolescent recruitment, I do think the Saṅgha could vastly improve its ranks by imposing more stringent criteria for admission. One measure that might be adopted at once is a longer probationary period before granting the novice ordination. For example, it might be made mandatory for boys intent on being ordained to live at training centres as lay postulants for a minimum of two or three years before they are considered eligible for novice ordination. This would give the Saṅgha elders an opportunity to observe them more closely in a wide variety of situations and to screen out those who seem unsuitable for the monk's life. If this is not practicable, then some other selective procedure might be applied. Whatever method is chosen, the standards of selection should be fairly rigorous—though not inhumane—and the elders should not hesitate to turn away unfit applicants. For one thing has become too painfully obvious to all concerned Buddhists alike, and also to non-Buddhists (both residents of Sri Lanka and foreigners) who judge the Dhamma by the conduct of its followers:

far too many youngsters are being draped in saffron robes who do not deserve to wear them. Such misfits only sully the good name of the Saṅgha and of Buddhism itself.

More rigorous screening of candidates for ordination is, however, only a preliminary measure aimed at sealing off the Saṅgha from those unsuited for the monkhood. What is equally essential is to offer those who do get ordained training programmes that will promote their wholesome, balanced development. This is truly a critical step, for if youngsters with the potential for the monk's life fail to receive proper training, they won't find fulfilment in the monastery, and if they don't find fulfilment, their future as monks will be in jeopardy. They will either become disillusioned with the Saṅgha and return to lay life, or from fear of the social stigma attached to disrobing, they may continue as monks in a perpetual state of frustration and discontent. This may explain why we see so many younger monks today involved in politics, business and other activities unworthy of their calling.

What is necessary above all is for the young monk to find meaning and happiness in his chosen path of life, a path that does not offer the immediate satisfactions available to his comrades who remain behind in the world. If so few monks today seem to show a real joy in the Dhamma, I suspect this is because the Dhamma is not being presented to them in a way that inspires joy. For the Dhamma to exercise a magnetic power that will draw the young monk ever deeper towards the heart of the holy life, it must address their needs and aspirations at a deep interior level. This means it has to be offered to them in a way that arouses an immediate, sincere, and spontaneous response.

Lay Buddhists often complain about a lack of discipline in the Saṅgha and appeal to the Saṅgha elders to impose stricter controls over their pupils. I do not want to slight the problem of poor discipline, and I agree that stricter enforcement of the Vinaya rules is essential, but I would also contend that poor discipline is more a symptom than a cause. What is primarily required is not so much stricter discipline as a far-reaching spiritual renewal that bubbles with vitality, and such a renewal cannot be instigated merely by imposing stricter disciplinary controls from above. This approach might even turn out to be counter-productive. If not conjoined with other measures designed to effect more fundamental changes in the quality of training it might turn the monastery into an open-door prison, with the monk's life made to feel like a lifetime prison sentence rather than a path to liberation. True discipline must be undertaken freely with understanding and appreciation, and this can come about only when one sees it as a source of joy and inner freedom, not as a clamp bringing fear and frustration.

If the Saṅgha is to rediscover its strength and vigour, it is necessary for those who receive ordination to find a meaningful role for themselves in their lives as monks. Such a role has to resolve two contrary demands. On the one side, it must remain faithful to the ancient ideals prescribed for the Saṅgha by the Buddha himself, ideals which express the governing purpose of the monastic vocation. On the other, it must respond to the fluid realities of life in the contemporary world, enabling the monk to feel he has a truly relevant role in relation to the wider community.

This last point is especially important. In present-day Sri Lankan society, as I explained earlier, tumultuous changes are taking place on every side, and one of their consequences is to place the monk in an ambiguous position, almost a 'double bind.' When he reviews his status from the standpoint of the Dhamma, he discovers himself to be, in theory at least, the paragon of Buddhist spirituality, a living representative of the Ariya Saṅgharatana, a 'field of merit for the world.' Yet, when he considers himself in relation to contemporary society, he finds himself to be deemed an anachronism, a relic from an earlier age: thus he finds his status and function stamped with profoundly disturbing question marks. These contradictory messages can precipitate a state of unbearable inner tension. One outlet from this tension is to accede to the archaic status of the traditionalist and thus become a spokesman of rigid conservatism, stubbornly resistant to change. The other outlet moves in the opposite direction: towards rebellion against all authority, including that of the Dhamma itself.

Precisely this, I believe, underlies the dilemma that confronts so many young, capable, intelligent and earnest monks once they graduate from novice status and face the prospect of a lifetime commitment to the Saṅgha. If one listens with one's inner ear, one can hear their questions, rarely expressed, hanging in the air: "Are we to pass our lives as mere symbols on which others can hang their sentimental piety, pushed to the sidelines in a secularized country that is running in blind pursuit of economic growth? Are we to spend our days marginalized, engaged in a ritualized routine of endless alms offerings, *pirit* recitations and *poojas*, functioning as religious decorations in the alcoves of peoples' lives, far removed from 'the real action'? Are we to go on preaching sermons in which we're expected to repeat only what the listeners have already heard a hundred times before, merely to tickle their sense of piety?" The rebellious and recalcitrant behaviour of so many younger monks, I believe, should be read as a silent protest against this fate, a way of saying: "Let us not be fashioned into somebody else's image of what we should be. Let our inalienable humanity not be sacrificed at the altar of social expectations."

If such messages are read correctly, we would see that the appropriate response should not be one of indignation but of compassion and a heartfelt desire to help. Those who wish to help the Saṅgha must be less quick to criticize and condemn. Instead, they should be ready to make a genuine effort to understand the aspirations of these younger monks and help them find a context giving meaning and value to their lives, confirming the correctness of their decision to ordain. The most important steps will have to be taken by the Saṅgha elders, who will need to review the whole process of monastic training. But one point should be clearly understood above all else. The quest for a meaningful role in relation to present-day society should never be used by the monk to justify adopting a lifestyle that betrays his special calling. This means that the monk must not seek to make his mark on society as a political activist caught in the interminable conflicts of party politics, nor should he be turned into a tonsured social worker or a specialist in worldly arts and sciences. The defining characteristic of the monk's life is renunciation, and this should never be undermined by a concern to find a relevant role in society. If properly undertaken, the life of renunciation is sufficiently relevant on its own: a perpetual reminder of where the true good for human beings is to be found.

Perhaps the best way to gain an insight into the kind of changes needed in the system of monastic training is to pose the question: "What is the role the monk should fulfil once he reaches maturity?" And this leads on to the next question: "What is the proper aim and purpose of the monk's life?" A meaningful programme of monastic education, which is at the same time a programme of monastic formation, should be formulated as answers to these questions.

When we look at the whole situation of Sri Lankan monasticism, we see that with a few noteworthy exceptions the monastic training in this country is sadly deficient. What underlies this deficiency is the lack of a clear conception of a monk's special vocation. Admittedly, in a country where some seventy percent of the population is Buddhist, monks are needed to cater to the religious needs of the people. But, we have to ask, does this justify the almost complete neglect of the unique system of spiritual training prescribed by the Buddha for the Saṅgha? Did he intend the Order to consist entirely of ritual specialists and cultural custodians, and to postpone the treading of his path to liberation to some future existence? To arrive at a correct conception of the goal of monastic training we have to pierce through the established social norms and popular conventions that govern Saṅgha life today, not stopping until we have recovered the original conception of the monastic calling sounded by the Buddha himself. It is this conception that must be drawn out from the massive volumes of Buddhist scriptures, rejuvenated with a breath of fresh air, and placed before the monk's inner eye as the real reason for his vocation.

It is towards the realization of this ideal that the monastic training should be directed. To work out the details of this is a task that must be given a great amount of careful and intelligent thought. Here I can only speak in generalities. The first, and overriding, generality is to recognize that the primary purpose behind the monastic path is personal growth and spiritual transformation in the direction pointed to by the Buddha: growth towards Nibbāna, final liberation from suffering: transformation guided by the clear-cut steps of the Noble Eightfold Path. Stated so baldly, however, this expression of the goal may be too abstract, too remote from the everyday concerns and aptitudes of a young monk who is just setting out in his training. So let us put it differently, into a language that is more immediate and concrete. The purpose of the monk's life is to train the mind, to purify the mind, to mould the mind in the direction of liberation from greed, aversion and delusion; to implant in the mind the purifying qualities of detachment, loving kindness, compassion and wisdom, and to share these aspirations with others. Whatever mode of expression is chosen is of secondary importance. What is of primary importance is a clear recognition that the guiding purpose of the monk's life should be the spiritual growth and self-transformation of the individual monk, and all other aspects of the training should be subsumed under this.

To follow through such a suggestion will require that the Saṅgha rediscover a discipline that has almost been lost, namely, the practice of meditation. Meditation, the methodical development of tranquillity and insight, was the original lifeblood of the renunciant life, yet for most monks today it has become only a word, perhaps a topic of sermons and seminars, or a ten-minute silence in the daily devotional service. In my view, a monastic life that does not centre upon the practice of meditation is merely a shadow of the genuine monastic calling, an evasion of the task entrusted to the Saṅgha by the Awakened One.

I am aware that not all who go forth are capable of a life of full-time meditation, and I certainly would not propose that all monks be obliged to follow such a lifestyle. Few in fact will be able to find happiness in a life devoted solely to contemplation, and throughout its long history the Saṅgha has had the flexibility necessary to accommodate members of diverse skills and temperaments. Within the Saṅgha there must be administrators, scholars, teachers, preachers, social advisers, counsellors, ritual specialists, and others, and the monastic training must prepare monks to fill these varied niches— what the Christian monastic tradition calls the 'active vocations.' The more intellectually inclined monks must also be exposed to the various branches of modern knowledge which will enable him to establish bridges between the Dhamma and the intellectual advance of humankind: philosophy and psychology, comparative religion, history, literature and art. But for the monastic life to remain faithful to its original calling, the practice of meditation must be restored to its rightful place: not at the fringes but at the centre.

The meditative life, however, must also be integrated with a wider sense of the universal, social message of the Dhamma; otherwise it can become self-enclosed and stagnant. In fact, one of the most regrettable turns taken in the historical evolution of Theravada Buddhism, not confined to Sri Lanka but quite pervasive here, has been the sharp division of the Saṅgha into meditating forest monks and non-meditating town-and-village monks. This fissure has deprived both groups of the healthy balance needed to make the Dhamma a spiritually nourishing force both in this country and in the wider world. The forest monks live almost entirely aloof from society, and thus, except by silent example, rarely contribute their meditative insights and refined moral sensitivity to resolving the profound ethical and spiritual dilemmas confronting the broader human community. Responsibility for upholding the social and communal dimension of Buddhist life devolves on the active town-and-village monks, who are only too prone to assume the role of custodians of a particular social and ethnic consciousness.

Today it isn't only Buddhism in Sri Lanka that is at the crossroads, but the Saṅgha as well, and the direction it takes will determine the future destiny of the Sāsana. The challenges of our age are unique and unprecedented, and they require intelligent responses governed by the wide, profound perspectives of the Dhamma. Mechanical repetition of the formulas of the past simply won't work. If the Saṅgha continues to adhere unthinkingly to established, self-stultifying structures and does not take up the urgent task of internal criticism and renewal, it will be condemning itself, and Sri Lankan Buddhism, to irrelevance. For both alert lay Buddhists and the world community as a whole, it will be just another antiquated institution struggling to hang on to its privileges. Today a cloud of moral and spiritual confusion hangs over humankind, a cloud that grows increasingly darker and thicker. It is the true task of the Saṅgha, and of Buddhism itself, to help dispel this confusion with the Buddha's own boundless wisdom and compassion. But if the Saṅgha is to rise up to this challenge, it must be ready to make some radical changes in its own system of recruitment, training, and practice. True, this will be a difficult task, but it is one that must be met.

From Facing the Future: Four Essays on the Social Relevance of Buddhism, The Wheel Publication No. 438/400, 2000. Originally published in the 1998 Centenary Issue of The Buddhist: Journal of the Young Men's Buddhist Association, Colombo.

52. PROMOTING BUDDHISM IN EUROPE

Prologue

My own personal acquaintance with Venerable Dhammanisanthi was limited to a few meetings mostly in the early 1980s, but I always felt a close bond with him through his life's guiding aim, the dissemination of Buddhism in Germany. Though I am not German myself, for twenty years I was closely associated with the great German scholar-monk Venerable Nyanaponika Mahathera, and I continue to live on at the Forest Hermitage established by his teacher, Venerable Nyanatiloka Mahathera, who was also German. Both these illustrious theras were always keenly interested in the spread of Buddhism in their native country. Though they had left Germany to lead the monastic life here in Sri Lanka, they worked with single-minded devotion to make the Buddha's teachings known throughout the world, and the many writings that flowed from their pens still bring to many readers in the West the Buddha's message of wisdom and inner peace.

In this respect they shared a common vision with Venerable Dhammanisanthi, which they expressed by their support for the German Dharmaduta Society. Earlier, when he was still known as Asoka Weeraratne and served as the Society's general secretary, Venerable Nyanatiloka was the first patron of the Society and Venerable Nyanaponika an advisor. I still recall that before he left for Germany in 1982 to take up residence at the Berlin Buddhist Vihara, Venerable Dhammanisanthi came to the Forest Hermitage to meet Venerable Nyanaponika and spent several hours with him discussing prospects for the spread of Buddhism in Germany. The discussion presented an interesting contrast between Venerable Dhammanisanthi's effervescent optimism and Venerable Nyanaponika's customary restraint and realism.

The topic of this seminar, "The Necessity for Promoting Buddhism in Europe," is in a sense very timely, as the opportunity for disseminating Buddhism in the West is much more ample today than it was fifty years ago when the German Dharmaduta Society was born. At the same time, however, we should not assume that Buddhism is barely known in Europe and has to be introduced almost from scratch. To the contrary, in the past two decades public awareness of Buddhism in the West has increased sharply. In many Western countries today Buddhism is the fastest growing religion. In North America, Western Europe, and Australia-New Zealand, hundreds of Buddhist centres have sprung up almost overnight, offering teachings and meditation retreats even in remote regions. Thus the challenge we face is not that of discussing how to introduce Buddhism to Europe as though it were an utterly unfamiliar creature, but of discovering how to promote the healthy growth of a Buddhism already sending down roots into European soil.

I will deal with my topic in three major parts. *First*, I will present a short survey of the historical development of Buddhism in Europe. This will necessarily be oversimplified and thus inadequate, but my aim is not so much to lay out all the facts as to show how Buddhism has arrived at its present stage of development in the West. *Second*, I will raise the question why Buddhism, at just this particular time, is exerting such a strong appeal on Westerners. Then, in the *third* place, I will briefly discuss a few special problems we face in trying to make our own Theravada form of Buddhism accessible to the West as a living and relevant tradition.

I. Historical Overview

I divide the history of the Western engagement with Buddhism into three major phases. These phases are not totally discrete, for they intersect and overlap, but the threefold division provides a useful way of determining general trends.

Phase I consisted in the academic study of Buddhist texts, aimed at discerning the broad contours of Buddhist history and doctrine. This project took place during the peak of the colonial period, when European countries were busy subjugating Asian peoples and incorporating their nations into their hungry empires. In many cases European interest in Buddhism was bound up with the Christian missionary enterprise of converting the native populations to Christianity.

Although reports about Asian Buddhist beliefs and practices had been drifting back to Europe since the thirteenth century, a clear picture of Buddhism as a unitary whole did not take shape in Europe until the middle of the nineteenth century, just a little more than 150 years ago. Before then, the sundry reports that had reached scholars in Europe were generally haphazard, inaccurate, and conjectural, if not utterly fantastic. The first person to comprehend Buddhism as a unitary tradition and establish its historical origins was the brilliant French philologist Eugène Burnouf. Burnouf had studied Pali, Sanskrit, and Tibetan manuscripts that had been sent to him in Paris from the East. Based on these texts, with barely no other clues, he wrote his 600-page tome, *Introduction to the History of Indian Buddhism* (1844), in which he traced in detail Indian Buddhist history and surveyed its doctrines and texts. Though later generations of scholars have greatly expanded upon Burnouf's work and filled in many missing pieces, they regard as essentially accurate the outline of Indian Buddhism he proposed in his groundbreaking study.

In the decades following Burnouf, there appeared throughout Europe a galaxy of brilliant scholars who opened up the treasures locked away in all the different branches of Buddhism. These scholars fall into three main schools. The scholars of the "Anglo-Germanic School" focused on the Pali tradition. Their work emanated from the Pali Text Society, founded by T.W. Rhys Davids, and their ranks included Caroline Rhys Davids, Oldenberg, Woodward, Hare, and Horner; the Danish scholars Trenckner, Fausboll, and Anderson; and the Swede Helmer Smith. The "Franco-Belgian School" investigated Indian Buddhism both Hinayana and Mahayana in Sanskrit, Tibetan, and Chinese texts; its luminaries were de la Vallée Poussin, Sylvain Levy, and Lamotte. The "Russian School"—represented by Stcherbatsky, Rosenberg, and Obermiller—concentrated on scholastic Indian Buddhism as preserved especially in Tibetan texts. Although these scholars usually remained reticent about their own religious beliefs, by collecting Asian manuscripts, publishing modern editions of these texts, and providing translations and scholarly studies of Buddhist thought, they laid the indispensable foundation stone for the spread of the Dhamma in the West, namely, access to the original Buddhist sources.

The academic study of Buddhism initiated by these pioneers has continued through to the present time, despite the setback of two world wars and frequent shortages in funding. In Western universities and institutes, scholars map in ever finer details and with broader sweep the entire Buddhist heritage—from Sri Lanka to Mongolia, from Gandhara to Japan. Thus what I call "Phase I" in the history of Western Buddhism is not so much a temporary stage superceded by its successors as a preparation for the further evolution of Buddhism in its Western setting.

Phase II in the European encounter with Buddhism I shall call "elite appropriation." By this, I mean the adoption of Buddhism as a living creed by an increasing number of intellectuals, writers, artists, and professionals. In the German-speaking world the catalyst for the transition from the mere academic investigation of Buddhism to its active appropriation was the philosopher Arthur Schopenhauer. Schopenhauer published the first edition of his philosophical masterpiece, *The World as Will and Representation*, in 1819, before he had come across reliable accounts of Buddhist thought. However, his philosophical intuitions showed such striking parallels to the Dhamma that several decades later, when Schopenhauer did gain access to accurate material on Buddhism, he at once recognized the affinity of his own thought to the Buddha's doctrine. Thus, in the second edition of his book, he hailed Buddhism as "the most perfect" of all the world's religions. Such was his admiration for the Buddha that he kept a small statue of the Master on his mantle alongside a bust of his philosophical hero, Immanuel Kant.

Schopenhauer did not become a Buddhist himself, which would have been almost unthinkable in the Europe of his day, but his writings had a profound impact on later European thinkers and guided many to the Dhamma. At least three major figures owed their discovery of Buddhism to Schopenhauer's influence: the Austrian Indologist K.E. Neumann, who translated the Dīgha and Majjhima Nikāyas and other Pali texts into German; the Bavarian judge George Grimm; and the Berlin homeopath Paul Dahlke. The last named pair, through their writings and promotional work, became the two leading proponents of Buddhism in Germany during the early part of the twentieth century. Their writings did not simply analyse Buddhism in terms of objective, impersonal categories, but tried to explain it from the inside, as experienced by one who had made the personal leap of faith.

In the English-speaking world, the primary impetus for the adoption of Buddhism by educated Westerners came from Sir Edwin Arnold's inspirational poem on the Buddha's life, *The Light of Asia*. Arnold depicted the Buddha as a figure of heroic stature whose personality combined deep compassion for all humanity with a masterly capacity for rational thought. These two characteristics dovetailed perfectly with the intellectual milieu of the period and aroused in Arnold's readers a new respect for the Buddha and interest in his teachings. Though conservative Christians were indignant at the poem's success, the British intelligentsia of the period were liberal enough not to feel constrained by Christianity's claims to sole possession of the truth. The Theosophical movement, founded by Madame Blavatsky and Henry Steele Olcott, also gave Buddhism a profile in the Anglo-American world. While their interpretation of Buddhism as a popular expression of esoteric wisdom bordered on the chimerical, the Theosophists helped to make Buddhism fashionable among those attracted to alternative ways of thought.

Inspired by the Dhamma, a few adventurous spirits, not content with mere book knowledge, left their homelands to travel to the East to learn Buddhism at its sources. Others like Childers and Rhys Davids, working in colonial administrations in Asia, already had access to native authorities on the Dhamma. By the turn of the century several Westerners took the decisive step of coming to the East to enter the Sangha. The pioneers in this development were the Englishman Allen Bennett, who became Venerable Ānanda Metteyya in Burma (1901), and Anton Gueth, who became Venerable Nyanatiloka (1903). Though Venerable Ānanda Metteyya later disrobed after a tentative mission to Britain, Venerable Nyanatiloka settled permanently in Sri Lanka, where in 1911 he founded Island Hermitage as a monastery especially for Western monks.

Within Europe, starting early in the twentieth century, Buddhist societies began to sprout, Buddhist journals commenced publication, and numerous books on Buddhism, of varying degrees of authenticity, attempted to bridge the gap between classical Buddhism and the Western intellectual heritage. During this phase of "elite appropriation" most proponents of Buddhism favoured the Pali tradition, as being far closer to the Buddha's original teachings than the baffling and ornate Mahayana sutras. What these thinkers emphasized in Buddhism was its rationality and realism, its ethical purity, its tolerance, its non-dogmatic approach to truth, and its compatibility with modern science. In this phase, with a few exceptions, the meditative, communal, and devotional aspects of Buddhism were left quietly on the sidelines. In other words, theory prevailed over practice.

Phase III in the spread of Buddhism in the West began roughly in the 1960s and continues through to the present. This third phase might be described as the popularization of Buddhism. During this phase, Buddhism comes to exert its appeal on an increasing number of people of different lifestyles and its following proliferates rapidly. At the beginning of this phase Buddhism was largely a counter-cultural phenomenon, adopted by those in rebellion against the crass materialism and technocratic obsessions of modern society: hippies, acid heads, disaffected university students, artists, writers, and anarchists. But as these youthful rebels gradually became integrated into the mainstream, they brought their Buddhism with them. Today Buddhism is espoused not only by those in the alternative culture, but by businessmen, physicists, computer programmers, housewives, real-estate agents, even by sports stars, movie actors, and rock musicians. Perhaps several hundred thousand Europeans have adopted Buddhism in one or another of its different forms, while many more quietly incorporate Buddhist practices into their daily lives. The presence of large Asian Buddhist communities in the West also enhances the visibility of the Dhamma. Thousands of books on Buddhism are now available, dealing with the teachings at both scholarly and popular levels, while Buddhist magazines and journals expand their circulation each year. Buddhist influences subtly permeate various disciplines: philosophy and ecology, psychology and health care, the arts and literature, even Christian theology. Indeed, already three years ago *Time* magazine devoted a full-length cover story to the spread of Buddhism in America, and at least five books on the subject are in print.

The transition in Western Buddhism from Phase II to Phase III was facilitated by two main factors. One was the increasing number of Asian Buddhist teachers who travelled to the West—Theravada bhikkhus, Japanese Zen masters, Tibetan lamas—either to give lectures and conduct retreats, or to settle there permanently and establish Buddhist centres. The second factor was the return to the West of the young Westerners who had trained in Asia in the late 1960s and early 1970s, and now came back to their home countries to spread the Dhamma. From the mid-1980s on we see even a new sub-phase of Phase III, or perhaps an incipient Phase IV: the emergence of a generation of

Western Buddhist teachers who have never been to Asia but have received their full training in the West.

What is characteristic of Western Buddhism in Phase III, in distinction from the earlier phases, is the focus on Buddhist practice, especially the practice of meditation. In this phase it is not the academic study of Buddhist texts and doctrines that dominates (as in Phase I), or the attempt to interpret the Dhamma through the prism of Western thought (as in Phase II), but the appropriation of Buddhism as a practice that can bring deep transformations in one's innermost being as well as in the conduct of everyday life. This does not necessarily mean that Buddhist practice is being taken up in accordance with canonical or traditional Asian models, nor that it is pursued to attain Nibbana in the sense upheld by classical Buddhist doctrine. Often Western Buddhists give their own twist to Buddhist concepts, sometimes in ways that depart drastically from canonical standards and from an Asian standpoint might border on "heresy." But in Phase III, Buddhism is viewed as in some sense a path to awakening, a way that brings deep understanding of the mind and makes accessible new dimensions of being. Hence at this stage Buddhism becomes a means of spiritual transformation through direct experience, through insights not arrived at by mere conceptual reflection.

In Phase III, we also find the arrival of various types of Asian Buddhism, which peacefully coexist, pursuing their own growth and cooperating with each other to secure common aims. With the passage from Phase II to Phase III a noticeable shift takes place in the type of Buddhism generally adopted by Western Buddhists. In Phase II, Pali Buddhism was dominant, though I must stress that this adherence to the Pali heritage did *not* entail a commitment to any form of Theravada Buddhism as practised in Asian lands. In fact, the elite Buddhists often looked upon Asian Theravada as a degeneration from the pristine canonical doctrine, which they believed was a unique possession of their own. But with the rise of Phase III the focus of attraction shifts away from the Pali tradition: first to Zen Buddhism in the 1960s and 1970s; and then to Tibetan Vajrayana Buddhism in the 1980s and 1990s. Further, new types of Buddhism come onto the scene, schools peculiar to the West, such as Thich Nhat Hanh's Order of Interbeing (based in France, but with a strong American chapter), the Arya Maitreya Mandala (centred in Germany), and the Friends of the Western Buddhist Order (based in Britain, but with several Continental chapters). These are partly syncretistic, partly innovative attempts to create new styles of Buddhist practice conformable to the Western temperament. Also the age range of Buddhist followers varies between the schools. Today in Germany most followers of the Pali tradition are in their 50s and 60s, while the followers of Zen and Tibetan Buddhism are in their 30s and 40s. This development is critically important for us, as followers of the Theravada, to understand, and I will therefore return to it later.

II. The Western Receptivity to Buddhism

At this point, I want to raise the question: How are we to understand the surge of interest in Buddhism among Westerners in recent years? How do we account for the eagerness with which so many today are ready to explore the Dhamma and often to deeply embrace it? It is necessary to address this question in order to begin to see the needs that we must fulfil as we try to make our own contribution to the spread of the Dhamma in Europe.

I think the answer to this question unfolds in roughly two distinct stages, corresponding to the last two phases in the Western adoption of Buddhism that I spoke of just before. During Phase II, "the phase of elite appropriation," intellectuals were drawn to Buddhism because it filled a vacuum that had been growing ever wider in Europe since the seventeenth century. This vacuum was the absence of any comprehensive body of wisdom teachings that could offer a key to the deeper meaning of human existence. The responsibility for shedding light on the meaning of existence had traditionally been assigned to philosophy, but from the seventeenth century onwards philosophy came to renounce this task in favour of other concerns. Besides, such guidance that philosophy did offer, as in Spinoza's *Ethics*, was usually embedded in systems of thought so subtle and complex that few people could understand them.

Of course, Christianity too staked out for itself a claim to hold the key to the riddle of existence, but the main thrust of orthodox Christianity has not been to show the way to wisdom. Its purpose is to offer the prospect of an eternal afterlife in heaven through faith in God and Christ the Saviour, and it was just such faith that was coming into question. Further, Christianity's own record as a defender of human values was far from impressive. Its legacy of crusades, inquisitions, forced conversions, and intolerance repelled rather than attracted ethically sensitive minds, while its alliance with the colonial regimes confirmed suspicions about its imperialistic designs. Moreover, as science strode boldly into one arena of knowledge after another, often in the face of staunch resistance from the Church, it discredited Christian claims to the infallibility of revelation. Thus for a growing number of independent thinkers the Christian religion had become irrelevant.

When translations of Buddhist texts and expositions of Buddhist thought began to appear in the late nineteenth century, they seemed to offer the West exactly what it was lacking: a system of spiritual wisdom that could give illumination and moral guidance yet did not demand unquestioning faith in theological dogmas. Instead, it rested its claims upon human reason and personal insight into fundamental truths and universal laws. The way Buddhism impinged on the Western mind during this period reveals both the strength and weakness in the Western perception of Buddhism. The strength lay in a deep and clear grasp of the doctrinal principles of the Dhamma, expressed in works that were utterly compelling in their insights, logic, and literary eloquence. The weakness was the understanding of Buddhism as primarily a rational, ideational system, to replace the tottering belief system of the Christian churches. Another limitation was that Buddhism in this phase still appealed mainly to the educated elite and thus could attract only those astute enough to break away from the cultural and religious mainstream, which was still predominantly Christian.

For the transition to Phase III to take place, that is, for Buddhism to spread more widely through the general population, certain additional conditions were necessary, and these only became sufficiently widespread in the second half of the twentieth century. One was the triumph of liberal democracy over autocratic political systems. Under the heading of democracy we must include not only political democracy, but also the democracy of the mind, an openness to new ways of thought and tolerance for viewpoints that differ radically from those of one's own intellectual heritage. This openness was encouraged by a partial change in the attitude of the Christian churches towards other faiths, which in the West after the Second Vatican Council (1963–65) swung towards greater respect and tolerance for non-Christian religions.

A second preparatory factor was a fair degree of economic affluence, which freed Europeans from excessive concern with material security and gave them the leisure to explore new avenues of thought. The rise of the consumerist society also helped them see the limitations to material development as a final solution to our quest for happiness.

A third factor was the relatively high standard of liberal education established in the 1960s, enabling a large proportion of young people to attend the university. Higher education exposed them to multiple viewpoints in all the domains of human knowledge, and also trained them to think critically and deeply about new ideas.

A fourth preparatory factor was improved means of transportation and communication, which facilitated contacts between East and West. Now curious Westerners could easily travel to the East to experience Buddhism first hand in its own native setting, while Buddhist teachers from Asia could move West to propagate the Dhamma.

The fifth factor, following naturally from the fourth, was the actual arrival in the West of Buddhist teachers, both Asians and Westerners trained in Asia. These teachers brought Buddhism as a dynamic faith that they embodied in their lives through years of serious training.

While the above five factors constituted the necessary conditions for Buddhism to become accessible to a sizable number of Europeans, they are not a sufficient explanation for the rapid escalation of Western interest in

Buddhism. To pinpoint the decisive cause for this phenomenon, I must refer back to the vacuum or void that had opened up right beneath the feet of European civilization, that is, the absence of a solid, authoritative spiritual tradition that could give guidance in the mastery of life. In the late nineteenth and early twentieth centuries this void was acutely felt only by the more discerning Western minds, disenchanted with both doctrinaire Christianity and economic materialism. Ordinary people were somehow able to balance their ancestral Christian faith with a bright optimism about the coming Golden Age, to be achieved through science and technology.

By the late 1950s, however, the picture had drastically changed. After two world wars and a prolonged cold war that threatened the whole world with thermonuclear destruction, countless people found their trust in the intrinsic goodness of human nature crumble into dust. Such horrors as the Nazi Holocaust and the Hiroshima atom bomb not only undermined faith in a benevolent God guiding the whole creation, but also brought to light the dangers in mere rationality not illuminated by a higher wisdom and staunch commitment to ethics. The most brilliant minds of the West, relying on the rational intellect, had twice plunged the whole world into barbaric irrationality, with death tolls numbering in the tens of millions. Now, with even more lethal weapons of destruction at hand, they threatened to do so again. Thus the void that sensitive nineteenth century thinkers had seen on the horizon had expanded until it had swallowed up almost everyone. And not only had it expanded, but for many it had acquired a sharp and compelling urgency that could not be quenched by any system of ideas, however noble. What they needed was a programme of action, which in many cases meant a deep personal engagement in the spiritual quest.

At the same time that the fear of nuclear war cast long shadows over the entire globe, unprecedented material affluence in the West brought into easy reach the comforts, conveniences, and sensory delights that earlier generations had only dreamt about. Yet while this consumerist paradise mesmerized many (and still continues to do so), at least a few people "with little dust in their eyes" realized that such mundane pleasures could bring no lasting peace to the heart. At this point, for such spiritually sensitive Westerners, the message embedded in the Four Noble Truths was no longer a splendid system of ideas, to be admired in the comfort of an armchair. The message had become, rather, a medicine for curing a terrible disease, the disease of suffering, and the one sensible thing to be done with it, as with any medicine, was to take it. Hence for the Buddhists in Phase III of Western Buddhism, the Dhamma presented itself as a path of practice pivoting on the training and mastery of the mind. As teachers and centres became available, growing numbers of Westerners took up the practice eagerly, ready to follow it wherever it might lead.

But Buddhism offered not only a method of mind training that could bring inner peace and deeper self-knowledge, it also fulfilled another profound need of the Western soul. As part of its deep intellectual heritage, Western civilization was committed to the idea that human happiness largely depends on the reformation of the social order in ways that eliminate political tyranny, economic oppression, and social injustice. The commitment to this premise was responsible for the rise of democracy in the West, as well as for less successful experiments with various forms of socialism. However, the experience of the nineteenth and twentieth centuries had shown that without some code of ethical guidance, mere aspirations for freedom and democracy could easily give birth to their opposites. Thus the French Revolution, launched under the motto of "liberty, equality, and fraternity," ended up with the guillotine. The Bolshevik Revolution, with its promise of a "dictatorship of the proletariat," culminated in the Soviet police state. Western idealists saw in Buddhism the foundations for a lofty social ethic devoted to world peace, social justice, and ecological sanity, yet internally protected by its moral code against the deformities to which secular political utopianism was prone.

To understand the appeal of Buddhism to many present-day Westerners, another factor we must consider is the general breakdown of community in modern Western culture. With increasing industrialization and urbanization, the older human-scale social structures that allowed each person to find a meaningful place in the whole gave way to huge, monstrous institutions that reduced individuals to mere cogs in an impersonal social order. People have come to feel isolated, alienated, cut off from the bonds of social solidarity, trapped in a system that fuels ruthless individualism. These destructive values have provoked a widespread psychological crisis marked by chronic stress, anxiety, and depression. The escape routes people seek are promiscuous sex, violent entertainment, alcoholism, and drugs; but these, of course, do not offer a real solution.

When Buddhism arrived on the scene it seemed to offer a counterweight to the loneliness and isolation so many people felt even in their overcrowded cities. For one thing, it stressed such values as universal love, compassion, cooperation, and altruism, half-forgotten ideals of the Christian legacy. But just as importantly, it ushered in a new sense of community. As Buddhist groups sought their own organizational forms, they gradually evolved towards the model of the Buddhist centre, where fellow practitioners meet regularly in a spirit of friendship to practise and study the Dhamma together, usually under the guidance of a teacher. Many Buddhist societies now have residential facilities where the more dedicated members live either temporarily or permanently. Some have urban centres accessible to people during the working week, and country centres some distance away to which members can resort for longer meditation retreats.

As I mentioned earlier, when Buddhism in the West enters Phase III, a shift occurs away from the Pali tradition towards Zen and Tibetan Vajrayana. One explanation for this might be the more attractive, more exotic surfaces of these schools of Buddhism; another factor might be the charismatic personalities of their teachers, the Zen masters and Tibetan lamas. But such an explanation is not complete. The main reason these traditions have gained in popularity over the Theravada is, I believe, because within their fold the lineage of meditation practice has been kept more alive than in mainstream Theravada. Certainly in the Pali Canon the Buddha repeatedly emphasizes the urgency of meditation above all else, and this message does live on in small pockets of earnest Theravadin practitioners throughout southern Asia. However, the European Buddhists of the older generations had set the pace by viewing Pali Buddhism largely in rationalistic terms, as a lofty ethic and impressive system of thought. Almost as if to confirm this, the few representatives of Asian Theravada to settle in the West have tended to present Buddhism largely in doctrinal and ethical terms. Rarely do they exhibit the same degree of spiritual vitality as the Mahayana and Vajrayana masters. Since present-day Western seekers are looking for a practice they can incorporate into their lives, not just a system of ideas they can admire and discuss, they naturally feel the appeal of the alternative forms of Buddhism—Zen, Vajrayana, and new Western Buddhist schools—over the Theravada.

This, however, is not to say that a meditation tradition rooted in the Theravada is lacking in the West. A number of Westerners who had come to Asian countries years ago to practise under qualified teachers later returned to the West to teach and establish Buddhist centres. But what we find, as an interesting development, is that often such Western teachers of Theravada-based meditation do not consider themselves adherents of Theravada Buddhism in its doctrinal sense. Instead, explicitly or implicitly, they distance themselves from Asian Theravada and call their style of Buddhism "the Vipassana tradition" or "the practice of mindful awareness." While they have evolved a rigorous system of training, they often lift Vipassana meditation out from its setting in Buddhist faith and doctrine, presenting it almost as an autonomous discipline of psychological insight and self-awareness. This is certainly a weak spot in the Western approach to the Dhamma, for the religious and philosophical dimensions of classical Buddhism are necessary for insight meditation to lead to its real goal, "the taintless liberation of the mind." Neglect of the textual and doctrinal side of Buddhism can result in a diluted, shoddy understanding of the Dhamma. But the stripped-down style of practice—non-religious, non-doctrinal, non-monastic insight meditation—is the dominant mode in which Westerners are taking up Theravada Buddhism. This development might induce us to examine our own tradition more closely to ask ourselves why the Dhamma is being approached in such a partial fashion, through such a pick-and-choose policy, instead of being embraced as an organic whole.

III. The Challenge of Bringing Theravada to the West

This brings me to the third major division of my talk, the special challenges we face in transmitting Theravada Buddhism to the West. When I ponder this issue, the question that immediately lodges itself in my mind is this: "What exactly is the type of Theravada Buddhism that we wish to spread?" For one thing, as I mentioned above, it is not merely texts and ideas that Westerners are looking for, not merely the Buddhism of the books. Books are certainly needed to introduce people to the Dhamma, to give them material for study and reflection. The point I wish to make is not that literature on Buddhism is dispensable, but that it is insufficient. For the Dhamma to take deep root in people's hearts, it must come to them, not between the covers of a book, but in living, breathing persons who display the truth of the teaching in their lives.

Thus when I raise the question, "What type of Buddhism do we wish to spread?" I am not thinking of the pure canonical Dhamma, which exists as such only in the books. In actuality, Buddhism has always been expressed in concrete practices, embedded in social structures, and embodied by real human beings. Thus we have to consider this aspect of Theravada Buddhism and not merely the doctrinal formulas of the Pali Canon. So when we ponder how to bring Buddhism to the West, we have to decide which of the many faces of Theravada we want to bring. To some extent, this is premature, since if Buddhism does eventually take root in the West, it will assume forms particular to Western social and cultural conditions. But to begin we need something to serve as a seed or nucleus.

Can we work with any of the established forms of Asian Buddhism? The predominant form of Theravada Buddhism in Sri Lanka, as in other Asian countries, is the religion of the temples. This revolves around such practices as alms offerings to the monks, *Bodhi poojas, pirith* chanting, and formulaic *bana* preaching. I do not want to demean the value of such practices, which can be important expressions of faith and a real means of shaping one's character under the aegis of the Dhamma. However, this is not the type of Buddhism that will appeal to Western seekers, who often come to Buddhism through disenchantment with the Christianity of the churches. In its modernized incarnation, Asian Theravada Buddhism finds itself charged with new tasks imposed by its communal setting: giving moral and social guidance to a newly affluent urban populace, preserving the Buddhist cultural heritage, and serving as a Buddhist lobby in political affairs. But again, this model of

Buddhism will have little relevance in the West.

The ideal form of Theravada to present would be one that fuses all healthy aspects of the tradition into an organic whole. The transmission would have to focus on the practice of meditation, yet it should include a strong emphasis on Buddhist ethics (including Buddhist perspectives on contemporary ethical issues), textual and doctrinal study, devotional practices, and, yes, a fair share of ritual, too; but ritual would have to be integrated into the spiritual path, not pursued in compliance with mere cultural norms. The meditation practice should be the heart of the transmission. Once students experience the beneficial effects of meditation on their lives, in time they will develop keener interest in the study of texts, in devotional practices, in the precepts, and in ritual. Ritual will then serve to cement these varied aspects of Dhamma into a coherent whole, animated from within by the meditative experience.

But now we come to the heart of the issue. Theravada Buddhism, in its orthodox mould, has always looked upon the monastic order, the Sangha, as the bearer of the Buddhist heritage. Thus, if Theravada is to take hold in the West it seems it should be through a monastic transmission, guarded and upheld by lay support. Without this, we would probably wind up with a watered down version of the Theravada, as we find today in the so-called Vipassana sanghas. A monastic transmission is needed to keep alive the stress on renunciation and restraint so characteristic of the true Dhamma, to sound the reminder that Nibbāna is to be won by relinquishing all points of attachment, not by reinforcing them with clever justifications.

The need for a monastic transmission, however, immediately runs up against a barrier stemming from the fact that, for most Westerners, monasticism is a strange and unfamiliar institution. To complicate matters, with a few exceptions, so far it is mostly non-monastics who have carried out the propagation of Buddhism in the West. Such has been the case with the Zen centres and even with most of the Tibetan Buddhist communities. In the Vipassana community, which looks to the Pali texts for inspiration, almost all the teachers are laypeople, who often travel and teach in male-female teams. This approach has proved highly successful with Western students, who can easily relate to teachers sharing their backgrounds and patterns of relationship. Inevitably, however, this laicized style of teaching blunts certain edges of the Dhamma which, from a canonical standpoint, should be kept sharp.

In such a setting, the Theravada bhikkhu, pledged to celibacy by his code of discipline and bound to a teaching that advocates the overcoming of sensual desire, inevitably finds himself swimming against the current. While in the home countries of Theravada Buddhism people regard a celibate lifestyle as a lofty virtue deserving of respect, Westerners look upon it as just a personal choice, even an odd choice that might arouse more suspicion than admiration.

With a few exceptions, it is unlikely to signify a superior spiritual status or commend itself as an ideal for others to aspire for. Thus, in such a novel setting, if he is to remain faithful to his vocation, the bhikkhu will require deep conviction in the wisdom of the Dhamma and exceptional inner strength. Otherwise he may either be tempted to disrobe or feel driven back to his home country. Not only must he uphold his own vows, but he must also be able to testify to the role of renunciation in the Buddha's full conception of the path.

Another problem confronting us in the task of spreading Buddhism to the West is more practical. In Sri Lanka today it is extraordinarily difficult to find monks who exemplify the personal qualities needed by a Buddhist "messenger of Dhamma" (*dhammaduta*) yet can also communicate the Dhamma in terms meaningful to people from a very different cultural and social background. This has negative repercussions for the whole project of propagating Theravada Buddhism abroad, making the Theravada something of a still backwater on the otherwise lively Western Buddhist frontier. So often, when Sri Lankan Buddhist vihāras are set up in the West, ostensibly to spread the Dhamma to Westerners, they wind up undergoing one of two fates. Either they turn into social and cultural centres for Sri Lankan expatriates, or, if there is no substantial Sri Lankan community around, they fall into a deep and heavy slumber, from which they are occasionally awakened by curious inquirers or a visiting school group. Once the Western seekers' interest in the Dhamma is aroused and they visit the vihara again in the hope of receiving spiritual nourishment, they may not find sufficient programmes to sustain their nascent interest. Thus they will either retreat into private study of the Dhamma or search for a centre belonging to some other school of Buddhism where a higher level of spiritual vitality prevails.

Of all the Asian Theravada communities, I feel the Sri Lankans have the strongest potential for transmitting the Dhamma to the West. From what I have observed, the Thai, Cambodian, and Burmese monks cater almost exclusively to their own communities and seldom even imagine that the Dhamma can have any pull on Westerners. It is the Sri Lankans who have been most inspired by the ideal of passing the Dhamma to the West, and again it is the Sri Lankan Sangha that includes monks ready to learn Western languages and translate the teachings into a message meaningful to Westerners. Yet, despite this, when we survey the Western Buddhist scene, the results are disappointing. We see a tremendous surge of interest in Zen and Tibetan Buddhism, in new Buddhist movements like the Order of Interbeing and the Friends of the Western Buddhist Order, and in Vipassanā as a secular practice. But apart from Ajahn Sumedho's Amaravati network, which consists of Western monks and nuns, the orthodox Theravada Sangha has had relatively little impact in the West. Of course, one might just interpret this as evidence that Westerners are too decadent to appreciate the true Dhamma. However, that interpretation would not only be uncharitable, but it would also be wrong. A sizeable number of Western Buddhists feel themselves powerfully drawn towards the Theravada tradition and are on the lookout for mentors to offer teachings. Thus the desire is there; it is just the resources to satisfy it that are in short supply.

Although I do not have an easy solution to this problem, it would be prudent to make a preliminary diagnosis of its origins. I would suggest, as a tentative hypothesis, that the fault lies partly in the system of monastic education that prevails here in Sri Lanka. This system is extremely inadequate and needs drastic revision from the ground up: revision with respect to the aim, depth, and breadth of monastic training. When monks trained in this system go overseas to expound the Dhamma, they find themselves facing severe handicaps. For one thing, they have to adapt to a society where social relationships are not governed by clearly defined roles and expectations. For another, they cannot get by with routine preaching and ceremonies, but must really strike at the personal existential concerns of Western students. They must also be able to cope with the tremendous increase in knowledge in so many fields that are in some way relevant to Buddhism.

The only way to meet these needs is by exponential improvements in monastic education. If a monk is to go abroad to spread the Dhamma, he must have not only a thorough knowledge of his own Theravada tradition, but some acquaintance with other subjects too. As a minimum, he needs a broad view of the history and schools of Buddhism, some knowledge of comparative religion, and fluency in English. He should also know, or be ready to learn, the language of the country in which he will work. Beyond these specific areas of competency, he will need the intellectual openness and acuity to comprehend the dispositions, attitudes, and worldviews of people from a different culture and relate to them in meaningful ways. He must also have some grounding in the real practice of the Dhamma, for knowledge of books and doctrines, however wide, will be fruitless if not coupled with dedication to the practice. Unfortunately, it is almost impossible to find a monastic institute that can impart the necessary training, and for some reason the Buddhist prelates, rather than initiate changes, seem bent on preserving the status quo. In this respect Buddhist educational institutions compare poorly with Christian seminaries, which equip their own missionaries with a thorough and wide-ranging education that often excels the Buddhist institutes even in the field of Buddhist studies.

However, the fault lies not only with the monasteries. It extends outward and reaches into Sri Lankan Buddhism as a whole, and concerns not merely education but an understanding of the purpose for which Buddhism itself is taken up and practised. It seems that at a certain point in its history, Sri Lankan

Theravada Buddhism largely forfeited its role of serving as a universal path to enlightenment and liberation. For most Sri Lankan Buddhists, with the exception of small numbers of earnest monks and devout householders, Buddhism has become primarily a means for constructing and sustaining a sense of ethnic and communal identity. Hence far too many Buddhists, including the monks, have lost a feel for the universality of the Dhamma, for the mind of non-discrimination and selflessness that is the key to the Buddha's own greatness and magnetic appeal. Instead, this universal attitude has become subverted by the use of Buddhism to shore up a social identity, thereby enclosing people in upon their own group instead of opening them to all humanity. The situation is quite different with the Tibetan Buddhists, for whom adherence to the bodhisattva ideal of liberating all sentient beings has kept that sense of universality and selflessness alive.

This constricted outlook also permeates the monasteries. As a result, the training of the monks focuses not so much on guiding them along the Buddha's path to awakening—towards the purity, freedom, and wisdom of the enlightened mind—as on teaching them how to serve as custodians of a distinct social and cultural heritage. I do not want to dismiss the value of this service, for within this country it is quite necessary to preserve the cultural and social pillars of Sri Lankan Buddhism, especially against the twin incursions of evangelical Christianity and materialistic consumerism. But this function should be subordinated to the more important one of showing the path to wisdom and peace; it should not become so domineering that the original path gets covered with mist and weeds.

These problems may also be aggravated by the sharp distinction, in the Theravada monastic tradition, between the so-called "village and town monks," devoted to preaching and community service, and the forest monks, devoted to full-time meditation. This division creates a situation where a monk not intent on winning the path to Nibbāna in this present life postpones the practice of meditative development to some future existence, justifying his life in robes as a service to society. Such social service, however, takes on a largely secularized colouring, and easily veers off into political activism, usually with an ethnocentric focus. Seldom is it integrated into a true path of spiritual development, except in pretext. On the other side, those monks who are keen on winning the paths and fruits in this life withdraw into the forest for full-time meditation and rarely show any inclination to share their insights with the wider community. Also, given their method of training, they will generally lack the linguistic and social skills needed to propagate the Dhamma in foreign countries. Thus we have this sharp dichotomy: educated town monks without deep personal insight into the Dhamma or experience in meditation, and meditation monks without much inclination to propagate the teaching. From the horns of this dilemma, it is hard to see an easy route of escape, but I can't help asking myself if this is really what the Enlightened One would want if he were alive today.

Since it would be inappropriate to prevail upon monks devoted to full-time meditation to take up a more active vocation, the remedy needed to redress this imbalance seems to require a revitalization of meditation practice within the bhikkhu training institutes. It is perplexing that the meditative side of the monastic training, which should be at the heart of the holy life, should ever have become lost in the first place. However, now that we recognize its loss as leaving a smarting wound in the whole system of monastic education, the one remedy that suggests itself is to restore it. This cannot be done merely by imposing meditation on the monks from the outside as a mandatory discipline. Meditation practice does not occur in a vacuum. It occurs under the impetus given by a clear understanding of the foundations and objectives of the Buddhist spiritual life, of which it is an integral part. So what is really needed is a rejuvenation of the spiritual challenge at the heart of the Buddhist renunciant life.

Personally, I do not think it is prudent to try to create institutions expressly for the purpose of training monks as *dhammadutas*. Such institutions would likely attract monks who want to go abroad for the wrong reasons—to gain prestige, to become popular, perhaps to find employment and disrobe. I feel it is wiser to strengthen programmes in the existing bhikkhu training centres. At the same time, we should keep an eye open for capable bhikkhus enrolled in these programmes who display the qualities needed to propagate the Dhamma in the West. We must also remember that the purpose in training monks is not to make them *dhammadutas*, but to lead them along the way to enlightenment. Thus the training should focus on the inner development of the monk, both in those qualities conducive to personal growth and in those that allow for a compassionate outflow of his spiritual development to others. Monks who have the special skills, and the inclination to work for the spread of the Dhamma, can then be chosen for *dhammaduta* assignments, providing they also display the inner maturity required by such a task.

I come to an inconclusive conclusion. At the present stage in its evolution, Buddhism in the West is taking on a form that focuses on the Dhamma as a path of inner transformation through meditation and contemplation, with other aspects of Buddhist practice subordinated to this concern. We should not immediately conclude that Western Buddhism is therefore an ideal model for Asians to emulate. Western Buddhists often lack a solid knowledge of the texts, and thus are prone to bend the teachings to fit their own agendas and expectations. It is here, I think, that Asian monks with a sound scholarly knowledge of the Dhamma can make a valuable contribution. But while corrective measures are needed in Western Buddhism to ensure right understanding, it is clear that the central focus of Western Buddhists will be on personal meditative experience as the way to inner peace and wisdom.

If Sri Lankan Buddhists are to make a significant contribution to the healthy growth of Buddhism in the West, we will need representatives of the Dhamma who are also living embodiments of the Dhamma. That is, we need monks—and nuns as well—who express in their lives and characters the potentials of the Dhamma as a way of life that brings real wisdom, purity, and peace within, and overflows in expressions of kindness and compassion for others. This is a difficult challenge, but it is an indispensable requirement if Sri Lanka is to contribute to the development of Buddhism in the West. Since the main responsibility for transmitting the Dhamma rests with the monastic order, the Sangha in this country must set its own house in order if it is to be qualified to perform this task. This will require some intense internal criticism and attempts at genuine reform, especially in the system of monastic training. If such changes do not take place, it is unlikely that Sri Lanka will be able to contribute much more to the growth of Buddhism in Europe than to maintain viharas that serve Sri Lankan expatriates.

I will end on a bright note. Despite the shortage of qualified *dhammaduta* monks, scattered across the West there are a few Theravada vihāras and Buddhist centres maintained by Asian bhikkhus who, in their own quiet and non-assertive way, are working to spread the Dhamma. Prominent among them we find Sri Lankan monks, who often must take up this task with much hardship and self-sacrifice. The hardship they face is not only external, but internal as well. They must maintain a delicate discipline amidst the temptations of the Western consumerist culture, and must also struggle against the weight of Buddhist tradition to find the clear and clean message of the Buddha hidden behind stultifying conventions. Such monks generally do not have large organizations behind them, or financial backing from home, but through their dedication to the Dhamma and compassionate concern for others, they actively seek to help Westerners find their way to the Buddha's path. Their selfless work deserves appreciation and support from all sincere Buddhists in this country.

From The Necessity for Promoting Buddhism in Europe, *a booklet privately published in 2000 by the German Dhammaduta Society, Colombo. It was the keynote address delivered at a seminar held on July 2, 2000 at the Mahaweli Centre Auditorium in Colombo to commemorate the first death anniversary of Ven. Mitirigala Dhammanisanthi, formerly known as Asoka Weeraratna.*

53. The Good, the Beautiful, and the True

The Quest for Happiness

All human beings, by their very nature, seek to be free from suffering and to find happiness. This aim, however, proves so elusive because our desire for happiness does not automatically entail knowledge of how to find it. If the knowledge of how to attain happiness automatically came along with the desire to be happy, there would be no need for a Buddha to arise in the world. We would all be able to achieve perfect happiness entirely on our own.

We need the guidance of a Buddha because, though we naturally wish to avoid suffering and to attain happiness, we have no clear conception of the path that can bring this desire to fulfilment. The root of our problem is thus one of knowledge, of clear comprehension. Despite our confidence in our own powers of understanding, our minds are in reality not reliable instruments of knowledge, but are subject to innate distortions that prevent us from gaining the type of knowledge we require. These distortions prevent us from understanding what we must avoid to overcome suffering, and what we must undertake to find true happiness and peace.

This lack of clear understanding is what the Buddhist texts call *avijjā*, ignorance or delusion. On account of ignorance we become victims of craving, of obsessive desire, and thus habitually engage in types of behaviour that are superficially pleasant but eventually bring discontent and suffering. There are other types of behaviour that seem to us difficult, painful, and challenging. These courses of action, we sense, might lead to stable happiness, but because they clash with our natural inclinations, because they involve effort, struggle, and inner change, we do not feel attracted to them. In short, we adhere to familiar ways of behaviour that bring immediate pleasure even when they are ultimately self-destructive; and we shun new, wholesome courses of behaviour even though, if we understood them properly, we would see that they ultimately lead to our benefit.

Many people identify happiness with the enjoyment of sensual pleasures. They assume that happiness comes from indulging the desire for delightful sights, sounds, smells, tastes, and tactile sensations. Thus they devote their energy to acquiring the means to obtain these objects of pleasure. Others are concerned not so much with the sensual pleasures that wealth can buy as with the wealth itself. For such people, wealth becomes a good in its own right. They evaluate themselves and others by the scale of their salaries, bank accounts, and holdings. They invest their time seeking to earn more, to acquire possessions, to increase their wealth. Seldom do they pause long enough to enjoy the pleasures their wealth might make available to them.

Other people devote their effort to the pursuit of power. They want to achieve high status so they can exercise control over others. They identify the attainment of happiness with high status and the exercise of political and social power. Still others are concerned less with wealth and power than with personal security. They do not attempt to climb the ladder of social status, but are content to settle for a lower rung: a secure and comfortable middle-class existence in which they conform to the general consensus of what a respectable life should consist in. They may have a nice house in the suburbs, a nice wife or husband, nice children attending a nice school. Everything in their lives seems as pretty as in a picture book, except that one thing is missing: a deep source of meaning that gives true nobility and value to their existence.

If we deeply examine the lives of people engaged in the pursuit of worldly goals, whether it be sensual pleasures, possessions, wealth, power, or security, we would find that in their heart of hearts they enjoy very little real happiness and contentment. Happiness eludes them because they assume that happiness consists in submitting to the dictates of craving. They fail to understand that craving in itself is insatiable. Thus, as soon as they achieve one object of desire, rather than finding contentment, they become obsessed by a new desire. This desire drives them on to the pursuit of new pleasures, more wealth, or higher positions of power. Thus the pursuit of worldly achievements moves in a vicious cycle, desire leading to gratification and gratification to new desire.

To convince ourselves that this is true, we need only consider the lives of those belonging to the so-called privileged élite. Such people seem to have everything one might desire: command of great wealth, high position, status, all the luxuries we might dream of. Yet though such people might be the envy of everyone else's eyes, we often find that within their hearts they experience no real serenity. If you visit their homes, you see a large house with many rooms, lovely furniture, and beautiful decorations. They may have servants and cooks, eat delicious food, and enjoy all the privileges of high status. But if you go into the bathroom and look into the medicine cabinet, you might find sedatives, anti-depressants, sleeping tablets, and stimulants: all sorts of psychotropic drugs to help them get through the stress and strain of their daily lives.

These reflections should convince us that real happiness is determined not by our material possessions and worldly success, but by our inner qualities of mind and heart: not by what *we have*, but by what *we are*. True happiness comes from a peaceful mind and does not depend primarily on our material conditions. Of course, to live happily we need some degree of material security. People oppressed by hunger, disease, and poverty cannot easily find happiness. Material security, however, is only a foundation, a starting point, for the development of our inner qualities. It is the development of these inner qualities, the development of the mind, that brings true happiness and peace.

The Buddha's teaching, in its classical formulation, speaks of the entire round of existence, *saṃsāra*, as *dukkha* or suffering. The teaching tells us that ultimate happiness is to be found in release from the 'wheel': by realizing Nibbāna, the ultimate truth, which brings freedom from the round of rebirth. However, the Buddha also speaks about types of happiness that can be experienced right here and now, in this present life. Thus I wish to examine what true happiness might mean according to the Dhamma without bringing in the classical framework of kamma, rebirth and Nibbāna as liberation from the round of rebirth.

I don't intend to say that we should put these teachings aside, for they are very essential to obtain a deep and comprehensive view of the Dhamma. The entire path to deliverance, as formulated by the Buddha, rests upon this philosophical framework, and to try to remove it or rationalize it is to wind up with an eviscerated version of the teaching. However, the Buddha himself says that one should examine the Dhamma for oneself in terms of one's own experience. Thus I want to begin with what is visible right before our eyes, what we can personally see for ourselves about the meaning of happiness and inner peace. By taking the visible types of happiness as the basis of our inquiry, we can gain confidence and trust in those aspects of the Dhamma that presently lie outside our range of vision.

In what follows, I will explore the concept of happiness, analyze it into its constituents, and inquire what must be done to achieve it. I will do this by taking three concepts that constitute the ultimate good according to the *Western* philosophical tradition and show how they can be achieved through the Buddha's teaching. These three concepts are Goodness, Truth, and Beauty, but I will examine them in a somewhat different sequence: Goodness, Beauty, and Truth.

Each of these concepts exercises dominion over a distinct sphere of human value: ethics, aesthetics, and knowledge. Goodness is the pinnacle of the ethical sphere. It is at once the underlying ground of right action, a quality that suffuses right action, and the inner state to which right action leads. Value in the ethical sphere is determined by the exercise of practical reason. To decide how we should act in the concrete situations we face in everyday life, we resort to a particular type of reflection as a regulative principle of our behaviour. In other words, to actualize Goodness we must respond to situations that demand a response in ways governed by ethical considerations.

Beauty is the highest value in the aesthetic sphere. The word 'aesthetics' usually suggests the appreciation of works of art, but I am using this word in a somewhat wider sense to refer to the whole range of experience in which Beauty is the dominant element. Art is considered the domain of aesthetics because great works of art arouse in us a sense of the sublime, a perception of transcendent beauty. But we can also gain a perception of the Beautiful by looking at breathtaking landscapes, by admiring great personalities, and by developing our minds towards exalted states of consciousness. For most people, the contemplation of art lifts their minds to crescendos of feeling unknown in normal life, and thus for most of us art is the primary means to awaken an experience of wonder and grandeur. But the encounter with the Beautiful can also be induced more intensely, and with greater potentials for spiritual achievement, by the direct transformation of consciousness in its affective and aesthetic capacities.

Truth is the ultimate object of our quest for knowledge. The whole purpose of the scientific enterprise is to uncover the truth about the world. Though scientific discoveries have practical applications, science is not entirely hostage to technology. Theoretical knowledge is widely regarded as a good in itself. 'Pure science,' the quest for a comprehensive and detailed understanding of the world, stirs our enthusiasm and drives much scientific research even when technological applications are unlikely. Yet the knowledge obtained by the scientific method always strikes us as terribly contingent. It is inseparably bound up with spheres that do not exhibit any trace of completeness; it is subject to constant correction and extension; it always seems to be scratching the surface of things. Our thirst for knowledge can only be satisfied by a sphere of Truth that confers upon us perfect knowledge, a knowing which penetrates to the profoundest depths of reality.

In sum, our quest for true happiness must combine three qualities: commitment to ethical Goodness, or the implementation of moral values in our active life; the contemplation of Beauty, the experience of elevated feelings that confer a sense of the sublime; and the realization of Truth, a knowledge that gives satisfaction and completeness to our intellectual life.

The Good

According to the Buddha's teaching, the necessary condition for any degree of true happiness is Goodness, that is, moral rectitude or virtue (*sīla*). Such Goodness is to be realized by ethical behaviour. In order to be truly happy, to experience true happiness in our lives, we must lead an ethically virtuous life. This means that we must adopt standards of behaviour by which we give consideration to the well-being of others in our bodily actions and speech. The moral life is a life in which we rise above the demands of self-interest and give heed to the interests of others as determinants of action.

Though in the Buddhist texts, morality is usually summed up in various codes of precepts, according to the Buddha the foundation for morality does not lie in any specific set of rules or precepts. It lies, rather, in a principle that we can apply in our relations with other living beings, especially with other human beings. This principle is the guideline of using oneself as the criterion for deciding how to act in relation to other people. When we have to relate to other people in particular situations, we have to step out of our own skin and place ourselves in the position of the other. If I feel driven to behave in a certain way towards another person, I must first consider how I would like it if somebody else were to behave towards me in such a way. This principle means, in effect, that we have to show respect and consideration towards other people, and not act merely on the spur of impulsive self-interest.

From this fundamental principle the Buddha derives the basic moral precepts of his teaching. Thus the Five Precepts (*pañcasīla*) are arrived at by applying the guideline of using oneself as a criterion to the most common situations amenable to an ethical point of view. By considering one's own feelings, we derive the precepts not to kill, not to misappropriate the belongings of others, not to engage in sexual misconduct, and not to speak falsely. To these four, the Buddha adds the fifth precept, to abstain from intoxicants, thus completing the Five Precepts. This precept is added, not because the use of intoxicants is directly harmful to others, but because one who indulges in intoxicants weakens the restraint imposed by conscience and thus becomes inclined to break the other precepts.

Practising morality by observing the Five Precepts leads to a type of happiness that the Buddha calls the happiness of blamelessness (*anavajjasukha*). When people engage in selfish, unethical behaviour, they may secure their own advantage in ways that make them appear to be successful, happy, and fulfilled, and we might even envy them for this. But when one acts against the basic principles of morality, deep within the mind one generates an underlying sense of discomfort—a recognition, dim or clear, that one has caused harm and suffering to others. This recognition brings along a gnawing sense of distress, which prevents us from finding happiness no matter how successful we might appear outwardly.

To see that this is so, imagine a big-time gangster who has earned vast wealth as the head of a heroin-smuggling ring, which he maintains by murdering off rivals and bribing officials. He drives around in a fancy car driven by a chauffeur, wears stylish suits, has a sexy woman at his side, and enjoys vacations at the costliest resorts. Yet we might ask, "Can he really enjoy inner happiness, aware that his success has been achieved by bringing misery to so many people?" Clearly, the answer to this question must be no.

When, however, we restrain our own selfish inclinations and regulate our conduct by ethical guidelines, we then achieve a clarity and purity of mind stemming from the realization that we are not deliberately harming any other living being. By subduing our selfish desires and abstaining from actions that might bring harm to others, we experience the happiness of blamelessness, the joy and ease rooted in a clear conscience. Such happiness arises because we recognize that we are not inflicting pain on any other living being. We do not cause fear in other beings, and thus we give them 'the gift of fearlessness' (*abhayadāna*). In our presence, all other living beings can feel secure: secure about their lives, secure about their belongings, secure about their personal relationships, secure about our communications. This is the first aspect of moral behaviour: to avoid inflicting harm and suffering on others.

But it is not enough merely to observe these principles of restraint. To fulfil the quest for Goodness, we must also cultivate the inner qualities of heart that correspond to these precepts. Thus the positive qualities we nurture, implicit in the precepts of abstaining from harmful deeds, are: kindness and compassion for others; honesty; respect for the marital rights of others; truthfulness in speech; and sobriety of mind. Those are the positive counterparts of the Five Precepts. If we undertake these two aspects of morality—restraint from evil actions, and the cultivation of wholesome attitudes of mind—then we are embodying in our lives the principle of Goodness, the first foundation of real happiness.

The Beautiful

According to the Buddha, Goodness or ethical purity is the basis, the indispensable basis, for real happiness. But in itself it is not sufficient. To discover a deeper and more substantial happiness than is possible merely through moral goodness, we must take a step forward. This brings us to the next constituent of happiness, which I call the Beautiful. I do not use this word to refer to physical beauty, to a beautiful face and a lovely figure, but to inner beauty, the beauty of the mind. In the Buddha's teaching, the true mark of beauty is beauty of the mind. That is why the Abhidhamma uses the expressions *sobhana cittas* and *sobhana cetasikas*, beautiful states of mind, beautiful mental factors, to characterize the qualities we must arouse in treading the path to happiness and peace.

To develop the beautiful states of mind, the beautiful consciousness, we begin with certain qualities that are fundamental to ethics. These qualities naturally inhere in the moral state of consciousness, and thus the moral consciousness is the launching pad in our quest for the Beautiful. True beauty cannot be reached by means of morally unwholesome states of mind. However, to travel further along the path to the Beautiful, we must deliberately propel the ethically purifying states of consciousness towards new pinnacles not accessible by the mere observance of moral precepts. In the process, these qualities of mind expand, becoming powerful, lofty, and sublime. They enter upon a whole new landscape, which in terms of Buddhist cosmology belongs, not to the realm of sensual experience (*kāmadhātu*) in which we normally dwell, but to the realm of pure form (*rūpadhātu*) accessible through the mastery of the *jhānas* or meditative absorptions.

The Buddha has taught many ways to develop the beautiful consciousness. These include meditation on certain coloured disks called *kasiṇas*, mindfulness of breathing, contemplation of the Three Jewels—the Buddha, the Dhamma, and the Saṅgha—and so forth. One group of meditation subjects often mentioned in the texts is the development of four lofty attitudes called the 'divine abodes' (*brahma-vihāra*): loving kindness, compassion, altruistic joy and equanimity. These are to be developed boundlessly, towards all sentient beings without distinction. They are considered the natural qualities of the divine beings known as the *brahmas*, and thus to develop them in meditation is to make one's mind the abode of inward divinity.

The first of these is the development of loving kindness, *mettā*, and that is the method I will explain here. The characteristic of loving kindness is the wish for the welfare and happiness of others, a wish that is to be extended universally to all living beings. This quality naturally underlies the moral precepts, too, but in this stage of practice we are not developing concern for the welfare and happiness of others merely as a ground for action. We are doing so to purify the mind, to make the mind radiant, beautiful, and sublime. Thus we cultivate loving kindness as a deliberate exercise in meditation.

To do so, one takes up for contemplation people belonging to four categories: oneself, then a dear person, then an indifferent person, and finally a hostile person.

One thinks first of oneself, and one directs the wish for well-being and happiness towards oneself, thinking: "May I be well, may I be happy, may I be free from all harm and suffering." You take yourself as an example of a person who wants to be well and happy, and you use yourself as a platform for extending the feeling of loving kindness towards other people. By starting with the wish for one's own welfare and happiness, one comes to understand how other people, too, wish to be well and happy; thus one learns to extend the wish for welfare and happiness to others.

One has to be able to generate a natural, warm, glowing feeling of kindness towards oneself. To make this practice easier, you can begin with your own visual image. See yourself as if in a mirror, smiling and happy, and pervade your image over and over with the thought: "May I be well, may I be happy, may I be free from all harm and suffering." When you gain some degree of proficiency in radiating loving kindness towards yourself—when you feel a warm beam of love going out from your heart and suffusing yourself—you then take other people according to their division into groups.

Begin with a friendly person, someone you consider to be a real friend. However, you should not choose a person with whom you have a close and intimate emotional relationship, such as a husband or a wife, a girlfriend or a boyfriend; nor should you select your own child. In such cases, emotional attachment can enter disguised as loving kindness and deflect the meditation from its proper course. Instead, you should choose somebody such as a respected teacher or a close friend, someone for whom you have affection and respect, but not a binding emotional relationship.

Invite this friendly person into your mind, and generate, strengthen, and cultivate a wish for the well-being and happiness of your friend. When you can successfully radiate the thought of loving kindness towards your friend—a deep and true wish for your friend's welfare and happiness—you should next choose a neutral person. This might be somebody that you pass each day on the street, or the postman, or the woman working in the supermarket, or the driver of the bus you take to work each day: somebody you see often enough so that you know his or her face, but with whom you have no personal relationship. Your attitude towards this person should be completely neutral: no trace of friendship, no trace of illwill.

You then consider this person to be a human being, just like yourself. To pave the way for the meditation, you might reflect, "Just as I want to be well and happy, so too this person wants to be well and happy." Metaphorically, you take your own mind out of your body and put it into the skin of the other person. You try to experience the world through the eyes of that neutral person. I don't mean to say that you should work a feat of psychic power, of mind-reading, but rather that you should use your imagination to feel what it is like to be this person that one considers neutral. This enables you to realize that this so-called neutral person is not just a nameless face, but a real human being just like yourself, with the same desire to be well and happy that you have, with the same aversion to pain and suffering that you have.

Having made this imaginary exchange of your personal identity with that person, you then come back into your own skin, so to speak, and radiate the thought: "May this person be well, may he or she be happy, may he or she be free from harm and suffering." You continue this radiation until you can pervade the neutral person with that warm, glowing, radiant wish for his or her welfare and happiness.

When you succeed in the meditation with the neutral person, you next choose a person you might regard as an enemy: a hostile person, a person whose very presence arouses anger in you. You take this person, and again try to feel the world from that person's standpoint. You apply the same technique of 'exchanging personal identities' as I explained in the case of the neutral person. Then, when your mind has been softened by such reflections, you radiate loving kindness towards the hostile person.

To radiate loving kindness towards a hostile person is often difficult, and for just this reason the Buddha has taught various methods for removing resentment towards such a person. If you apply these methods skilfully, with the right balance of patience and effort, you will eventually overcome your aversion towards the hostile person. Then you will be able to radiate the wish for the real happiness of this person, even if that person is temperamentally mean and cruel. You should persist with your effort until you feel a deep, genuine concern for that hostile person's welfare and happiness, then radiate loving kindness towards that person, over and over, until you can feel the enemy as your friend.

Thus one has learned how to radiate loving kindness towards oneself, a friendly person, a neutral person, and a hostile person. Through practice, one reaches a point where one can radiate loving kindness towards them all equally, without distinction, without discrimination. The Buddhist texts call this stage "the breaking down of the boundaries," for one no longer erects boundaries between oneself and others, or between one's friends, neutrals, and foes. After consolidating this stage of non-discrimination between different people through repeated practice, one next starts to extend that feeling of loving kindness wider and wider until it embraces all sentient beings. One radiates it over one's town, over one's country, over one's continent, over the other continents, over the entire world. One radiates the mind of loving-kindness universally towards all humans in the world: white, brown, black, and yellow; men and women and children, without reservation; then one includes all sentient beings as well, in all the various planes of existence.

In the famous Mettā-sutta, the Buddha says that just as a mother loves her only son even at the cost of her own life, so one pervades all living beings with this sense of loving kindness. In this way, one transforms loving kindness from the stage of non-discrimination into a truly universal, all-embracing quality of the heart.

This development of loving kindness brings inner beauty to the mind, and beauty of the mind is one of the components of true inner happiness and peace. Suffering, discontent, and dissatisfaction originate from the mental defilements, or *kilesas*. As one develops the meditation on loving kindness, this wholesome quality of pure love expands until it becomes boundless, dispelling the darkness of the defilements. As the defilements are dispelled, many other pure, wonderful qualities of mind emerge and blossom: faith, mindfulness, tranquillity, concentration, equanimity. These pure qualities bring along joy, happiness, and peace even under difficult external conditions. Even if other people treat you harshly, even if you are living in difficult straits, your mind still remains happy and calm. So, this second component of happiness is the Beautiful, beauty of the mind, and one effective way to develop beauty of mind is through the meditation of universal loving kindness (*mettā-bhāvanā*).

As one's mind becomes settled and clear, one learns how to sustain attention on a single object, and through this effort the mind enters into stages of deep concentration called *samādhi*. By persistent practice, if one has mature faculties, one might attain those exalted states of consciousness known as the *jhānas*, the meditative absorptions. There are four such states, characterized by sublime joy, bliss and tranquillity, and their attainment elevates consciousness to exalted levels far above the sphere of sensory experience. These states are the apex of the beautiful consciousness, and their mastery marks the full actualization of Beauty as a living experience. To treat them adequately would require a detailed discussion, but it is enough to say that the practice of meditation on loving kindness helps to prepare the mind for their attainment.

Truth

Now we come to the third component of happiness, Truth, or more precisely, the realization of Truth. The Buddha says that even when one's moral virtue is well established and the mind well purified by concentration, one has not yet reached the highest happiness and peace. The meditative absorptions bring ineffable bliss and calm, they suffuse the mind with radiance and light, they lift one up to divine heights, but they still do not fully resolve the problem of suffering. Whatever bliss and calm they induce is imperfect, incomplete, unstable. To reach the highest happiness and peace, one must go a step further. What one needs is wisdom, the direct realization of Truth.

Realization of Truth is so essential to true happiness because wisdom alone is capable of cutting off the defilements at the root, and it is wisdom that realizes Truth. The development of loving kindness suspends the defilements from the mind tentatively, so that they cannot invade consciousness and obsess our thoughts. However, though we may experience peace and purity by developing loving kindness and other such worthy qualities, the defilements continue to subsist deep in the foundations of the mind. If we are not diligent, they might gain an opportunity to rise up and infiltrate consciousness, causing affliction and distress.

According to the Buddha, the deepest underlying root of all the defilements is ignorance (*avijjā*). So long as ignorance remains, the defilements persist, though perhaps in a dormant rather than active condition. To make the mind completely impervious to the machinations of the defilements, we thus have to eliminate ignorance. When ignorance is eradicated, all the defilements vanish along with them, permanently and irreversibly.

Ignorance, according to the Buddha, means not understanding things as they really are, that is, not understanding the true nature of the phenomena comprised in our own experience. For each of us the world, in the ultimate sense, consists of our own 'five aggregates' (*pañcakkhandha*)—form, feeling, perception, volitional formations and consciousness. The world is 'the all' of the senses, their objects and the corresponding types of consciousness. The instrument we must use to eliminate ignorance is wisdom (*paññā*). Wisdom therefore means the correct understanding of things as they really are, the correct understanding of our world: the five aggregates, the six sense spheres the various types of consciousness.

This wisdom is not reducible to mere conceptual knowledge, but must be direct and perceptual. It is not arrived at by a process of objectification, by standing back and distancing ourselves from our experience, but requires us to take a highly personal 'insider's view' in which we remain at once utterly immersed in our subjectivity yet unidentified with it. This view can only be obtained through systematic training. To arrive at the wisdom that cuts off the roots of suffering, one has to enter the stage of Buddhist meditative training called the development of insight (*vipassanā bhāvanā*). Insight means seeing directly into the true nature of our own body and mind, into the constitution of experience, and that is precisely what is aimed at by the practice of insight meditation. First, we have to develop a capacity for concentration, for sustained attention, by collecting the mind into one point through such practices as loving kindness meditation, the *kasiṇas*, or mindfulness of breathing. Then we use the concentrated mind, focused and unified, to explore the nature of experience as it unfolds from one moment to the next.

The key factor in generating insight is mindfulness (*sati*): close, careful attention to what is happening to us and within us on the successive occasions of perception. Mindfulness does not attempt to manipulate the content of experience. It simply observes what is happening at each moment as it is actually happening. When we investigate our own experience with this concentrated, collected mind, observing everything with bare attention, we begin to understand the real nature of all conditioned things, for the nature of all conditioned existence is laid bare in our own mind and body. Within our own body and mind, within our five aggregates, we know and see the nature of the entire world.

As mindfulness deepens, as we attend to the five aggregates, we see that they all share three characteristics. They are impermanent (*anicca*), arising and passing away countless times at every moment; they are vulnerable to suffering (*dukkha*); and they are empty of any substantial core that might be identified as a self (*anattā*). These three characteristics inhere in everything conditioned. They are the true nature of all formations (*saṅkhārā*), of all things formed by causes and conditions. We can observe that everything within our experience arises and passes, and we thereby know that everything that comes into being everywhere must also pass away: whatever begins must end. We can observe that whatever aspect of our experience totters and collapses exposes us to suffering, and we thereby know that there is nothing in the conditioned world that is worth clinging to, for to cling is to suffer. We can see that all the constituents of our own being, our own five aggregates, are insubstantial, devoid of intrinsic essence, and we thereby know that all phenomena everywhere are without substance or selfhood. This direct experiential knowledge of the personal domain opens the door to universal knowledge. By knowing the nature of reality within the complex of our own five aggregates, we gain a certitude about the entire conditioned world throughout boundless space and time.

But the truth about the conditioned world, in its full extent, is still not the ultimate truth. It is still a truth bound up with what is conditioned, formed, and perishable, and thus a defective truth. It is, in fact, only half the truth accessible to us, half the truth we must come to know. The Buddha says, "First comes insight into the real nature of phenomena, afterwards comes knowledge of Nibbāna" (*pubbe dhammaṭṭhitiñāṇaṃ pacchā nibbāne ñāṇaṃ*; Saṃyutta Nikāya 12:70). As we contemplate the five aggregates, the mind becomes poised in unruffled equanimity, gaining a vantage point from which it can observe with crystal clarity the three characteristics stamped on all the constituents of being. When insight wisdom reaches its culmination, it strains the limits of the conditioned, and then the mind breaks out from conditioned phenomena into the unconditioned. By penetrating the nature of the conditioned world, it comes out on the other side of that world, steps into the domain of the unconditioned, the transcendent truth. And it is this supreme or ultimate truth (*paramasacca*) that the Buddha calls Nibbāna, deliverance from all suffering: "This is the supreme noble wisdom, the knowledge of the destruction of all suffering. One's deliverance, being founded upon truth, is unshakable. For that is false which has a deceptive nature, and that is true which has an undeceptive nature, namely, Nibbāna. Therefore one who possesses this, possesses the supreme foundation of truth. For this is the supreme noble truth, Nibbāna, which has an undeceptive nature" (Majjhima Nikāya 140).

A Triadic Unity

It is important to note that until Truth is fully realized and embedded in our being, our accomplishments in the pursuit of Goodness and Beauty are partial and fragile. Without the realization of the transcendent Truth, Goodness, as moral virtue, has to be maintained with diligence. We are tempted to transgress the precepts, and if our determination to follow the decrees of morality falters, we may throw conscience to the wind and submit to our raw impulses. Thus Goodness not founded on direct realization of Truth is permeable by its opposite. The Buddha says that it is only with the first breakthrough to ultimate truth, the attainment of stream-entry (*sotāpatti*), that commitment to the Five Precepts becomes inviolable; and it is only the arahant or liberated one who has eradicated the deep tendencies from which immoral conduct springs. Thus the realization of Truth is necessary to secure, stabilize, and perfect the achievement of Goodness.

The same applies to Beauty. The beautiful mind, attained by cultivating such divine qualities as love and compassion, must be kept beautiful by constant vigilance. Like any well-kept garden, if we don't water it, weed it, and prune it day by day, it will become wild, disorderly, unsightly. The calm, bliss, and radiance of the concentrated mind are the rewards of earnest effort, and we cannot take these rewards for granted. Without heedfulness, the defilements will again break through into the topsoil of consciousness, distorting our thoughts and perverting our emotions. By attaining the jhānas we might enjoy bliss and peace for aeons, but that bliss and peace will not be unshakable. In the absence of Truth, our attainments may decline, fade away, and vanish. It is only through the realization of Truth that the defilements are "cut off at the root, made baseless, annihilated, unable to arise again in the future." Thus it is only through the realization of Truth that Beauty becomes for us an enduring achievement.

So we see that among the three strands that make up true happiness—Goodness, Beauty, and Truth—Truth stands on a level of its own, incommensurate with the other two. It is at once the ground upon which Goodness and Beauty are stabilized, and the apex upon which they converge when taken to their furthest limits. Truth anchors Goodness and Beauty in the mind so they can never be lost, while at the same time it brings to perfection their own inherent potentials for excellence.

To sum up, when we analyze closely the concept of happiness, we see that it consists of three strands: Goodness, Beauty, and Truth; or ethical purity, beauty of mind, and realization of truth. We begin embodying Goodness in our lives by observing the precepts, the codified principles of ethical behaviour. Then, with Goodness as the foundation, we strive for Beauty. We develop a beautiful mind through one of the exercises of mental development that lead to the purification of mind, of which I have discussed only one, the development of loving kindness. Then, when the mind becomes pure, calm, and radiant by means of concentration, we strive for the realization of Truth. We use the concentrated mind to investigate the nature of our own experience. First, we realize the nature of conditioned reality as manifested in our own 'five aggregates' of bodily and mental phenomena, and then we realize the unconditioned reality, Nibbāna, the supreme truth. The realization of Nibbāna brings to fulfilment all three components of the goal, Goodness, Beauty, and Truth, merged into a triadic unity, an indissoluble whole. This whole confers upon our lives peace, harmony, and the highest happiness, what the Buddha called the unshakable liberation of the heart.

From Bodhi Leaves No. 154; first published in 2001.

THE BUDDHIST PUBLICATION SOCIETY

The BPS is an approved charity dedicated to making known the Teaching of the Buddha, which has a vital message for all people.

Founded in 1958, the BPS has published a wide variety of books and booklets covering a great range of topics. Its publications include accurate annotated translations of the Buddha's discourses, standard reference works, as well as original contemporary expositions of Buddhist thought and practice. These works present Buddhism as it truly is—a dynamic force which has influenced receptive minds for the past 2500 years and is still as relevant today as it was when it first arose.

For more information about the BPS and our publications, please visit our website, or write an e-mail, or a letter to the:

Administrative Secretary
Buddhist Publication Society
P.O. Box 61
54 Sangharaja Mawatha
Kandy • Sri Lanka
E-mail: bps@bps.lk
web site: http://www.bps.lk
Tel: 0094 81 223 7283 • Fax: 0094 81 222 3679